Lawyers Working to End Homelessness

Edited by
Amy Horton-Newell

Defending Liberty
Pursuing Justice

Commission on Homelessness & Poverty

Printed in the United States of America.

ISBN: 1-59031-690-8

Discounts are available for books ordered in bulk. Special consideration is given to state and local bars, CLE programs, and other bar-related organizations. Inquire via e-mail at *homeless@abanet.org* or via telephone at (202) 662-1694.

Contents

Foreword

As President of the American Bar Association I have had the honor and pleasure of traveling throughout the United States and many nations of the world to meet with members of the legal profession. I am continually impressed by the tireless work of lawyers and judges to improve the law and the human condition, both at home and abroad. That dedication serves to advance the ideals that guide our shared vision of equal justice for all.

It is in that spirit that I have called for a *Renaissance of Idealism* in our profession, a recommitment to the noblest principles that define the profession: to provide legal representation to assist the poor, disadvantaged and underprivileged; and to perform public service that enhances the common good. The importance of providing legal representation to those who have great need for legal services but limited resources, and to the most vulnerable among us, cannot be overstated. It is a lifeline that can make the difference between stability and poverty, between hope and despair.

Lawyers Working to End Homelessness evidences the will and determination of lawyers across the nation and abroad to take the vital and important first step in addressing chronic poverty by working to overcome a seemingly insurmountable problem—homelessness. The dedication and efforts of these lawyers illustrate that there is hope and opportunity for people living and working on the streets, in our communities and courts.

The Homeless Court Program, supported by the ABA Commission on Homelessness and Poverty, is one of the most timely and important projects of our Association. This important program, which I observed first-hand during a two-day visit to San Diego where it originated, helps homeless people address lingering legal problems that can prolong and exacerbate an already desperate situation. The Commission is partnering with judges, lawyers, court employees, and advocates who are working tirelessly to make the justice system more accessible for homeless people. The Commission is a leader in fostering replication across the country of this innovative program that expands access to justice, reduces court costs, and helps homeless people move towards self-sufficiency. I commend the work of the members of the Commission and its innovative chair, Steven Binder, in developing and expanding the concept of Homeless Courts throughout our nation, and I urge your support for this very important and needed program.

This is but one of many innovative initiatives examined in this publication. Readers will find inspiration for action from this publication whether it is "Law Students Dedicated to Justice for Street Youth" (Trupin), a "Private Law Firm Tackling a Public Problem" (Simes) or a "Holistic Eviction Diversion Project for Elderly Disabled Tenants" (Dahlman). I urge you to read and be enriched by each chapter, and then take the time to use what you have learned in your community to help homeless people with legal problems.

The work of the ABA Commission on Homelessness and Poverty and the authors herein underscore the need for an idea whose time I believe has come: a defined right to counsel for poor people facing serious civil legal problems, parallel to the right to counsel guaranteed to indigent persons with criminal legal problems in the 1963 U.S. Supreme Court decision in *Gideon v. Wainwright*. This idea is based on the premise that poor people facing loss of shelter, threats to family integrity, or serious threats to their health should have access to a lawyer provided by the state if they cannot afford a lawyer.

If we are to fulfill the eloquent promise of equal justice under law that is carved above the entrance to the United States Supreme Court building and countless courthouses nationwide, we must ensure that poor people who face life-threatening civil legal problems are provided with counsel to help them. *Lawyers Working to End Homelessness* is an important contribution to that effort.

Michael S. Greco, *President*
American Bar Association
2005-2006

Acknowledgments

An impressive number of lawyers collaborated on a year-long project to put together "Lawyers Working to End Homelessness." Attorneys from across the country conceived, drafted, reviewed and edited the articles for the book. Perhaps more importantly, these same lawyers are working to end homelessness and making a difference in their communities. Some of the authors are full-time public interest attorneys, others work at big firms and donate their legal expertise through pro bono initiatives or impact litigation—all of them are working for justice. The American Bar Association Commission on Homelessness and Poverty is tremendously grateful to them for sharing their stories.

Thanks to the members of the Commission—both past and present—who served as authors and reviewers. Their comments and support were invaluable. Thanks are also owed to Mary Jordan Mullinax, Staff Assistant to the Commission, and ABA intern Julia Choe, for the many hours they spent reading and rereading the articles.

Finally, a very special thanks to Amy Horton-Newell, Staff Director of the Commission on Homelessness and Poverty, who came up with the idea for this project, and who, through countless hours, shepherded the book from idea to reality. Amy envisioned a book that would appeal to all those who work in the legal field—students, staff and attorneys—and would inspire them to take action to address homelessness in their community. This vision has come to fruition and we hope it will be a resource for lawyers interested in advocating for homeless people for years to come.

ABA Commission on Homelessness & Poverty

Executive Summary

*"**obstruct...1** to block or stop up (a passage) with obstacles or impediments; dam; clog* **2** *to hinder (progress, an activity, etc.); impede* **3** *to cut off from being seen; block (the view) — SYN. HINDER..."*

*"**obstruction...1** an obstructing or being obstructed* **2** *anything that obstructs; hindrance —**SYN.** OBSTACLE"*[1]

Imagine, if you can, a continuous supply of permanent and adequate housing coupled with self-sufficiency and stability for all those in need of housing. In more concise words, imagine ***The End to Homelessness***.

Unfortunately, the End to Homelessness must be imagined, as it has not been achieved. Numerous "obstructions" encase and surround the end and have thwarted this achievement to date. These "obstructions" are very formidable and thickly layered, and they include the following:

- The deprivation of rights, respect, dignity, and equal treatment for people who are homeless;
- The criminalization of people who are homeless, which includes sweeping them off the streets and burdening them with multiple citations for misdemeanors;

---

1 *Webster's New World Dictionary, Third College Edition (1988 Simon & Schuster, Inc.), p. 936.*

- The lack of available and adequate education, transportation, medical assistance, health insurance, child care, temporary housing, food, and clothing for people who are homeless;
- The impact of mental health issues and substance abuse problems on people who are homeless;
- The impact of domestic violence and physical, mental, and sexual abuse of people who are homeless;
- The inability to obtain identification for people who are homeless;
- Not In My Back Yard (NIMBY), zoning, permitting, and other land use restraints;
- The lack of available property locations;
- The marketplace economics related to developing and purchasing adequate permanent housing; and
- The absence of financing, tax assistance, and other forms of financial incentives for the creation of adequate permanent housing.

These obstructions are formidable, but they are not insurmountable against tools like time, passion, perseverance, conviction, and effort—with the right approaches, the obstructions can be removed. This is what some members of the legal profession are doing today. Using an equally impressive number of approaches and tools, they are working to remove the obstructions to ending homelessness.

These members of the legal profession differ from those who view helping people who are homeless as a non-starter or from those who view ending homelessness as incomprehensible. They do not sit back and ignore or overlook people who are homeless. They are not reluctant to help these people. Some provide assistance on an individual basis; others do it through governmental entities, legal services, bar associations, law schools and clinics, nonprofits, other organizations, or private firms. Some do it on a pro bono basis as volunteers. They use multiple and various approaches, including litigation, education, legislation, policy formation, and advocacy.

They create new legal structures—new courts and new governmental programs—to remove the obstructions. To date, these members of the legal profession have touched only a small portion of the overall homeless population, but every day they are working to reach more.

Who makes up this small portion of the homeless population? To begin with, they are without appropriate permanent homes. Some are fortunate to have merely temporary roofed housing (perhaps staying in a shelter or with family or friends); however, the majority live without any acceptable roof above their heads—quite possibly, in a doorway, alley, or park, or on a sidewalk, bench, or beach.

Some are individuals. Others are families. Some are adults. Some are children. Some are veterans of military service. They are typically impoverished and without regular jobs. Their clothes may be torn, worn, and not suitable for their climates or climate changes. They often struggle with hygiene maintenance and appear unkempt. Some suffer from substance abuse or other forms of disabilities or mental illnesses. Some may have been abused, neglected, impacted by violence, or victims of violence. They may be in need of medical assistance and most likely lack health insurance. They may need child care. They may use outside areas as their restrooms. They may have encountered unfriendly or inaccessible judicial systems. They may have been swept off the streets by governmental authorities. They may have received multiple misdemeanor citations.

This book is a six-chapter compilation of articles by and about just a few members of the legal profession who are successfully and continually implementing approaches and efforts to remove the "obstructions" to end homelessness. What follows below is a flavor of the articles.

CHAPTER 1: INDIVIDUAL LAWYERS WORKING TO END HOMELESSNESS

Individual lawyers are helping people who are homeless. Chapter 1 shares examples of these individual efforts.

Casey Trupin's piece entitled "Staking the Tent: Fighting for the Right to Not Be Overlooked" demonstrates how individuals working with people who are homeless can cause neighboring populations to be accepting of them by discovering the humanity that they all share. Specifically:

> Now, locals are increasingly excited about Tent City. Residents are met with offers of help and curiosity, not fear. A suburban couple wrote their councilmember earlier this year describing their experience with Tent City as "incredible." They shared meals with the residents and worked together to decorate the church for Christmas. They lauded the occupants after "seeing their patience and endurance as they take the bus to work, attend their camp meetings, do their patrols and work together in this opportunity to ***transition into the larger community***." As for Hunter's concern about the deep prejudice regarding communities with people who are homeless, the couple responded, "We have been blessed and transformed, having a chance to see what their lives are like, finding the humanity that we share, though we all have different faces and opportunities in life…We would be poorer for not having the experience of Tent City Four in our midst."

In her piece entitled "Breaking the Cycle of Poverty: Providing Pro Bono Legal Services in the U.S. and Abroad," Patricia Julianelle writes about her sabbatical from the National Law Center on Homelessness & Poverty. As part of her sabbatical, she joined on as pro bono counsel to the National Association for the Education of Homeless Children and Youth ("NAEHCY"), drafting language for statutes and regulations, helping implement its legislative strategy, and providing technical assistance to service providers, legal services attorneys, and schools. Julianelle also discusses her pro bono work in Chile, which is where she is living while on sabbatical.

In a third piece, Maria Foscarinis discusses her motivation to enter public service and to end homelessness. Foscarinis states that she was inspired to create the National Law Center on Homelessness & Poverty at a time when homelessness was becoming the face of the most extreme form of American poverty. She began by helping people who are homeless while she was in private practice, and since the time she formed the Center, she has addressed a number of issues, including shelter, welfare, lack of beds, zoning laws, military bases, education, *Homeless Eligibility Clarification Act, Homelessness Housing Act,* criminalization of the homeless, Social Security disability benefits, and state and local plans to address homelessness.

In a fourth piece, Cassandra Goldie, the Director of the Homelessness Legal Rights Project, Gilbert + Tobin Centre of Public Law, University of South Wales ("Homelessness Legal Rights Project"), writes about the deprivation of human rights of people who are homeless in Australia, and in part, her passion and efforts to use the "law and human rights tools" to address the needs of people who are homeless in Australia.

In a fifth piece, Will Hoch, a partner in the Oklahoma firm of Crowe & Dunlevy and the immediate past chair of the American Bar Association's Commission on Homeless and Poverty, discusses various ways in which individual lawyers can play a role in ending homelessness. Mr. Hoch covers a broad spectrum of activities—from serving on a board at the local shelter to starting a legal clinic or a homeless court.

In a sixth piece, Kassandra Perez, a Pepperdine Law School student, reflects on a tour of housing facilities and shelter units she took with the Honorable Harry Pregerson, a Ninth Circuit Court of Appeals judge, and her simultaneous interview of him. During her time with Judge Pregerson, Ms. Perez learns that, in significant part, Judge Pregerson's persistence, passion, conviction, and toil led to the establishment of a number of shelters and housing facilities for those who are homeless.

Finally, in this chapter, J. Peter Sabonis shares his story of working with a community-organizer in Baltimore to address low wages and employment issues faced by the working homeless.

CHAPTER 2: LAW STUDENTS AND PROFESSORS WORKING TO END HOMELESSNESS

Chapter 2 contains pieces promoting the roles of law students and professors and the benefits that their efforts provide.

In one article, Casey Trupin, the co-founder of Street Youth Legal Advocates of Washington (SYLAW) and a Staff Attorney with the Columbia Legal Services, and Corey Fitzpatrick, a third year law student at the University of Washington Law School in Seattle, discuss how their Seattle program has provided outreach, advocacy and, in conjunction with Columbia Legal Services, advice and service to homeless youth. For them:

> The missing component was that of legal assistance. While most street youth have other basic needs, there is often a legal issue which, if remedied, can expedite the transition to a positive and healthy adulthood.

The piece entitled "All About Dignity: A Collaboration in St. Louis to Defend the Rights of the Homeless" by John Ammann, Professor of Law at St. Louis University, presents a successful litigation which challenged a July 4, 2004 removal and arrest of homeless people without probable cause, challenged downtown community courts as unconstitutional private courts, and advocated to ensure proper service was available for the homeless and to enforce a prior litigation decree. In that case, the U.S. District Court in St. Louis issued a preliminary injunction in favor of the plaintiffs regarding the removal and arrest without probable cause and a state court issued an injunction enjoining the use of a community court. Lawyers from Legal Services of Eastern Missouri collaborated with law students on the matter. The U.S. District Court wrote a 41-page decision recognizing the dignity of the homeless and chastising the police and city officials for depriving them of their rights. A significant consequence of the case was "**A Legacy of Dignity**":

> Homeless men and women were noticed and respected by middle-class lawyers and law students who not only

> represented them, but ate with them, shared Christmas parties with them and became friends with them. Homeless men and women were noticed and respected by a federal judge. Homeless men and women were noticed and respected by the local media who reported on the case, and interviewed them about their circumstances. They had been able to get the City and Police Department to acknowledge in writing that new policies would be instituted protecting the rights of the homeless, and for that matter, everyone, to be in public places and to be free from unreasonable searches and seizures of their person and property. Most importantly, the legal team hopes that the general public became a bit more sensitive to the issues of homelessness from this effort.
>
> ***The litigation perhaps has shown that by using our system of justice to recognize and enhance the dignity of the homeless, we have the opportunity to enhance the dignity of us all.***

Krista Kauper, Director of Development for the ABA Fund for Justice and Education, discusses the importance of the John J. Curtin, Jr. Fellowship Program. She highlights a number of Curtin Fellows (all of whom are law students) who are working to address homelessness and poverty-related issues. In one case, a Fellow was working with a client who:

> needed shelter for the night, but he had been told that all shelters were full. San Francisco's mayor had recently declared that homeless people were not to sleep in the streets or in doorways. Frustrated, Lee went straight to the top and called the mayor's office to remind them of promises and to demand that the mayor's staff find her client a bed. Suddenly, there was a bed available.

Finally, Bob Whitman, a professor at the University of Connecticut School of Law, discusses People Advocating Therapeutic Homes ("PATH"), a program and type of home designed to assist people who are homeless and who are in need of mental health and addiction recovery. In his piece entitled: "Law Schools Can Play an Important Role in Helping the Homeless," Mr. Whitman focuses a significant portion of his article on the role law students play with PATH, including securing 501(c)(3) status for the organization, addressing legal issues of people involved with the program, and publishing a book about operating a PATH-type home.

CHAPTER 3: LAW FIRMS WORKING TO END HOMELESSNESS

Chapter 3 focuses on the role of law firms: large and small, on their own and in conjunction with other entities, in addressing the needs of those who are homeless.

Jeffrey Simes, a Partner at Goodwin Procter LLP, presents a New York education case in which a class of homeless parents struggled to be permitted to have their children attend schools because the parents were continually moving outside of the school district. In his article, "Private Firms Tackling a Public Problem: How Law Firms Can Help Fight Homelessness," Mr. Simes discusses how his firm used litigation to successfully resolve this problem.

While Mr. Simes' piece is about litigation, a piece written by Laurel Glassman, counsel with Dewey Ballantine LLP, and Carol Weiser, a Partner with Sutherland Asbill & Brennan LLP, talks about how law firms can assist in the formation of a 501(c)(3) (in this case Gifts for the Homeless, Inc.) and through such a 501(c)(3) do fundraising and in-kind gift raising. Specifically, Gifts for the Homeless, Inc. focuses on obtaining clothing, sleeping bags, blankets, toiletries, and winter items, in addition to cash donations. The article details how the organization taps volunteers at law firms throughout the DC metropolitan area to coordinate donations. The authors also discuss the organization's highly successful fundraiser—its annual battle of the *law firm* bands.

Comparatively, Robert Downs describes ways in which lawyers in solo and small firms can use their broad based understanding of the legal practice to provide assistance to people who are homeless by identifying domestic violence and education issues they may be facing, referring them to appropriate social services organizations, and donating to and volunteering time with service organizations that address their needs.

Finally, in pieces from both Maria Foscarinis, the Executive Director of the National Law Center on Homeless & Poverty, and Paul Freese, from Public Counsel in California, the authors demonstrate the benefits of having nonprofit public service organizations partner with law firms to meet the needs of people who are homeless.

CHAPTER 4: BAR ASSOCIATIONS WORKING TO END HOMELESSNESS

This chapter talks about the role of the bar associations—on national/international, state, and local levels—in the effort to end homelessness.

The American Bar Association ("ABA") has been a national leader in the effort to end homelessness. Amy Horton-Newell's piece about the ABA's Commission on Homelessness and Poverty highlights its formation, some of the policies that have been adopted by the ABA's House of Delegates, its education and advocacy materials (for example, "Representing the Poor and Homeless: Innovations in Advocacy" and "NIMBY: A Primer for Lawyers and Advocates"), its partnerships with other ABA and non-ABA organizations, its addressing homeless youth issues, and its work to promote the creation and implementation of homeless courts throughout this country.

On a state level, Jane Shaeffer, a Member of the Florida State Bar, talks about how a Florida State Bar Committee was formed to help address homelessness. She points out that to date, the committee's activities have been "to educate, activate and advocate." The committee members have sponsored seminars and have lobbied in support or opposition to legislation. She believes that by:

> [w]orking on the premise that there is strength in numbers, it is felt that a committee recognized as part of the Bar gives advocates for the homeless credibility not obtainable by any other way. By working together we develop a structure and direction for this advocacy, and comfort knowing we are not out there all alone.

At the local bar level, Judge Jay Zainey's article entitled "Homeless Experience Legal Protection (HELP): Attorneys' Outreach Program for the Homeless" discusses the benefits and impacts of the HELP program in New Orleans. The program brings lawyers to shelters and homeless centers in an effort to provide pro bono legal services. The program's goal is to secure for the homeless access to legal services, and consequently, to help the people who are homeless escape homelessness, "rebound as productive members of society," and restore their "dignity." HELP focuses on a wide variety of matters, including identification cards, qualification for SSI, and matters related to Katrina. Judge Zainey describes an example of a success story in his essay when he talks about what one volunteer lawyer had to say:

> When the person came in to see me, his face was downcast. After he and I discussed his legal issues, and came up with solutions, he looked up to me and thanked me for treating him as a human being—and with dignity and respect…he walked out the door…I felt like I won the biggest case of my career. I would like to see this person again and to thank him for giving me the opportunity to really make a difference in his life.

Of critical importance, Judge Zainey points out that the Lafayette Parish Bar Association has successfully replicated this program.

Finally, in an article about the Lawyers Clearinghouse on Affordable Housing and Homelessness, Josephine McNeil and Maribeth Perry talk about how in the late 1980s, several different groups in the Boston area, including the Boston and Massachusetts' Bars, formed a Clearinghouse to address homelessness in Boston. The goal of the Clearinghouse was to mobilize attorneys willing to provide pro bono legal services to affordable housing developers, tenant groups, advocacy groups for the homeless, and other organizations involved in addressing the issue of homelessness.

CHAPTER 5: NONPROFIT LEGAL ORGANIZATIONS WORKING TO END HOMELESSNESS

This chapter focuses on the efforts of lawyers at nonprofits and legal services organizations.

Shelbi D. Day, an Equal Justice Works Fellow with Southern Legal Counsel, Inc., writes about the work of Equal Justice Works Fellows in "Equal Justice: Working for the Rights of the Homeless." This article specifically talks about how Equal Justice Works Fellows are addressing, among other things, civil rights abuses of the homeless, criminalization, anti-sleep ordinances, and the prohibition of solicitation on public streets and right of way issues. Her piece motivationally concludes:

> My fellowship, and the stories shared with me by other Equal Justice Works Fellows working with homeless individuals, has had an impact on my career and person. I am inspired by the courage and perseverance of individuals who struggle daily to survive life's circumstances that most of us could not even imagine. I have been touched by individual stories of survival and perseverance of the human spirit through even the worst adversity. Over the past year-and-a-half, I have constantly run up against the cruel stereotypes people have of homeless individuals, and have been taken back by the way homeless people are treated by fellow citizens,

> police officers and governments. Plainly, homeless individuals are treated in inhumane and unfair ways that no human being should have to endure. The biggest lessons that I have learned are that a little respect and empathy go a long way; even the smallest gesture of kindness is met with gratitude and appreciation; and everyone has a story worth listening to. I am regularly humbled and reminded how fortunate I am.

Edward Hoort, the Executive Director of Legal Services at Eastern Michigan (LSEM), writes about the traditional and non-traditional efforts to address homelessness in his piece "Traditional and Non-Traditional Homelessness Prevention." On the traditional side of the equation, Mr. Hoort includes addressing eviction proceedings, mortgage forfeiture, bankruptcy, SSI, SSDI, food stamps, TANF, Medicaid, childcare, and unemployment. On the nontraditional side, he talks about a tax reversion program, a tax foreclosure program, helping tenants stay in tax reversion property, working to preserve housing stock, protecting tenants from becoming homeless, and LSEM's innovative GAIN$ program.

Also included is an article by Emiko Ryan, an AmeriCorps Attorney at the Homeless Legal Advocacy and Prevention Project of the Legal Aid Society of Hawaii-Kauai. In it, she describes how the Kauai Office designed and then implemented Holistic Services for the Homeless (HLSH). The program was designed to assist all people who are homeless, not only those living in their vehicles or at the beach, but also those in the women's shelter, in transitional housing, and those living on the couches and floors of friends and family (the 'hidden homeless'). The means of implementation included reaching out to and representing people who are homeless. After a successful beginning, the program has expanded and changed its name to the Homeless Legal Advocacy and Prevention Project ("HLAPP"). In May of 2006, a further addition to the program occurred with the creation of a Center for Equal Justice. Among other things, this Center provides computers, a typewriter, copy and fax service, and research materials to the homeless.

In an article by Maria Foscarinis, the founder of the National Law Center on Homeless & Poverty, she describes the history of this Center and focuses on its programs related to Katrina, children and youth housing, income, civil rights, human rights, and domestic violence. The Center applies a multi-faceted approach to address homelessness, including impact litigation, public policy advocacy, education and outreach, and the mobilization and engagement of lawyers. At the conclusion of her piece, she lists by chronology the Center's significant efforts for the homeless. One of those efforts is what is described as a long-term solution—"Beyond McKinney." This solution, created in 1992, is described as:

> a nationwide effort to establish long-term solutions to homeless: affordable housing, adequate income, social services and civil rights. Policies developed through "Beyond McKinney" launched the homeless persons' right to vote campaign and prompted a suit filed against the U.S. Census Bureau for failing to include homeless people in the national census; the under counting of homeless people deprives many regions of much-needed federal funds to help combat homelessness.

In a comparable piece about Public Counsel, Paul Freese, Director of Litigation & Advocacy at Public Counsel, describes its Homelessness Prevention Law Project. Through it, Public Counsel has engaged literally thousands of volunteers to advocate on behalf of these vulnerable individuals in a variety of settings, including street outreach, legal clinics at shelters and drop in centers, and advocacy sessions in county social service offices. It has evolved from calling itself the "Homeless Assistance Law Project" to "The Homelessness Prevention Law Project" to reflect Public Counsel's philosophy that homelessness is not an acceptable condition for any human being.

Finally, Robin Runge, the Director of the American Bar Association's Commission on Domestic Violence, provides an article about innovative programs in Maine and Delaware whereby lawyers address the housing issues of domestic violence victims.

CHAPTER 6: COURTS WORKING TO END HOMELESSNESS

This chapter highlights the benefits of problem-solving courts and governmental programs.

Judge Steve Leifman describes the Eleventh Judicial Circuit Criminal Mental Health Project (Miami, Florida) in "Making Jail the Last Resort." As basis for the project, Judge Leifman points out that homeless people with mental health issues appear to be twice as likely to be arrested and jailed and therefore more likely to reuse the judicial system. Through this alternative court program, the court system has been able to reduce recidivism and help the homeless with housing.

Similarly, Steve Binder, the current Chair of the ABA's Commission on Homelessness and Poverty and a Deputy Public Defender for the City of San Diego, describes the Homeless Court Program and how it works to help the homeless clear their existing offenses and warrants for misdemeanors, without conviction, after they have successfully participated in a shelter program. According to Binder, "the Homeless Court Program brings the law to the streets, the court to the shelters, and the homeless back into society."

Finally, in another type of diversionary project, Rhonda Dahlman talks about how AARP's Legal Counsel for the Elderly is working to prevent homelessness through its holistic eviction diversion project for the elder disabled tenant. It seeks to train housing providers on how to address the needs of elderly tenants by involving social workers, service providers, and volunteers. The program also seeks to educate the courts on alternatives to eviction. Ms. Dahlman encourages communities to prevent the homeless elderly situation from worsening by not allowing more elderly to become homeless. According to Dahlman, the project allows elders to live independently and with dignity.

In summary, these chapters and their motivational articles highlight the tremendous efforts of just a few members of the legal profession. For them, the means to end homelessness require removing the "obstructions" to the End to Homelessness.

It is the hope of the ABA Commission on Homelessness and Poverty that this book will motivate you to reach out to the people who are homeless and, in doing so, build on what these members of the legal profession are already doing to achieve ***The End to Homelessness.***

ABA © DAVID SHERMAN

James L. Forman *Partner*
Rider Bennett, LLP
33 South 6th St. #4900 Minneapolis, MN 55402
612.340.8922 jforman@riderlaw.com

James (Jamie) L. Forman is a partner with Rider Bennett, LLP in Minneapolis, Minnesota. His practice is business and commercial litigation, with a particular focus on cases involving temporary restraining orders, injunctions, or other forms of equitable and extraordinary emergency relief. He has been active with the American Bar Association as he is a Fellow of the American Bar Foundation, a Fellow of the ABA's Young Lawyer's Division, former member of the ABA Commission on Homelessness & Poverty, a past chair of the ABA Steering Committee on the Unmet Legal Needs of Children, and a former member of the Editorial Board of the ABA Business Law Section's Business Law Today. Additionally, he served on the Minnesota State Bar Association's Katrina Relief Fund Task Force. Furthermore, he has been involved with a number of nonprofit organizations, including currently serving as a Director of the Lawyers Committee for Civil Rights Under Law (Washington, DC) and as a Director of the Loan Repayment Assistance Program of Minnesota (Minneapolis, MN), recently being named a Trustee of Lewis & Clark College (Portland, OR), and having served in the past as a Trustee of William Mitchell College of Law (St. Paul, MN) and as a Director of the Minnesota Organization of Adolescent Pregnancy, Prevention and Parenting (St. Paul, MN).

CHAPTER 1

Individual Lawyers Working to End Homelessness

Staking the Tent:

Fighting for the Right to Not Be Overlooked

Casey Trupin

Beneath his office is the original street of broken dreams. To the east, Yesler Way disappears near the end of Lake Washington in one of Seattle's most upscale residential neighborhoods. As it runs west over one hill, it comes to a peak near Harborview Hospital, where scores of adults who are homeless seek out emergency care for lack of preventive care. There, on top of First Hill, Yesler Way looks out on one of the most spectacular urban views. The Smith Tower, which stood for 48 years as the tallest building in the West, is guarded on either side by Elliot Bay and the Olympic Mountains. Commerce literally floats behind the building as ferries take business people to and from the Puget Sound islands where they live. For almost three decades, attorney Ted Hunter has watched it all happen in this area. And now his career has brought him to this place, Pioneer Square, above which his office sits.

Looking closely, Yesler Way does not disappoint. From the top, you can almost see it all, the mountains and the water and the ferries. The view from there is almost enough to make you forget you are on a Skid Row. The Skid Row, in fact—this is the birthplace of that term. Before Yesler Way, Skid Rows and Skid Roads didn't exist. It's not until you walk down this way that you can see the extreme poverty and homelessness refusing to relinquish its grip on this street.

In the mid 19th century, Henry Yesler built a lumber mill at the foot of the street, just across from where Hunter works. Yesler Way was made of logs known as skids, and timber was hauled down the greased skids to the mill. For the next 150 years following the building of the mill, Yesler Way survived the worst. The area burned down in 1889. The Depression hit the area hard in the late Twenties and Thirties. An earthquake in 1949 (and again in 2001) did significant damage. In the 1970s, a hotel fire and subsequent strict housing codes caused numerous low-cost and single-room-occupancy (SRO) hotels to close down, leaving low-income people nowhere to sleep.

In the mid 1970s, Hunter was a law student at the University of Washington in Seattle. The war was over before he started law school, and homeless veterans already started to populate the streets. The year he graduated, 1978, Microsoft quietly moved to the city, and decades later it would inject great fortunes into the economy. That same year, the city council struggled to address homelessness, proclaiming a goal "to realize, as soon as feasible...a decent home and a suitable living environment for all...citizens." Twenty-seven years later, the city has yet to realize that goal.

Above the street, Ted Hunter's five-attorney firm, Driscoll and Hunter, sees a significant number of cases while working as land use hearing examiners. One case in particular—Hunter's favorite and most rewarding—involves major land use deals and lawsuits over plots of land in expensive neighborhoods. Unlike his other cases, however, this case sustains housing for dozens of people, with nobody making a dime of profit.

For the past seven years, Hunter has represented a local organization as it fights against cities and counties to ensure that people without homes have a safe place to live and are not forced to hide in anonymity. His clients, the Seattle Housing and Resource Effort and the Women's Housing, Equality and Enhancement League (SHARE/WHEEL), comprise a group formed to advocate for the rights of Seattle's homeless population. SHARE/WHEEL has never backed down from a legal fight, whether it be challenging the city for implementing an anti-homeless sidewalk sitting ordinance or taking on the United States Postal Service for its unfair treatment of people who are homeless, which makes this partnership a perfect fit. Hunter, too, does not back down.

Hunter's decision to become a defender of people who are homeless wasn't as much personal as it was political. Ever since Hunter graduated from law school, he has worked on issues involving the use of land. While he found his work for the Legislature on energy and environmental matters interesting, he felt torn, getting paid with public money without doing anything to give back. After leaving the Legislature, he worked as a Land Use Hearings Examiner—an Administrative Law Judge at the municipal level often dealing with large builders working on mixed use developments. He had training as a mediator and liked the fact that his job allowed him to take advantage of these skills. However, he grew less and less able to stomach the constant subdivision of property while the cost of developing housing went up. The houses got bigger and bigger, and affordable housing began to disappear. The community began to develop an attitude towards housing density, towards the smaller homes they used to occupy. And he watched the lines at the shelters and missions near Yesler grow longer. As an ALJ, he was part of the process of dividing up the land in ways that could reduce affordable housing. "I started asking, 'Am I part of the problem?'" he says. He motions in the direction of the two stadiums located just south of his office building. "We're putting thousands of cars in parking lots where we could be building homes."

Prior to 1999, Hunter wasn't working specifically on homelessness. He volunteered at the local King County Bar Association, taking family law and general legal cases. One day, SHARE's coordinator, Scott Morrow, called the bar association, seeking help for Tent City.

Tent City is the aptly named collective of tents where dozens of homeless men, women, and families live, on average, for six weeks. The fact that couples and families can live there sets it apart from most of the area's shelters—where family units are banned. Seattle's tent cities probably first formed their roots during the Depression. As in other cities, a Hooverville sprung up near Pioneer Square in the Thirties. But the nation recovered, and the very visible display of concentrated homelessness changed into slightly less obvious scenes like that of modern day Yesler Way. In 1999, frustrated with the city's poor response to homelessness, a Seattle community organization, El Centro de la Raza, invited a group of individuals who were homeless to stay in tents on the organization's grounds. El Centro, which itself had been formed through a takeover of an abandoned building, was not afraid of pushing the envelope when it came to anti-poverty strategies. The city and some neighbors were nonplussed about bringing homelessness out into the open, and began fining El Centro 50 dollars per day. "There was, and is, a deeply embedded prejudice that homeless people are not an asset to the community," notes Hunter. Ultimately, however, the city and the neighbors' fears did not materialize. In fact, neighborhood police reports showed a decrease in crime. Business revenue in the neighborhood actually increased, shattering the theory that local businesses would be hurt.

Unfortunately, the city was undeterred by this data and pressed on with penalties for El Centro, which, along with SHARE/WHEEL, took the matter to court. After more than 23 years of practice, the City of Seattle challenge to Tent City would be "one of the high points of [Hunter's] career." In September of 2001, the judge found that the case "crie[d] out for compassion," ruling that "tents are obviously habitations" and that the use of tents was not in itself sufficient reason for declaring a zoning violation or refusing to grant a land use permit. Tent cities, the judge explained, were needed in times of crisis—and this was one of those times. In March of 2002, the Seattle City Attorney's office signed an agreement with SHARE/WHEEL recognizing the legality of Tent City and setting standards for its operation similar to those that SHARE/WHEEL had been practicing.

Contrary to the public image of homelessness, about half of Tent City residents work full-time, and many of the remaining residents have part-time jobs or are in educational programs. The two tent cities (Tent City 3, which moves around the city, and Tent City 4, which moves around the county) have strict rules banning abusive language, drugs, and alcohol. Additionally, all residents must participate in the governance and maintenance of Tent City, doing chores and attending weekly meetings. Hunter continues to be impressed by the way Tent City operates—the way it polices itself and the way everybody pitches in, commenting that "It is run like a German hostel." A suburban resident recently echoed Hunter's comments in a letter. "What struck me during my two dinners with Tent City 4 was how orderly the 'city' is run. They each have jobs and take them seriously. There is also a strong care ethic among the residents." At one point in his career, Hunter might have been surprised by this, but no longer: "Individuals who are homeless and have the capacity to give back also have the desire to do so."

Tent cities are generally, although decreasingly, met with ire and fear. Cities and counties set up extra police presence. In the past, hyper-vigilant neighbors complained to everybody that would listen. Lawsuits to ban Tent City have become par for the course. One anti-Tent City website argues that "[c]riminal activity is rampant in and around Tent Cities" and that there is "clear evidence that the local [c]ommunity's concerns are based on facts not fear." It is unclear where these facts are from, given that the data from Tent City host cities show no increase in crime. In addition, an independent investigation by the *Seattle Times* showed the same outcomes. The point of Tent City, other than to provide housing, explains Hunter, is to make citizens come to the conclusion that "once you live next to people who are homeless, you realize they're not that bad."

Two benches face Hunter's office building and the triangular cobblestone park contains another ten benches. All of the seats are inhabited by people who appear to be homeless. Some are young, some are old, some talk to each other, some talk to themselves. One man kicks at pigeons and seagulls. Across the street, people sell the local Real Change *newspaper produced by people who are poor or homeless. On the right of the steel and glass pergola is a memorial to Chief Sealth (Seattle), for whom the city is named. It reads "Chief Seattle: Now the Streets Are Your Home." It rarely goes unnoticed that many of the people who are homeless in the park are American Indians, sitting on benches next to the revered Chief who didn't believe people should own land to the exclusion of others. At various times, tourists walk towards and disappear into a building next to Hunter's to visit Seattle's underground city, the remains of the Great Fire, now buried underneath Pioneer Square.*

Ted Hunter in Pioneer Square—Seattle's Skid Row

ABA © CASEY TRUPIN

Public forums have been aplenty. Tent City attackers and defenders have been vociferous. Proponents face an uphill battle. Attackers, Hunter notes, seem to believe "that people who are homeless will rape your wife and kidnap your daughter." At one public forum, King County Executive Ron Sims spoke of the value of Tent City and of the value of people who are homeless. The County Executive has been open about the 8,000 people homeless in his county on any given night, almost half of whom cannot find any shelter. He laments that "[D]espite the more than $24 million King County spends annually to assist the homeless, there are not enough shelter beds or affordable housing for everyone." He sees Tent City as a step towards a permanent solution, commenting that "[E]mergency situations demand emergency actions." This type of talk does not always go over well at public forums, and at this forum, Sims was met with a chorus of boos. Public forums, Hunter says, are not enough. They are chaotic and do not allow you to use the "grip of law." "Legal forums are necessary," he urges. "They allow you to transform a forum from chaotic to one that brings some order to the chaos of human life and to how people perceive people who are homeless."

Legal arguments advanced by the churches and synagogues that host Tent City have centered around the First Amendment rights of the places of worship as well as the general civil rights of the residents. They are beginning to win, not just in court, but in public debate as well. Hunter, who has seen the law from both sides of the bench, explains that "Law might be an avenue to address prejudice." His theory bears out in some public letters. One family recently wrote to urge consideration of the rights of the homeless in Tent City zoning decisions: "We are on a new frontier of civil rights… Isn't it abhorrent to assume that the poor are ignorant, prurient or felonious?"

In 2004, Hunter and SHARE/WHEEL faced another huge challenge. The suburb of Bothell sought to evict Tent City from the grounds of its host, a local Catholic church. The city argued that Tent City was an illegal encampment and sought an injunction barring it from the church grounds. But Hunter and his client prevailed in court, showing that the city failed to prove that the city's zoning laws and duty to protect the welfare of residents outweighed the church's right to exercise its religion by providing shelter to the homeless.

Now, locals are increasingly excited about Tent City. Residents are met with offers of help and curiosity, not fear. A suburban couple wrote their councilmember earlier this year, describing their experience with Tent City as "incredible." They shared meals with the residents and worked together to decorate the church for Christmas. They lauded the occupants after "seeing their patience and endurance as they take the bus to work, attend their camp meetings, do their patrols and work together in this opportunity to transition into the larger community." As for Hunter's concern about the deep prejudice regarding communities of people who are homeless, the couple responded, "We have been blessed and transformed, having the chance to see what their lives are like, finding the humanity that we share, though we all have different faces and opportunities in life… We would be poorer for not having the experience of Tent City Four in our midst."

Tent City's mission of exposing citizens to homelessness so that they respond with resolve instead of fear seems to be working. However, local governments continue to balk, requiring Hunter and others to broaden their work. "Anyone who tries to attribute homelessness to one cause," he remarks, "is missing the mark."

"Homelessness has as many solutions as it has causes." His excitement is palpable when he speaks of a new tax on the transfer of property that will help fund counties' ten year plans to end homelessness. In the 2005 Legislative session, he helped to design a bill, the *Homelessness Housing and Assistance Act,* which contained a creative approach to funding anti-homelessness initiatives. Counties and cities that develop plans with specific components will benefit from the additional tax. The new law is expected to bring in between 12 and 16 million dollars per year to combat homelessness in Washington State.

Meanwhile, Hunter is bringing in no money from working on these projects. "It can be a real struggle," he admits. "But I'm old school when it comes to work. I grew up in a church system where you tithe 10 percent. I believe that you tithe your time and you tithe your talents." He has the math all worked out. Two-thousand work hours in a year. Ten percent of two-thousand is 200 hours. "Four to five hours a week is really not that much," he reasons. The lost wages don't trouble him. "I own my own business," he explains, which gives him the freedom to do this and also gives him perspective. "Look at the blessings I have. I am blessed to be in a profession that is supported by the community in terms of the rates we charge," rates which he laments can be "outrageous." The money ultimately means little to him. "All of us want to feel like we're making a difference in real peoples' lives. With this work, I feel that way."

Fear of the unknown has a long history here. In 1948, Yesler Way was the northern edge of an area known for jazz and frequented by people of color, and thus, officially off limits to servicemen housed nearby. Skid Row had adopted a new personality — a color line. These days, outside Hunter's office building, it isn't uncommon to hear people bemoaning the effect the "bums" have had on the street. Fear of the unknown is rampant. People are too focused on this to see the plaque memorializing the young man who died in the doorway of Hunter's building while trying to save a woman from people rioting over a Fat Tuesday celebration. They are too focused to notice the beautiful pergola across the street that had to be rebuilt twice, once in 1973 and once in 2002 when it was pulled down by a semi. Hunter notices the people that others call "bums," but has a different response. He under-

stands the fear, having had to confront it when he thought about the people who slept near his home in Seattle's Woodland Park. "Would I want people sleeping in tents there?" he asked himself. He is sure that he wouldn't, but also knows that "People are *sleeping there. And frankly, I'd rather have them sleeping in tents than out in the cold."*

Hunter and his colleagues won't run out of work anytime soon. Even now, the attacks keep coming. Other lawyers have joined in the fight. Big firms have represented the churches and synagogues, missions have hired attorneys to help, and the local bar's young lawyers group has spearheaded a task force to help as well. This year, he and his clients had to keep close watch on a bill that would set minimum housing standards for all homeless shelters equal to the state requirements for housing migrant agricultural workers. The bill could have had a drastic effect on tent cities. Frustrated,

ABA © CASEY TRUPIN

Casey Trupin *Staff Attorney*
Columbia Legal Services
101 Yesler Way, Ste 300 Seattle, WA 98104
206.287.9665 Casey.Trupin@ColumbiaLegal.org

Casey Trupin is an attorney at Columbia Legal Services in Seattle, where he advocates for at-risk, homeless and foster youth as well as homeless adults. In 1997, Trupin co-founded Street Youth Legal Advocates of Washington (SYLAW) and went on to direct the program until 2005. He is also a member of the ABA's Commission on Homelessness and Poverty. Trupin has worked extensively with, lectured on, and written about troubled youth. In 1995-1996, he conducted a year-long study of resources for homeless youth throughout Latin America as a Thomas J. Watson Fellow. Trupin graduated with honors from the University of Washington School of Law in 1999 and was inducted into the school's Public Interest Law Association Hall of Fame in 2006. In 2005, Trupin was nominated by Senator Maria Cantwell and recognized by the Congressional Commission on Adoption Institute as an Angel in Adoption for his work on behalf of homeless and foster youth.

Hunter was fearful that "all this bill is going to do is put more people on the street." In all likelihood, the "street" he is referring to will be the one that runs in front of his office. Through his work, perhaps one day it will once again be known only as "Yesler Way" because its historical name will no longer fit. And some days, he sees signs that this may, indeed, happen. Hunter occasionally runs into people he has seen previously living on or near Skid Row. They approach him and tell him things have changed. While they are still technically homeless, they say "I got a home now." They are quick to clarify: "I now got a home at Tent City."

Breaking the Cycle of Poverty:

Providing Pro Bono Legal Services in the U.S. and Abroad

Patricia Julianelle

In the spring of 2004, I left my position at the National Law Center on Homelessness & Poverty (NLCHP) to take a sabbatical in Chile. I hoped to learn Spanish, experience Chilean culture, and have some fun. After 12 years of working with juvenile offenders, foster children, students with special needs, prisoners, and children in homeless situations, it seemed like a good time to rest and refuel.

However, like many attorneys, I found resting and refueling to be somewhat tedious. I missed the intellectual challenges of my work. Yet, it was the emotional draw that ultimately made a sabbatical impossible for me. To put it simply, it was fairly unsatisfying to rest and refuel while children and youth were living in cars, tents, bus stations, motels, and shelters.

To respond to this malaise, I decided to restructure my year off; I would keep working, only now I would do it for free. Only a public interest lawyer could devise such a perverse sabbatical. Telecommuting from Chile, I enlisted myself as the pro bono counsel of the National Association for the Education of Homeless Children and Youth (NAEHCY), headquartered in Minnesota. NAEHCY is the only organization of educators dedicated to supporting the school enrollment and success of children and youth experiencing homelessness. Its members are actually ending homelessness and breaking the cycle of poverty, one student at a time. I had collaborated with NAEHCY for four years prior to moving to Chile, and joining its fledgling staff of one as pro bono counsel was a natural fit.

As NAEHCY's Latin American legal affiliate, I drafted language for statutes and regulations, helped implement our legislative strategy, and provided technical assistance to service providers, legal services attorneys, and schools. NAEHCY's staff and members were highly effective as lobbyists and educators, yet lacked a lawyer's skills and perspective. I rounded out our team, which also collaborated with NLCHP, local legal services groups, foster care and disability advocates, and law firms. Our collaborative effort won important legislative victories in 2004 and 2005, including: increased funding to support homeless students; advances in increasing public housing services for homeless families and children; new protections for homeless students with disabilities in the *Individuals with Disabilities Education Act* (IDEA) and its implementing regulations; increased requirements for collaboration between schools and programs for runaway youth; a strong beginning to the reauthorization of the *Head Start Act* and the *Higher Education Act*; and the defeat of efforts to waive the education rights of homeless students following Hurricane Katrina.

In addition to supporting NAEHCY in the United States, I have been able to put my skills to use in Chile as well. Through a contact

You can make a difference!

Attorneys across the country have worked in their communities to raise awareness and advocate on behalf of children, youth, and families experiencing homelessness. Whether forming a project dedicated to homelessness, incorporating advocacy into existing projects, or simply serving as a resource, these attorneys are working to end homelessness in their communities.

with a Jesuit priest, I found myself in one of Santiago's roughest neighborhoods at midnight, participating in a Catholic mass for men and women living on the street. It was a profoundly moving experience that led to my collaboration with Hogar de Cristo, the largest (of the very few) homeless services providers in Chile.

The main cause of homelessness in Chile is the same as that in the U.S.: poverty. Low-income jobs, where available, don't pay enough to afford housing. The contributing factors are also the same: injury or illness can result in unemployment and loss of housing; substance abuse and mental illness contribute to the homelessness of some adult men and women; and domestic violence leaves many women and children without adequate incomes to house themselves. Family culture in Chile is such that extended relatives will often share housing, which helps limit the number of people forced to live on the street.

How to get started...

For ideas about pro bono needs in your community and to get involved in supporting children and families experiencing homeless, contact:

- Your school district's homeless education liaison (contact information is available from the district office or the National Center for Homeless Education, (800) 308-2145);
- Your local homeless coalition (a listing of coalitions is available at **www.nationalhomeless.org/resources/state/index.html**);
- NAEHCY (**www.naehcy.org** or (763) 545-0064);
- The Le Tendre College Scholarship Fund for homeless youth (**www.naehcy.org/about_letendre.html**);
- Local shelters, runaway youth programs, or legal services programs; or
- The National Law Center on Homelessness & Poverty, (202) 638-2535.

It is a very exciting moment in homeless advocacy in Chile. For many years, Hogar de Cristo was the only organization that worked with people in homeless situations, and its philosophy of charity concentrated on providing food and basic shelter, without addressing the causes of homelessness. Recently, a change in administration at Hogar de Cristo has revolutionized this approach. Hogar de Cristo now leads a coalition of agencies that emphasizes the humanity of *gente en situación de calle*: people in homeless situations. The coalition has won some legislative victories, including eliminating barriers to social services for people in homeless situations and working with the government to conduct Chile's first census of homelessness.

Recently, the coalition has begun concentrating on children and youth experiencing homelessness. I have been able to provide technical assistance based on my experiences in the United States. For example, I have provided advice on legislative strategy and outreach to the legal community, model programs for youth, and best practices for education. I supported Hogar de Cristo's efforts to derail a government plan to establish separate schools for youth experiencing homelessness. I spoke on legal strategies to end homelessness, legislative initiatives, and model programs at Chile's first *Seminario de la Situación de Calle.* When NLCHP's Executive Director Maria Foscarinis came to Chile on vacation, she volunteered to share her wisdom as well; we co-presented at a conference organized especially for us by Hogar de Cristo.

One of the most important aspects of my work with Hogar de Cristo has been respecting their priorities and the culture within

Homelessness in Chile

Roughly 15 million people live in Chile, with almost half concentrated in and around the capital, Santiago. No one knows how many are homeless; the first ever census of homeless people in Chile was recently completed, but the results are not yet tabulated. Hogar de Cristo serves 1,000 people daily in its homeless programs.

which we are working. My previous advocacy prepared me well for this, as I have always found that successful local advocacy requires approaching the community humbly, listening attentively, and being willing to follow the lead of local organizers. Using this approach in Chile has allowed me to support their efforts, while creating an environment where my opinions and priorities are also respected.

My efforts with Hogar de Cristo require very little time and energy, but are extremely valuable for the coalition. In fact, I have often found that simply sharing our knowledge is an easy, yet important, way for lawyers to help end homelessness. It can also be deeply fulfilling.

In addition to the opportunity to support NAEHCY and homeless advocacy groups in Chile, my "sabbatical" has led to a new kind of public service work. I recently started and am now the Executive Director of a new nonprofit organization. Again, my free time is to blame. When I finally put my foot down and took off an entire month last year, I traveled to Torres del Paine, Chile's most famous national park. I was struck by the awesome splendor of the park, but also by the fact that among the thousands of tourists I saw, only eight were Chilean. In Chile, as in most of the world, people with limited incomes seldom have the opportunity to visit their country's most beautiful treasures.

Pro Bono Advocacy Abroad

Even in a country where a U.S. bar membership is nearly worthless, there are ways to support the fight against homelessness and poverty. The mere fact of being from the U.S. carries a certain amount of weight and privilege that can lend strength to local advocacy efforts. Consider:

- Legislative advocacy;
- Sharing the U.S. experience;
- Technical assistance on model programs and best practices;
- Assistance with press outreach; and
- Financial support.

After a day of trekking in the park, I sprawled out in my tent and wrote, in a fit of inspiration, what has become the strategic plan of a new nonprofit organization, *Escalando Futuros*. *Escalando Futuros* will collaborate with a group of students from a struggling public school in Santiago to develop the strengths and resources they need to achieve their professional goals. The program takes a comprehensive approach to ending the cycle of poverty for these young people through academic support, English classes, preparation for the college entrance exam, conflict resolution and emotional development activities, and social services and basic needs assistance for their families. Each year, from 6th grade to high school graduation, we will also take two outdoor excursions to national parks.

Before beginning *Escalando Futuros*, I visited public schools in Santiago and talked to many teachers, administrators, psychologists, and low-income parents and young people. Again, I did not want to impose my goals and values on the local community, where they might be inappropriate or unwelcome. Together with a Chilean board of directors, we have started raising money, developing our program, and publicizing our views on public education reform in Chile's main daily newspaper. It is an exciting, challenging, and engaging new adventure.

> Starting a nonprofit is not for everyone, but there are many ways to support nonprofit organizations whose work you admire. As corporations, nonprofits need legal assistance with many issues, including labor, taxes, real property, contracts, and others. Your pro bono legal assistance allows them to dedicate more resources to programs and services. Financial donations are also always needed. You can even help fight poverty and support public education in Chile through a donation to Escalando Futuros. Visit **www.escalandofuturos.com**.

I have been fortunate to find many interesting, exciting, and fulfilling opportunities for pro bono activities in the U.S. and Chile. The fact that those opportunities ultimately have led to a new career in nonprofit management has been an unexpected gift. However, similar opportunities exist in every community. Your skills and resources can help fight poverty and homelessness in the U.S. and abroad: litigation and representing individual clients; providing legislative support; technical assistance; sharing research capacities; financial contributions; press research; and building coalitions are a few ideas. Together with the rest of the ABA Commission on Homelessness & Poverty, I invite you to find and enjoy the pro bono work that best suits you.

Patricia Julianelle *Pro Bono Counsel*
National Association for the Education of Homeless Children and Youth (NAEHCY)
P.O. Box 26274 Minneapolis, MN 55426
pjulianelle@naehcy.org

Patricia Julianelle is the pro bono counsel for the National Association for the Education of Homeless Children and Youth and a former staff attorney at the National Law Center on Homelessness & Poverty in Washington, DC. She advises educators across the country on the rights of children and youth experiencing homelessness and works to enforce those rights through direct advocacy, education and outreach, and legislative advocacy. She has written articles for the *Children's Legal Rights Journal, Journal of Negro Education,* and *Clearinghouse Review* and has co-authored two books. Patricia's work includes partnerships with the U.S. Department of Education, the National Center on Homeless Education, and other national groups. Currently, she is starting a nonprofit education organization in Santiago, Chile.

Finding A Way:

A Firm Lawyer Changes Careers and Creates a Law Center Dedicated to Ending Homelessness

Maria Foscarinis

Introduction

When I first got involved in legal advocacy on homelessness, the explosion that has since become modern day, 21st century American homelessness had just begun. This was in the early 1980s, and the country was witnessing a profound change in the nature and scope of homelessness. What had been a problem affecting primarily single, white men on the skid rows of large cities was fast beginning to affect families and children, racial and ethnic minorities, and residents of suburban and rural areas. Fueled by rising housing costs, stagnant or falling wages, and cuts to social welfare programs—including health and mental health care, welfare, food stamps, and, most of all, low-income housing programs—homelessness was becoming the face of the most extreme form of American poverty.

At the time, I was a young lawyer in the litigation department at Sullivan & Cromwell in New York, focusing on securities and other commercial litigation. I had gone to law school with the fairly amorphous goal of using the law to work for justice—to make an impact on the world. After completing law school at Columbia and a federal clerkship, I arrived at the law firm hoping to learn how to be a lawyer and vowing to seek out pro bono work as a way of eventually transitioning to a public interest career. My plan worked.

I got involved as a pro bono lawyer for a class of homeless families challenging the denial of emergency shelter by Nassau County and New York State in a case brought initially by advocacy groups and nonprofits, such as the Coalition for the Homeless. Going out to Long Island, a wealthy suburb of New York City, to visit class members and seeing their destitution and almost complete lack of resources was my first glimpse into the difference that I as a lawyer could make. Going back to my office and corporate clients—and the overabundance of resources devoted to their needs—brought home the difference that legal advocacy could make for those whose voices and needs would otherwise be unrepresented and, indeed, unheard.

My firm supported my pro bono work, and I also continued my full load of regular clients. I very much appreciated the training and opportunity the firm gave me; I maintain my relationship with friends there and the firm itself to this day. But after working on the case (successfully) for about two years, I had an opportunity to pursue my original plan to become a public interest lawyer, and I took it.

I moved to Washington, DC to lead an advocacy campaign to get the federal government to respond to homelessness, working with the national offshoot of the groups I'd been working with in New York. I established an office in DC for the National Coalition for the Homeless, putting my fine legal skills to work as I rented office space, bought a telephone, and taught myself to use a word processor. I went from having every conceivable form of assistance to being completely on my own. At the time, there was virtually no federal response to homelessness: in fact, the official Administration position was that homelessness was not an issue for the federal government. Rather, it was a matter for private charity or, at most, for local government.

Thus, I launched my career as a do-it-yourself lawyer, as I sometimes call it. While law library research gave me a few leads and led to a couple of lawsuits, there was no surplus of federal statutory authority on the rights of homeless people. Legislative advocacy was clearly critical, as was following up legislative success with outreach to inform intended beneficiaries (whether homeless people, providers, or both) of their new rights, close monitoring in collaboration with local groups, and, when necessary, litigation to enforce those rights.

In 1989, I founded the National Law Center on Homelessness & Poverty (NLCHP), a not-for-profit organization dedicated to ending and preventing homelessness in America (see article in Chapter 5).

Advocacy for a National Response: Federal Legislation

By the early to mid-1980s, homelessness was clearly a national crisis. But the Administration then in office initially denied that homelessness was a national concern— or even an appropriate concern for government. Rather, according to President Reagan, homeless people were so "by choice" (*Boston Globe* 1984). Funds for emergency food and shelter through the federal disaster relief program were appropriated for homeless persons on an ad hoc basis beginning in 1983, but no permanent legislation had been authorized (Foscarinis 1993, 1994). In this context, legal advocacy began to focus on eliciting a national response.

This was my mission when I arrived in DC in late 1985, and I developed a two-part legal strategy: litigation to enforce existing federal laws and force the federal agencies to action, and legislative advocacy to spur Congress to action and help make new laws. On the legislative end, I worked with a coalition of legal service lawyers and groups (including the Mental Health Law Project, the National Housing Law Project, and the Center for Law and Education) that had developed proposed legislative remedies to problems their field staff saw repeatedly in serving their homeless clients. From these proposals, we organized a legislative agenda, and I took on the task of lobbying for it, with pro bono legislative support from a large firm and a large coalition of national and local level supporters.

Efforts to secure sponsors to introduce and champion the legislation in the US Congress initially met with steep barriers. Nevertheless, in October 1986, part of this proposed legislation was enacted as the *Homeless Eligibility Clarification Act*. This new law provided that homeless people could receive benefits under a series of federal programs, including Supplemental Security Income (SSI), Medicaid, Aid to Families with Dependent Children, and food stamps, without having to supply an address.[1] It also established a pre-release program to allow persons confined in institutions such as mental hospitals and prisons to apply for food stamps and SSI benefits, in order to prevent their becoming homeless upon release. Also enacted in 1986 was the *Homeless Housing Act*—legislation creating and funding two small 'demonstration' programs to fund emergency shelter ($10 million) and transitional housing ($5 million).

Then in 1987, following a concerted campaign involving a broad coalition and including multiple strategies (such as community organizing and public protests) in addition to legislative advocacy, another, larger part of our proposal became law. On July 22, 1987, part one of our proposal became the first, and still only, major federal legislation addressing homelessness: the *Stewart B. McKinney Homeless Assistance Act*, now known as the McKinney-Vento Act, 42 U.S.C. Secs. 11301-11472. As then enacted, the legislation primarily provided federal funding for shelter, transitional housing, and permanent supportive housing, and it also established certain legal rights including rights of homeless children to education and rights of providers of services to homeless people to priority in applying to use certain vacant federal properties at no cost.

Our coalition was diverse. My primary colleague in the legislative advocacy was Mitch Snyder, a controversial figure well-known at the time for his attention getting tactics, which included civil disobedience, hunger strikes, and sleep outs. Michael Stoops, then a Portland Oregon advocate, sometimes joined us, as did Rod

1 *It did not, however, ensure that they could* apply *without an address; that requirement, originally part of the legislation, was removed from the final bill.*

DeArment, a partner at Covington & Burling, a major Washington law firm (Rod had also been a member of Republican Administrations). We were an odd group: Mitch was living on a heat grate outside the Capitol that winter as a protest in support of our legislation; he was often joined there by Michael Stoops. When we went on lobbying visits together, Mitch was in a battered Army jacket, unkempt, looking like a homeless person, and I was in my lawyer's suit looking like, well, a lawyer. (When he joined us, Rod sometimes made a point of noting that he was with me, an observation Mitch did not appreciate.) But we were all saying the same thing, and I believe that the diversity in our group strengthened us and made us more effective.

Our coalition also included the American Bar Association, a partnership that sometimes caused surprise on the Hill, but one that added weight to our cause. Along with the ABA and Arlene Kantor at the Mental Health Law Project (now the Judge David L. Bazelon Center for Mental Health Law), I worked on draft ABA policy on homelessness. The ABA House of Delegates adopted the policy in August 1986, authorizing the ABA to lobby on legislation to address homelessness and leading to the creation of the Representation of the Homeless Project, which later became the Commission on Homelessness & Poverty.

Advocacy for a National Response: Federal Litigation

Federal litigation proceeded parallel to this legislative advocacy. In DC, I spent time in the law library looking through the statute books. Eventually this laborious process paid off, and we brought a federal court action against the Department of Defense (DoD), with pro bono support from a large Washington firm and a smaller firm and in collaboration with service providers and homeless people. The court ordered DoD to issue regulations implementing an obscure federal program to make surplus defense department properties available to service providers to use to aid homeless people

(*Bruce v. DoD*, No. 87-0425 (D.D.C. June 17, 1987)). This case established an important precedent: the plaintiffs—a homeless person in need of shelter, a shelter provider without sufficient space to meet demand, and a national advocacy organization—were able to demonstrate a causal connection between the defendants' failure to implement the program and the situation of the plaintiffs that was sufficient to establish standing to sue to enforce the program. This early victory also focused the attention of a major federal agency on homelessness as a national and federal concern.[2]

After the McKinney Act passed, we worked with service providers and advocates across the country to monitor implementation of the new law. When we discovered non-compliance, we filed several quick suits (with significant pro bono support) to require the federal agencies to disburse funds according to the urgent timetable established by Congress. Subsequently, we brought additional, more complex suits to implement the new law, beginning a long process of litigation, legislative change, and more litigation. In 1988, together with grass roots advocates and pro bono law firm support, we brought a suit to enforce compliance with Title V, the Federal Surplus Property Program. The suit resulted in a permanent injunction against five federal agencies, requiring them to make available free of charge "suitable" real property, by deed or lease, to providers of services for homeless people. To date, several enforcement motions have been filed successfully against the federal agencies to enforce the order (*National Law Center on Homelessness and Poverty v. Veterans' Association*).

Fighting the Criminalization of Homelessness

Beginning in the early 1990s, my colleagues at NLCHP and I noticed an increase in the number of calls and requests for help from local level advocates about city efforts to criminalize homelessness. In a trend that rapidly gathered steam in the 1990s, cities were begin-

2 *The underlying law was subsequently superseded by the passage of much stronger provisions in Title V of the* McKinney Act, *discussed below.*

ning to increasingly enact laws that punished homeless people living in public spaces. Ironically, at the same time many of these local governments also cut back on homeless people's rights and benefits, including those involving shelter and other rights obtained earlier. In response, in 1991 NLCHP produced our first national report documenting the trend in the law and marshalling policy arguments against that kind of city policy. As the trend continued and grew, so did our reports. Since 1991, we have published nine increasingly comprehensive reports, first alone and later sometimes in collaboration with the National Coalition for the Homeless. On a parallel track, we also developed a program at NLCHP to fight such laws through policy and litigation, typically working with pro bono law firm lawyers to support local advocates who would call us for help.

But as the trend continued, it seemed to me that we had to do more than just fight it. I have always felt very strongly that the issues raised by the criminalization of homelessness go beyond civil liberties and rights: We are not arguing for a right to sleep on the street or live in public places. Fundamentally, we are arguing for a right to be somewhere inside—to have a home. We are arguing for the human right to housing.

So we began focusing on what we call "constructive alternatives" to the criminalization of homelessness. Acknowledging that we, like cities, do not think that people should be living in public, we proposed solutions that would help create alternatives to the streets. Essentially, we tried to put a proactive, positive frame around the issue, instead of a reactive, negative one. So far, we've had some success with this approach. At the same time, however, I felt that we had to be prepared to fight in court when this approach did not work. So we continued our litigation work, often in partnership with other organizations and pro bono lawyers.

Advocating for Relief Beyond Shelter

A similar concern led me to focus our national policy work on long-term solutions to homelessness. From the beginning of my work on homelessness, I (like many advocates) understood that shelter was only a short-term solution. True solutions to homelessness had to include permanent housing as well as adequate income, and access to health care and other social services, as well as civil rights safeguards. In short, systemic reform, not just emergency crisis response, was needed.

As a result, we began to engage in advocacy efforts, in concert with others, to amend federal law in the direction of longer-term solutions. For example, we worked to amend the emergency shelter grants program (under the McKinney Act) to allow funds to be used for homelessness prevention. The McKinney-Vento education program was amended to help give parents of homeless children and youth a voice regarding their children's school placement and to require educational authorities to coordinate with housing authorities. Outreach materials widely disseminated by national advocacy organizations coupled with follow-up assistance helped local level groups understand and implement the law for their clients. These groups also helped NLCHP and other legal advocates monitor compliance with and, when necessary, litigate to enforce the law.

Like other advocates, I saw addressing the needs of children, who make up some 25% of the homeless population, as being critically important. Helping to stabilize homeless children not only alleviates their immediate suffering, but also helps prevent them from growing up to become homeless adults. I was lucky to serve on the ABA's Steering Committee on the Unmet Legal Needs of Children, a group that drew attention to the needs of poor children or homeless children and the McKinney-Vento education program. In 2002, the ABA Commission on Homelessness & Poverty published "Educating Children without Housing: A Primer on Legal Requirements and Implementation Strategies for Educators, Advocates and Policymakers." Publications, although not a traditional legal tool, can be a powerful complement to litigation and legislation.

My career has also taught me the importance of ongoing vigilance. Some issues continually resurface again and again. The case and issues at the beginning of my advocacy career in Long Island's Nassau County recently gave rise to yet another lawsuit some twenty years later, this time in neighboring Suffolk County. To help ensure access to school and school services for homeless children in the County, NLCHP filed a lawsuit against the school district, the County, and the State, seeking to enforce the education provisions of the McKinney-Vento Act. As usual, this was done in conjunction with local legal services and a team of lawyers and paralegals in Goodwin Procter's New York office that was led by partner Jeffrey Simes (see related article in Chapter 3). Following a favorable court ruling, an important consent decree benefiting homeless children has now been finalized. We are still continuing our work in New York, though, to ensure compliance with the order. Constant monitoring of how communities respond to homelessness is critical, as attitudes and elected leaders change.

Current Trends and Work by Lawyers

Over the years, I have become convinced that the law is a critical tool not only in addressing homelessness, but also in preventing it. Because I see homelessness as an extreme form of poverty, I believe that marshalling the resources of anti-poverty programs—not just programs aimed specifically at homelessness—must be part of the solution. In the past few years, NLCHP has increased its focus on legislation beyond the confines of the McKinney-Vento Act. For example, advocacy in 2004 by NLCHP and allied groups successfully pressed for amendments to the federal laws governing special education to address the special needs of homeless children; successful work on implementing regulations followed in 2005. Currently, as a result of work by NLCHP and allied groups, amendments to include homeless children in mainstream early childhood programs are pending. In a similar vein, legal advocacy for access to mainstream programs has also focused on disability benefits

"Over the years, I have become convinced that the law is a critical tool not only in addressing homelessness, but also in preventing it." **Maria Foscarinis**

under the Social Security Act, for which many homeless people are eligible; because of the difficulty of the application process, few actually receive them.

At the local level, a number of states and localities have adopted plans to end and prevent homelessness. Although these plans vary greatly in specificity and thus quality, I think they are an important advocacy opportunity. As lawyers, we can help put legal teeth into the plans, making them more meaningful. To help do this, NLCHP has published a guide called "Adding Legal Teeth to Plans to End Homelessness." At the same time, however, many cities continue to enact laws and pursue practices that criminalize homelessness, and litigation to challenge them is also ongoing. An initiative to involve courts and judges in helping homeless people unfairly affected by such laws was initiated by San Diego Public Defender Steve Binder, currently Chair of the ABA Commission on Homelessness & Poverty. Most recently, lawyers have worked in a range of ways to respond to the dramatic increases in homelessness resulting from hurricanes Katrina and Rita; this work includes a class action suit brought by NLCHP and others. These efforts have helped to remind me of the large numbers of attorneys creatively working to address homelessness, but they have also highlighted the effect that we, as lawyers, could have if more of us worked in this area.

These initiatives are important and make a real difference in the lives of the people they touch. Yet I feel that we also need—at the same time—something more. We need to say, clearly and directly, that homelessness and poverty have no place in the richest country on earth. And as lawyers, we need to marshal the tools that can help us move towards a vision of a world without such brutal injustice. This is why I have recently begun working on using human rights law and strategy as an additional tool to supplement our other strategies. Unlike purely domestic law, human rights law recognizes housing as a basic human right and outlines strategies for implementing this right over time. Our work at NLCHP is providing leadership to advocates interested in adding human rights law to their strategies. We are also part of a small but growing movement of legal and other advocates who believe that human rights apply not just elsewhere, but here at home as well.

Conclusion

Lawyers, legal advocacy organizations, law firms, and the organized bar have played a leadership role in efforts to end modern American homelessness. The legal profession as a whole can be proud of the talent, energy and commitment that we, as lawyers, have demonstrated in putting our skills to work on behalf of the poorest members of our society and, indeed, on behalf of the good of all of us. Clearly, we still have a long way to go. I feel incredibly privileged to have the opportunity to use my legal career to make a

ABA © NLCHP

Maria Foscarinis *Executive Director*
National Law Center on Homelessness & Poverty
1411 K Street, NW Washington, DC 20005
202.638.2535 mfoscarinis@nlchp.org

Maria Foscarinis is founder and executive director of the National Law Center on Homelessness & Poverty, a not-for-profit organization established in 1989 as the legal arm of the nationwide effort to end homelessness. Ms. Foscarinis has advocated for solutions to homelessness and poverty at the national level since 1985. She is a primary architect of the *Stewart B. McKinney Homeless Assistance Act,* the first major federal legislation addressing homelessness, and she has litigated to secure the legal rights of homeless and poor persons. Ms. Foscarinis writes regularly about legal and policy issues affecting homeless and poor persons, and her work has appeared in legal journals, general audience publications, and books. Ms. Foscarinis is a 1977 graduate of Barnard College and 1981 graduate of Columbia Law School, where she was an editor of the Law Review; she also holds a Masters of Arts degree in Philosophy. After clerking for the Honorable Amalya L. Kearse of the U.S. Court of Appeals for the Second Circuit, she was a litigation associate at Sullivan & Cromwell. In 1985, she led the establishment of the Washington office of the National Coalition for the Homeless until she founded the National Law Center on Homelessness & Poverty.

difference in the lives of homeless and poor Americans. But sometimes I also despair at the need that is still unmet. My journey, to date, has challenged me to celebrate victories, without forgetting the work that still remains; to face setbacks head on, without losing hope; to persevere in a vision of a more just world despite continuing injustices. More than anything, the growing number of attorneys and other advocates working to end homelessness and poverty gives me hope. As lawyers, we must continue our vigorous efforts until, after working with our non-lawyer colleagues, we bring an end to the injustice of homelessness. If history is any indication, we are up to the challenge.

Using the Law and Human Rights to Challenge Injustice for People who are Homeless: An Australian Lawyer's Story

Cassandra Goldie

Introduction

It is the best and the worst of times in Australia. The nation enjoys continuing strong economic growth with private wealth accumulation at record levels. Unemployment rates are the lowest they have been in 30 years. John Howard, the Australian Prime Minister, has recently celebrated 10 years in office, and critiques of his leadership highlight economic management as one of his major achievements. According to the UNDP Human Development Index, Australia ranks No. 3 in the world, after Norway and Iceland, and if you walk down the inner city streets of Sydney or Melbourne, you will probably nod your head in agreement. It all looks pretty good.

Yet, the number of people who are homeless in Australia continues to be at unacceptable levels.[1] The gap between the rich and poor grows. Services for people who are in poverty and homeless strug-

1 *As at the last Australian Census in 2001, the number of people experiencing homelessness was 99,900. See Chris Chamberlain and David MacKenzie, "Counting the Homeless 2001" (ABS Catalogue No 2050.0, Australian Bureau of Statistics, 2003).*

gle for funding, and overall community sector funding deficits continue to rise. Legal Aid federal funding has been cut, and policies have been implemented that reduce the ability of the statutory legal aid bodies in Australia to undertake public interest test cases and to engage with coalitions and social movements to promote social justice and human rights.

Perhaps as a result of these opposing trends, there has been a growing interest in the use of a rights-based approach to homelessness in Australia both in legal and non-legal settings, including the use of international human rights tools.

My own experience is one illustration.

A Personal Note

For almost five years, from 1992 until 1997, I worked as a manager and legal practitioner with Legal Aid Western Australia, the state-based independent statutory authority with primary responsibility for delivery of legal aid services in that state. It was during this time that I first became involved in advocacy efforts to promote the fundamental human right to adequate housing.

Between 1994 and 1995, the Western Australian public housing authority, Homeswest, increased the serving of Termination Notices on public housing tenants from a monthly rate of 221 tenants to 929 tenants, representing a 320% increase in eviction rates in just 12 months. There was clearly a crisis, and the legal aid and community sector groups were endeavoring to respond. Legal Aid had traditionally provided very limited legal assistance to people facing eviction, yet the demand for help intensified as a result of these changes in public housing policy and practice.

Homeswest had developed a practice of using "no cause" eviction notices under Section 64 of the *Residential Tenancies Act 1987* (WA) to terminate tenancies. Section 64 provides that a landlord may terminate a tenancy using a 60 day eviction notice without providing any reasons for the termination. Homeswest did not need to prove any breach of the tenancy agreement to obtain an eviction order. Section 64 was being used when there were allegations of "anti-social behavior" against the tenant but neighbours did not wish to give evidence. Homeswest was not providing families with procedural fairness to respond to specific allegations. In some cases, Homeswest was using Section 64 to evict families who were in intense housing need, sometimes with babies and small children, to appease neighborhood complaints. Anecdotal evidence suggested that Indigenous families were being targeted and that direct or indirect racism was a significant factor. There were no procedures to ensure that evicted families would not become homeless following their eviction. It was clear to me that the Western Australian government policies and practices were operating in violation of international human rights standards, including the right to adequate housing and the prohibition against forced evictions.

In collaboration with a large number of civil society groups, I participated in the formation of the Anti-Section 64 Coalition to advocate for the cessation of no-cause evictions in public housing tenancies. The Coalition consisted of Legal Aid, the Aboriginal Legal Service, and community legal centres, together with church groups and other community welfare groups. Through the Coalition, Legal Aid became involved in providing community education and training to community workers about ways to challenge eviction notices. We met with Homeswest public officials, the State and Commonwealth Ministers responsible for housing policy, the Western Australian Equal Opportunity Commissioner, and the Federal Human Rights and Equal Opportunity Commissioner. Media advocacy was undertaken. I delivered a paper on the ways in which the Western Australian government was acting in violation of Australia's international human rights obligations, and we facilitated tenants to make Legal Aid applications for legal representation to challenge their evictions. A number of test cases were commenced. Legal Aid also documented individual eviction case studies to form the basis of a submission to the Equal Opportunity Commission or the Human Rights and Equal Opportunity Commission. At the peak of Legal Aid's involvement in the Coalition, a number of positive developments had been achieved. Homeswest had retreated from using Section 64 to evict tenants, and both State and Federal

Ministers had committed funds and resources to establish an Evictions Project. The purpose of the Evictions Project was to develop recommendations about appropriate early intervention strategies and alternative actions to reduce eviction proceedings against public housing tenants.

I do not recall the specific event that led to the call from the Minister, but it came. I was told that the Minister for Housing had contacted the Chairperson of Legal Aid Western Australia and questioned the use of legal aid funds for these activities. I was advised that I was to discontinue my membership and involvement in the Anti-Section 64 Coalition and the Director of Legal Aid was to provide the Legal Aid Board of Commissioners with a report about the number of eviction cases involving public housing tenants that were being funded at that time. Legal Aid went on the public record expressing reservation about the appropriateness of Legal Aid staff participating in public lobbying activities, such as the Anti-Section 64 Coalition, or being involved in "expensive" test cases.

> *It is at least questionable whether the expenditure of the Commission's resources (i.e. its salaried staff) in assisting the work of the [Anti-Section 64] Coalition is an activity coming within the statutory description of the Commission's duties and responsibilities...However, that question aside the real issue is whether the Commission can afford to expend its resources in this way, when there are so many applications for legal assistance from persons who qualify financially for such assistance, unable to be met due to the shortage of funds and resources...The Commission's decision is in no way to be taken as either a lack of sympathy with the aims and objectives of the Coalition, or a decision that it will not provide legal assistance to evicted tenants, judged on a case-by-case basis, on an assessment of the individual case and the financial position of the applicant...*[2]

2 *Letter from Chairperson of Legal Aid to Anti-Section 64 Coalition, 4 March 1997.*

One of the factors in my decision to resign from Legal Aid was the increased political interference by the Government of Western Australia in the activities of Legal Aid and the significant limitations that had been placed by both Federal and State governments on the role of Legal Aid to support important social justice and human rights movements, such as our effective efforts to stem the flood of evictions of public housing tenants.

In 1998, I moved from Legal Aid Western Australia to take up the position of Coordinator and Principal Solicitor of Darwin Community Legal Service (DCLS) in the Northern Territory of Australia. When I was interviewed by the Management Committee for DCLS for the position, it became clear to me that the Committee was strongly supportive of the Centre performing an activist role using law and human rights tools and expected that I would support and lead that role with the staff and volunteers. It was this commitment that swayed me to accept the position, and I moved some 3500 km north to the tropical lands of the Northern Territory.

I recall well the day that Stella Smith walked into the DCLS office in Darwin, the capital city of the Northern Territory, and I sat with her as she demanded help. Stella is a local non-Indigenous community activist, film-maker, mother, and generally beautiful soul on this planet. She demanded that we had to "do something." Stella had spent many hours sitting with and acting in support of Indigenous families living in the "longgrass" around the urban centre of Darwin. There is a large number of mostly Indigenous people who camp in and around the urban areas. This is a common feature of many rural and remote towns in Australia with high Indigenous populations, as well as the capital cities. Some people, living in public space, have done so for most of their lives. In Darwin, people living in this way have been described as "longgrassers" or "itinerants." In other places, people are described variously as fringe dwellers, parkies, "goomies," and "drones."

Stella shared with me the story of one particular family group, headed by a senior elder, Johnny Balaiya, who had been camping around Darwin for many years. The family group was now being served Trespass Notices and "moved on" to make way for development without any offer of a suitable alternative home. Their history was one of constant eviction, harassment, and persistent inhuman and degrading treatment. Stella had been to a number of legal services without success. I agreed to help, although I was not exactly sure how. In the days, weeks, and months that followed, I came to learn about the daily experiences of the Indigenous family groups who were faced with intense poverty, yet who were constantly harassed and moved on under a range of local council bylaws or policing legislation. I also learned that, whilst many people used alcohol in self-harming ways, they also lived lives of defiance and dignity. For many people, their practice of living in public areas around Darwin was their best attempt to live in the way of their Indigenous culture in the context of ever expanding dispossession through urban development.[3] I also learned that if you lived in public places in Australia, you effectively lived in a "human rights wasteland."

The Darwin City Council uses a local government anti-sleeping by law to ban sleeping in public places between sunset and sunrise. The by law is rigorously enforced either by moving people on or by issuing infringement notices, despite the reality that the Northern Territory has the highest rate of homelessness in the country. The bylaw creates a minor regulatory offence[4] with a small fine of $AU 50 imposed for infringement. The impact of the enforcement of this seemingly trivial offence on the lives of people living in public spaces amounts to daily evictions from peoples' homes, decimation of family networks, constant loss of meager possessions, feelings of outrage, resentment, and resultant perpetuation of exclusion and dispossession. In collaboration with Indigenous communities and non-Indigenous activists, DCLS undertook a wide range of activities in support of the human rights of longgrassers, including commencement of several test cases, media advocacy and public

3 *For detailed research about this way of life, see W. Bartlett Day, Aboriginal Fringe Dwellers in Darwin, Australia: Cultural Persistence or a Culture of Resistance? (PhD Thesis, Department of Anthropology, University of Western Australia, 2001).*

4 *A regulatory offence means that the usual defences to a criminal charge, such as insanity, honest and reasonable mistake or justification or excuse, are not available.*

protests, research, and community education, with the aim of seeking the repeal of laws that criminalize people living in public space and to promote the development of more culturally appropriate models of public housing.

I became passionate about how the law and human rights tools could be used to promote the human rights of people facing homelessness, particularly those who live in public space, which has led to my current PhD research and the establishment of the Homelessness Legal Rights Project at the Gilbert + Tobin Centre of Public Law at the University of New South Wales.[5]

The Bigger Picture: Australian Homelessness Legal Advocacy

Historically, in Australia, there has been a tendency for legal functionaries to see the "problem" of "homelessness" as an area to which law has little to offer. Homelessness has more typically been perceived as a "non-legal" welfare problem, linked to lack of employment, abuse of alcohol, mental health issues, and other individual circumstances, rather than the result of a lack of protection of basic human rights and a legal regime that fails to protect those rights. This attitude is likely due to a range of features of the legal profession and legal frameworks in Australia: a general lack of understanding about international and comparative human rights law; restrictions on the statutory legal aid system, as demonstrated by my own personal legal aid experience; the lack of a bill of rights in Australia; and a legal profession that largely reflects the broader community attitudes towards people who are homeless.

Even in human rights areas of legal practice and advocacy, homelessness has often been seen as an issue confined to economic, social, and cultural rights discourse, in particular the "right to adequate housing" contained in Article 11 of the *International Covenant*

5 *Go to* http://www.gtcentre.unsw.edu.au/projects_partners/projects/hlr/index.asp.

on Economic Social and Cultural Rights.[6] Economic, social, and cultural human rights, including the right to adequate housing, have not been comprehensively incorporated into the domestic legal system of Australia. Accordingly, in Australia, homelessness has been too easily dismissed as a problem not amenable to legal intervention at the domestic level.

Community and welfare groups have also seen the legal system as a tool of oppression of people who are homeless rather than as a tool for change.[7] Accordingly, links between legal functionaries and community activists have not been developed and consolidated. Until recently, there has been relatively limited debate in Australia amongst legal functionaries or community activists about the legal and human rights of people facing homelessness, and how people might pursue those rights to assert greater control and legitimacy, inside and out of the domestic courts and at the international level. There have also been scarce efforts by legal aid services to provide specialist legal assistance and advocacy for people experiencing homelessness.

In 1975, Justice Ronald Sackville delivered his seminal report, *Homeless People and the Law.* Over the years, significant papers and reports have been written, particularly the Human Rights and Equal Opportunity Commission National Inquiry into Homeless Children,[8] and there have been important legal and social campaigns in support of people facing homelessness, such as the *Rent Watchers* campaign leading up to the 2000 Olympics in Sydney and the campaign against loitering offences in Port Kembla. However, most

6 *International Covenant on Economic, Social and Cultural Rights, opened for signature 16 December 1966, 999 UNTS 3 (entered into force 3 January 1973).*

7 *Di Otto, "Rethinking Homelessness" (2004) 17(1) Parity 6, 6: "[T]he language of human rights was not part of the social justice vocabulary of [the 1970s and 1980s]. We spoke of empowerment, self-help, community participation, and holding governments accountable, but without resource to the law to legitimate these claims, or to enforce them. This blindness to the potential of legal strategies to assist social justice goals was attributable to the widely held view that the law worked against the interest of marginalised groups, operating as an instrument of the wealthy to maintain structural disadvantage, rather than providing a means to challenging inequalities."*

8 *Human Rights and Equal Opportunity Commission, "Our Homeless Children: Report of the National Inquiry into Homeless Children" (Canberra: Australian Government Publishing Service, 1989).*

early debates lacked a human rights analysis, and reports and campaigns tended to be localised endeavours without the capacity to launch a broader campaign of community and legal activism to define and secure legal protection of the basic human rights of people facing homelessness.

However, recent events in Australia evidence a seismic shift in this approach with a special historical link to developments in the United States. The rest of this article will share with readers that story.

A Short History of Legal Aid in Australia

Australia now has a well-developed legal aid system, consisting of four major components. Established in the 1970s, statutory legal aid commissions exist in each of the seven States and Territories, jointly funded by the Commonwealth and State and Territory governments, with a total of 75 offices and over 2,000 staff. Legal Aid Commissions are the primary providers of direct legal services to people who are not in a position to pay for legal assistance. Statutory legal aid commissions focus on legal assistance to defend serious criminal charges and assist family law problems, with attenuated civil law services.[9] There are no specialised programmes for people who are homeless.[10]

Secondly, there are now over 200 community legal centres operating around the country. Community legal centres are civil society organisations that are managed by volunteers and receive funding from a wider range of sources whilst relying primarily on Commonwealth funding with supplementary funding from some State and Territory governments. In addition to direct casework, community legal centres also provide, to a greater or lesser extent, legal education and training to the community and are actively involved in policy and advocacy efforts. Centres provide general

9 *For example, in 2004/5, the breakdown of types of cases funded by Legal Aid Western Australia was: criminal law 66%; family law 28%; and civil law 6%. See Legal Aid Western Australia, "Annual Report 2004/5 " (2005).*

10 *The notable exception is Legal Aid Queensland that has recently conducted a six month Homelessness and Street Offences Project, discussed further below.*

and specialist legal services in a wide range of poverty-law areas. Some centres provide specialist services that are important to people facing homelessness, particularly in the area of social security law and tenancy. However, until recently there were no centres specialising in supporting people who are homeless.

Thirdly, the Commonwealth government also provides funding on a tendered basis to specialist Indigenous legal services in each state and territory. These services are also significantly underfunded, with the majority of effort taken up in responding to the inordinately high rates of arrest and imprisonment of Indigenous people in Australia.

Particularly since policy changes have been implemented by the Howard Government, there is significantly less independence and flexibility in the way in which these publicly-funded legal aid services are provided. Under the influence of government policies, legal aid services have limited capacity to address systemic problems faced by homeless people using legal tools such as test cases and public advocacy.

Pro bono legal services are again becoming an increasingly significant fourth component of legal aid service delivery, with private lawyers undertaking controversial public interest cases in areas such as refugee and discrimination law.

Given this legal aid environment, whilst existing legal aid programmes have been providing important legal services to people who are homeless for over 30 years, the need for additional services remains:

> *There is a need to ensure better access to legal advice for homeless clients and a capacity to effectively deal with a wider range of legal issues and problems. This could include challenges to discrimination practices in the private rental market, to rules and administration of Centrelink,[11] to State government housing programs and to unreasonable or discriminatory local government by-laws.*

11 *Centrelink is the federal agency of the Commonwealth Department of Human Services that delivers the social security payments and services in Australia.*

> *Homeless clients and their support workers could be better serviced, and perhaps even grasp the law as a weapon, if the legal profession and homeless agencies put their minds to the development of more flexible and innovative programs for delivery of legal services (footnote added).*[12]

The Development of Specialist Legal Services for People who Are Homeless

In 1999, Caitlin English, who was then the Executive Director of the Public Interest Law Clearinghouse (PILCH) in Melbourne, Victoria, travelled to the United States as part of a Churchill Fellowship to study the delivery of pro bono legal services in public interest cases for people who are poor and marginalised. PILCH was established in 1995 as a clearinghouse for pro bono services, basing itself on innovative models in the US. The English study concluded that "the United States was considerably further advanced in the provision of pro bono services than we were in Australia" and noted "the leadership role of the American Bar Association in developing Bar pro bono schemes throughout the country."[13]

As part of her tour through the US, English visited a number of specialist pro bono programmes for people experiencing homelessness, including Volunteer Lawyers for the Homeless and Public Counsel's Homelessness Prevention Law Project, which provides outreach services to people experiencing homelessness, drawing on summer clerks from the Public Interest Project at UCLA. English also highlighted the work of the National Law Center on Homelessness & Poverty, the "Adopt a Shelter" program in Hollywood and Santa Monica, the Homeless Youth Project in Los Angeles, and the Lawyers Clearinghouse on Affordable Housing and Homelessness in Boston. She urged "Australian

12 *Denis Nelthorpe, "The Law - A Shield or a Sword?" (Paper presented at the Homelessness and the Law Forum, Melbourne, Victoria, 2000).*

13 *Caitlin English, "Churchill Report" (1999), 1.*

lawyers and community advocates seeking to increase the rights and legal services to homeless people [to] benefit from examining further the activities of public interest lawyers in this field in the United States."[14] A key finding from the English study was that "the location of services at the point of contact with homeless or at-risk groups was the most effective way of providing legal services to the homeless."[15]

In response to the findings of the English study, in October 2001 the first Homeless Persons Legal Clinic was established by PILCH in Melbourne, Victoria in partnership with the Council to Homeless Persons, the peak advocacy group for homelessness services and people who are homeless in Victoria. The Clinic commenced as a 52 week project providing legal services at two Clinics based at welfare agencies, supplemented by legal assistance provided by private law firms on a pro bono basis. The Clinic was explicitly "based on similar schemes in the United States which have proved of considerable worth to homeless people in dealing with the civil legal issues which may impact on their ability to access accommodation, employment or social security payments."[16] The Clinic made an important commitment to training legal practitioners and welfare agency staff to increase the success of the integration between the work of agencies and the relevance of the law to supporting people who are homeless.

The Clinic is a highly respected legal service provider as well as a strong and effective advocate for the legal and human rights of people who are homeless. The Clinic provides legal services at seven welfare agencies through weekly clinics staffed by pro bono lawyers from eight law firms. In addition, the Clinic is active in policy and law reform work, with significant impact. The success of the Homeless Persons Legal Clinic in Melbourne, Victoria was the catalyst for similar initiatives in another four of the seven jurisdictions in Australia.

14 *Caitlin English, "Legal Services to Homeless People in the United States" (Paper presented at the Homelessness and the Law Forum, Melbourne, Victoria, 2000)*

15 *Public Interest Law Clearing House and Council to Homeless People (Victoria), "2000/2001 Funding Submission to the Victorian Department of Human Services" (2000), 5.*

16 *Public Interest Law Clearing House and Council to Homeless People (Victoria), "Homelessness and the Law - Towards a Workable Solution" (2000).*

On December 10, 2002, the Queensland Public Interest Law Clearing House (QPILCH) launched the Brisbane-based Homeless Persons' Legal Clinic as a six-month pilot project based on the Melbourne model. The Coordinator and Solicitor for the Clinic was originally a part-time seconded employed solicitor from private law firms.[17] In September 2005, QPILCH was successful in receiving a one-year grant from the Queensland Department of Communities in order to expand its services and employ a full-time solicitor. The Clinic provides pro bono legal help through seven legal clinics operated at a range of welfare and emergency accommodation centres. There are ten participating law firms, and legal assistance is provided in all areas of law (with limited services in criminal and family law matters). The Clinic is also involved in community education, training activities, systemic advocacy, and law reform initiatives, as well as providing ongoing training to participating pro bono solicitors. The Clinic is the first legal service in Queensland that is specifically designed to address the legal needs of homeless people.

In May 2004, the New South Wales Public Interest Advocacy Centre and Public Interest Law Clearinghouse also set up a Homeless Persons Legal Service, based in Sydney. The Service was modelled on the Victorian and Queensland Clinics, although the specific design was informed by a detailed consultation process with a wide range of community and legal groups. The Service received twelve months' funding support from the Commonwealth Department of Family and Community Services under the National Homelessness Strategy and the Public Purposes Fund administered by the New South Wales Attorney-General's Department. It relies on pro bono services from seven private law firms, and provides legal help at six community locations. As with its counterparts in other States, the Service has also been actively involved in systemic legal and policy research and advocacy.

In Perth, Western Australia, the first steps have now been taken to set up a specialist Homeless Persons Legal Clinic. In October

17 *Blake Dawson Waldron provided the first seconded solicitor in 2002/3, then Minter Ellison Lawyers seconded several solicitors until 2005.*

2004, Labor Lawyers (Western Australia) and Human Rights WA held a public forum on "Homelessness and the Law," opened by the Honorable David Malcolm, Chief Justice of the Supreme Court of WA and addressed by Philip Lynch, Coordinator of the PILCH Homeless Persons Legal Clinic in Melbourne, Victoria. Arising out of that Forum, a funding application to establish a Perth-based Clinic was submitted to the Attorney General of Western Australia. The application was declined in favour of a small grant for a Scoping Study to be conducted. The initiative is now being driven by an informal Steering Committee of volunteers and supporters in collaboration with a private law firm. The Scoping Study will assess the legal needs of people who are homeless with a view to formulating recommendations about the model for a specialist service that would be suitable for local conditions.

Finally, in South Australia, a coalition has been formed to develop a specialist legal service for homeless people, again inspired by the success of the services in Victoria, Queensland, and New South Wales. The Coalition recently sought $AU 80,000 from the South Australian government to establish the Clinic but, despite the support of the South Australian Council of Social Services and Homelessness, the funding application has been declined. Efforts continue.

At around the same time as the first specialist legal service for homeless people was created in Melbourne, Victoria, the Asia Pacific Programme of the Centre on Housing Rights and Evictions (COHRE) opened its doors in Napier Street, Fitzroy—Melbourne, Victoria in 2000. COHRE is an international human rights non-governmental organisation that specialises in the international human right to adequate housing. The COHRE Asia Pacific Programme was established by Ken Fernandes, a long-time housing rights community activist with a history of working with local communities in a wide range of countries. COHRE's presence in Australia has acted as an additional catalyst, bringing a strong human rights-based perspective to a wide range of initiatives to promote access to justice for people who are homeless. Since 2003, the role of COHRE in Australia has been complemented by the presence of Alison Aggarwal in Sydney. Aggarwal is the Research Assistant to the UN Special Rapporteur on Adequate Housing on women and housing rights.

Since 2000, there has been an explosion in publications and academic interest regarding the legal and human rights issues experienced by people who are homeless. On a recent count, prior to the year 2000, about ten journal articles and publications had been published by Australians dealing with legal and human rights concerns associated with homelessness, with only one article published prior to the 1990s. Since 2000, at least 60 articles have gone to print! Over the last five years, papers, forums, and training courses have been delivered in a range of contexts, and in 2003, the Homelessness Legal Rights Project was established at the Gilbert + Tobin Centre of Public Law, University of New South Wales involving maintenance of a web site and publication of e-bulletins dealing specifically with the Australian legal and human rights of people facing homelessness.[18]

A Human Rights-Based Approach

The strong influence of human rights discourse on debates about the needs and interests of homeless people in Australia arguably commenced with the creation of the Australian Social and Economic Rights Project (ASERP)[19] which was formed in 1999 by a broad coalition of local activists, the Victorian Council of Social Services, and COHRE to produce the first-ever NGO Shadow Report to the United Nations Committee on Economic, Social and Cultural Rights (CESCR) in preparation for the 2000 review of Australia's compliance with its international obligations under the *International Covenant on Economic, Social and Cultural Rights* (*ICESCR*) including the right to adequate housing. The NGO Shadow Report was crucial to the incisive critique that the CESCR brought to bear on the Australian Government's Report, which dealt with Australia's com-

18 *Go to* http://www.gtcentre.unsw.edu.au/projects_partners/projects/hlr/index.asp. *Contact Cassandra Goldie at the Gilbert + Tobin Centre of Public Law, University of New South Wales.*

19 *Go to* http://members.ozemail.com.au/~rmclc/ASERParchive2000.htm#vwg.

pliance for the years 1990-1997. The Concluding Comments of the CESCR criticised Australia's performance against treaty obligations in a number of key areas, including failure to incorporate the *ICESCR* into the domestic legal system, the disproportionate disadvantage of Indigenous people in all key areas of economic, social, and cultural rights fulfilment, particularly employment, housing, health, and education, and the lack of a National Housing Strategy or legal protection from forced evictions.

The use of human rights standards, jurisprudence, and tools to analyse failings and promote solutions for people who are homeless is a recurrent theme amongst the wide range of systemic rights-based law reform initiatives that have been developed over the last five years. Specialist homelessness legal services have often acted in collaboration with other community legal centres, Legal Aid Commissions, community welfare agencies and advocacy groups, and the private legal profession to generate a critical mass in human rights-based advocacy for people who are homeless in one of the wealthiest nations in the world.

The Victorian Clinic has developed submissions regarding reforms to vagrancy and begging laws, the protection of homeless people's right to vote, and reforms to anti-discrimination laws to include "social status" as a prohibited ground of discrimination. The Clinic contributed to the incorporation of human rights-based recommendations in the Report of the Senate Select Committee on Mental Health, and through Clinic advocacy efforts, the Victorian Magistrates Court has established a Special Circumstances List for sentencing of people with special needs, such as being homeless or experiencing mental health issues. On November 15, 2005, the Victorian Government introduced into the Victorian Parliament the *Infringements Bill 2006* (Vic). The Bill contains provisions that provide that "homelessness" is a "special circumstance" that must be taken into account for the purpose of determining whether a fine should be issued or, once issued, withdrawn. The Clinic has also prepared a proposal for the establishment of a Homeless Persons Court. Lobbying and formal submissions by a coalition of legal and community groups including the Clinic were successful in opposing reforms to the *Disability Discrimination Act 1992* (Cth) that would have permitted discrimination in the provision of housing against people with a drug addiction.

In 2004, the Victorian Council of Social Services in collaboration with the Homeless Persons Legal Clinic, Shelter Victoria, Women's Housing Ltd, and COHRE conducted the Housing as a Human Right Project, with publication of *The Human Right to Housing in Australia*,[20] consultations with 21 focus groups of 185 people across Victoria about their experiences of being denied the right to adequate housing, and the convening of a Housing Rights Tribunal, enabling people to tell their stories in public to an eminent panel of legal and human rights experts.

In the Australian Capital Territory ("ACT"), the ACT Council of Social Services, ACT Shelter, and the Welfare Rights Centre have initiated the Housing as a Human Right Campaign, publishing a poster and series of postcards to tell the stories of people in need of adequate housing. A coalition in the ACT is also lobbying for the adoption of a Homelessness Charter of Rights that is underpinned by human rights standards.

In collaboration with Dr. Tamara Walsh from the Faculty of Law at the University of Queensland, the QPILCH Homeless Persons Legal Clinic is also involved in research and systemic advocacy to address the many barriers to justice for people who are homeless in that State. In 2004, Walsh published *From Park Bench to Court Bench: Developing a response to breaches of public space law by marginalised people*,[21] in association with the QPILCH Homeless Persons Legal Clinic and the Rights in Public Space Action Group (RIPS), a coalition of community organisations that formed to achieve legal and policy reforms to the legal regulation of human behaviour in public space. *From Park Bench to Court Bench* is a detailed analysis of current

20 *Dan Nicholson, "The Human Right to Housing in Australia" (Centre on Housing Rights and Evictions, 2004).*

21 *Tamara Walsh, "From Park Bench to Court Bench: Developing a response to breaches of public space law by marginalised people" (Faculty of Law, University of Queensland, 2004). To download a copy of the Report, go to* http://www.law.uq.edu.au/staff/tempprofiles/publications/Walsh_T_ParkBenchToCourtBench_Combined.pdf.

trends in the regulation and policing of public space offences in Queensland, making the connection between offending behaviour and the realities of living in poverty. It provides a range of recommendations for reforms to legislation, policing policies and practices, sentencing approaches and fines enforcement procedures, drawing on best practice and lessons learned from both Australia and comparative jurisdictions. Dr. Walsh recently released a further study into the prosecution of offensive language and behaviour offences in Queensland. The Rights in Public Space Action Group has also organised public forums and law reform submissions to push for repeal of offences criminalising people living in public spaces. With community legal centres, there has been collaboration on a research initiative to undertake court observations about the backgrounds of people who were being charged with public order offences. The court observation research has combined with a six month legal representation project by Legal Aid Queensland to highlight the failure of the courts to adequately take into account the personal circumstances of offenders, the uniform trend of guilty pleas for public order offences even in circumstances where a defence may be available, and the almost uniform imposition of fines on people who are not in a position to pay, at a rate slightly higher than those who have a greater capacity to pay.[22] This research and advocacy has been partially successful, with the repeal of the offence of vagrancy. The Queensland Government has also implemented a two-year pilot programme to create a "Special Circumstances" list for the purposes of sentencing homeless people and others experiencing disadvantage in relation to these kinds of offences. The program is designed to enable the courts to refer people who are homeless to accommodation and support services.[23] However, the Queensland Government has also introduced a new *Summary Offences Act* that re-criminalises begging and public drink-

---

22 *For details of the six month project by Legal Aid Queensland which provided legal representation to 60 people before the Brisbane Magistrates Court, see Legal Aid Queensland, "Homelessness and Street Offences Project" (2005). Go to* http://www.legalaid.qld.gov.au/newsevents/whats_new/docs/HomelessnessProject.pdf.

23 *Karen McLeod, "The Homelessness and Street Offences Project" (2006) 19(1) Parity 62.*

ing and significantly increased the fines associated with these public order offences.

The New South Wales Homeless Persons Legal Service (HPLS) recently released its first major systemic research and advocacy report dealing with the various ways in which the current fines enforcement system in New South Wales disproportionately impacts and discriminates against people who are homeless. The Law and Justice Foundation of New South Wales has also undertaken an extensive legal needs study regarding people who are homeless, concluding *inter alia* that services such as the HPLS operating from a community setting are a highly effective way to make justice accessible to people who are homeless.

In October 2002, Philip Lynch, Coordinator of the Homeless Persons Legal Clinic, collaborated with Associate Professor Dianne Otto from the Faculty of Law at the University of Melbourne to prepare a first submission to the UN Special Rapporteur on the Right to Adequate Housing on *Women and Adequate Housing in Australia.* This submission was followed by workshops in 2004 coordinated by the Research Assistant to the Special Rapporteur about how to use mechanisms of the Special Rapporteur to promote housing as a human right in Australia. The workshops were instrumental in raising awareness amongst housing activists about approaching housing and homelessness from a rights-perspective and resulted in the development of a further national submission to the Special Rapporteur on *Women and the Right to Adequate Housing in Australia,* a process that was overseen by a Steering Committee consisting of National Shelter, Victorian Council of Social Services, People with Disabilities, Women with Disabilities Australia, WESNET, Centre on Housing Rights and Evictions, community legal centres, community housing associations, and tenancy services. These efforts have directly led to the impending visit of the UN Special Rapporteur on Adequate Housing in July 2006.

The effort that is now solidly underway to promote a human rights-based approach to supporting people who are homeless in Australia is not without its significant challenges. The Howard Federal Government is particularly hostile to a human rights agenda. Australia is now only one of five nations in the world to lack a national bill of rights, and the Prime Minister is openly opposed to such reform. Public housing stocks have fallen from 372,000 in 1995-96 to about 345,000 in 2006, with increasingly lengthy waiting lists, and a number of State and Territory governments have introduced laws to remove security of tenure in public housing tenancies. There has been a spate of law reform at State and Territory level to expand police powers to move on people occupying public space. Ongoing reforms to the social security system continue to unravel any notion of access to minimum subsistence income as a right, and radical changes to the industrial relations system have now also removed security of employment for many Australian workers. In December 2004, the Commonwealth Government announced its intention to cut funding to the Supported Accommodation Assistance Programme (SAAP) which is the primary source of funding for crisis accommodation services in Australia.

However, activist efforts and alliances to promote a human rights framework for people who are homeless in Australia are now stronger than ever before, as demonstrated by the depth and range of activities described in these pages. Arguably, the most significant impact to date has been the development of a human rights culture amongst Australian communities. Genuine systemic change can be achieved by political engagement that is in response to broad-based community demands. It is significant that a number of Australian State Governments have recently introduced statutory bills of rights or are investigating their adoption. It is also significant that in March 2005, the Victorian Homeless Persons Legal Clinic wrote to the UN Special Rapporteur on the Right to Adequate Housing, Miloon Kothari, calling for urgent action to be taken regarding Australia's retrogressive measure to cut funding to SAAP services, a proposal that is simply unjustifiable given Australia's current economic prosperity and its obligations under the *ICESCR* to protect the right to adequate housing which includes a core obligation—at the very least— to not make the situation worse for people who are homeless. The Special Rapporteur has written to the Howard Government, and this funding cut has now been partially reversed.

The Special Rapporteur is visiting Australia in July 2006 to investigate the country's compliance with its international obligations to fulfill the human right to adequate housing, and a broad coalition of legal and community groups is organising a national effort to use this opportunity to continue to place pressure on Australian governments to fulfil their human rights obligations.

Watch this space.

ABA © HADASS SHLAGMAN

Cassandra Goldie *Director*
Homelessness Legal Rights Project
Gilbert + Tobin Centre of Public Law
University of New South Wales, Australia
P: +61 8 9335 1180 M: +61 418 851 014
c.goldie@unsw.edu.au

Cassandra Goldie is Director of the Homelessness Legal Rights Project at the Gilbert + Tobin Centre of Public Law at the University of New South Wales, Australia, where she is undertaking a PhD into the legal and human rights of people living in public space. She also works as a consultant on economic, social, and cultural rights, particularly the right to adequate housing. Cassandra was formally Senior Legal Officer with the Centre on Housing Rights and Evictions and Coordinator and Principal Solicitor of the Darwin Community Legal Service. She has also worked as a manager and solicitor with Legal Aid Western Australia and is admitted to practice in Western Australia and the Northern Territory. She has a Master of Laws from University College London focusing on public international law and the use of international human rights legal resources by local communities.

Because We Can:

Using Our Legal Skills to End Homelessness

William H. Hoch III

When I was contacted and asked to prepare this article, I inquired as to why I had been chosen and what earthly contribution I could make. The other contributors to this publication have a greater knowledge of the statistics, the causes of homelessness, the methods to help and assist the homeless, the lack of affordable housing, the lack of mental health care and other resources—basically, I am humbled by their knowledge and dedication to the cause.

Being asked, I inquired as to the purpose of any contribution I could make. The response: explain what "regular" lawyers (i.e., non-advocates) can do to assist in the fight against homelessness. I was also asked to explain those actions I had taken to assist the homeless. Because of the awkwardness of talking about myself, I have largely ignored the latter and attempted to focus on the former.

I first came face-to-face with homelessness in the mid-1980's when I arrived in Washington, DC to attend college at the Catholic University of America. At that time (much as it is still today), our Capitol City was awash with homeless men and women—most were mentally ill. Following the lead of many of my fellow students, I volunteered to help at S.O.M.E. ("So Others Might Eat," an interfaith, community-based organization that serves people experiencing homelessness in DC) and other "soup kitchen" type programs.

After college, I had the pleasure of working as a Legislative Assistant and later as a Legislative Director for a Member of Congress from my home state of Oklahoma. The McKinney-Vento Act passed in 1987, and one of my many areas of legislative responsibility included homelessness. Because the Member I worked for was from a rural Oklahoma district, I became interested in issues of rural housing and homelessness, rural economic issues, and farming crises (chapter 12 bankruptcies). After completing more than five years on Capitol Hill, I returned to Oklahoma to work for a United States bankruptcy judge and later began my career as a "regular lawyer."

I began participating through my church in serving the homeless at local shelters. This service turned into advocacy when I was asked to serve on and later chair the ABA Commission on Homelessness and Poverty. This advocacy work has been the most rewarding work of my entire legal career. I am humbled by those with whom I have had occasion to work who have dedicated their entire lives to the cause. I am inspired by the likes of Steve Binder, the catalyst to the Homeless Court Program; Casey Trupin, whose legal career is dedicated to assisting homeless youth in Seattle, Washington; Maria Foscarinis, who is a tireless advocate for people who are homeless; Jamie Forman, another "regular lawyer" who has dedicated much time and insight to the Commission; and Amy Horton-Newell, the ABA staffer for the Commission, who keeps us focused and moving forward. My work on the Commission and with my fellow Commissioners has introduced me to advocates across the country who have made an indelible mark on me because of their common-sense approach to those issues facing the homeless. The "ideas" in this essay are theirs—not mine. I have profound respect for these individuals who I speak of, and I am honored and humbled to call them my friends. The following are just some of the things that "regular lawyers" can do:

Volunteer

Visit a shelter in your hometown and inquire as to what their needs are. Let's face it—as "regular lawyers" we are busy with billable hours, firm-related commitments, and family obligations. It is hard to find the time. But I can tell you that it will change *your* life when you change another's life. Visit a shelter. Find out what the needs of your community are. Look into the face of a homeless child and their mother and after assisting them with a simple legal matter, try not to feel it. It will change you.

Start a Legal Clinic

People who are homeless have a host of legal problems. They include obtaining identification; accessing housing; securing VA or Social Security benefits; criminal matters; custody; divorce; protective orders; and related services. As lawyers, we have a great ability to bring about change and are entrusted with a wealth of contacts—use them. Whether it is through your law firm or through a law school or other means, we have the contacts and ability to make it happen. Start a clinic. Get law students involved. Because we can.

Start a Homeless Court in Your Community

In 2003, the ABA House of Delegates (the Association's legislative body) endorsed the innovative Homeless Court Program (HCP). The HCP is designed to assist a homeless individual's transition from the streets to self-sufficiency by removing legal barriers—such as outstanding warrants—to desperately needed services such as housing, treatment, and public benefits (see article in Chapter 6). Despite what one might hear from politicians, I have never met anyone who desires to be on the streets. It is usually through a series of devastating setbacks that individuals or families find themselves without housing. Lack of affordable housing, financial difficulties, job loss, disabilities, domestic violence, mental illness, and substance abuse cause homelessness—it is not a personal choice of the individual or family to be on the streets. Additionally, many cities in our country are hostile to those that have found themselves in this predicament, and most cities fail to provide the necessary services to prevent and end homelessness.

Rather than addressing the root causes, such as failure to provide affordable housing or drug counseling, some communities criminalize homelessness through ordinances. I continue to be ashamed as a lawyer of the proceedings I observed in New Orleans in which homeless individuals were thrown in city jail without a preliminary hearing for over 90 days for public urination, sharing a sandwich on the street corner (seriously), jaywalking, or sleeping on a park bench. The last three are things that anyone can do without concern for incarceration so long as he or she doesn't "look" homeless—but not in New Orleans. What about your community? Do you know? If not, find out what's going on in your community. If you can help an individual move from homelessness to self-sufficiency because of your efforts in establishing a homeless court, you will be rewarded many fold. I recall the personal testimony of one formerly homeless veteran who said he owed his *life* to Steve Binder and Al Pavich (President and C.E.O. of Veterans Village of San Diego) and that he would keep moving forward because of them. I doubt anyone reading this has received a similar testimony from one of their corporate clients. Why a homeless court? Because we are lawyers and we can establish a program that removes legal barriers to self-sufficiency.

Serve on a Board of a Shelter

Lawyers can contribute in many ways. One is serving on the board of directors at your local nonprofit, service provider, or coalition that assist the homeless. Many shelters are run by overworked well-intentioned individuals that either don't have time or are not adept at maintaining corporate minutes, by-laws, financial statements, and related corporate requirements. Lawyers can be a tremendous help in this regard. Lawyers also have clients that they can contact to "get involved." Let your clients know what you are doing and suggest that they join the fight to combat homelessness. It will improve the image of lawyers, and, I bet, improve your relationship with your client. Why? Because we can.

ABA © CROWE & DUNLEVY

William H. Hoch III *Shareholder/Director*
Crowe & Dunlevy
1800 Mid-America Tower Oklahoma City, OK 73102
405.239.6692 hochw@crowedunlevy.com

William H. Hoch is a shareholder in Crowe & Dunlevy's Oklahoma City office where he has practiced since 1995. Mr. Hoch is a graduate of the Catholic University of America (B.A, 1988; J.D. 1993) and concentrates his practice in the areas of bankruptcy, commercial litigation, copyright and trademark infringement, antitrust, and related litigation. He is a former Law Clerk to the Honorable Richard L. Bohanon, United States Bankruptcy Judge for the Western District of Oklahoma, and the Honorable Marion Opala, Justice of the Oklahoma State Supreme Court. Mr. Hoch was also Legislative Director to former Congressman Glenn English (D-OK), where he handled issues related to telecommunications, rural electrification, civil rights, rural development, housing, and homelessness. He served on The Catholic University of America's Board of Governors. Mr. Hoch is the former chair of the American Bar Association's Commission on Homelessness & Poverty from 2001 to 2005. He is currently a member of the American Bar Association's Standing Committee on Governmental Affairs. He also chairs the Oklahoma City Chapter of the Federal Bar Association's Pro Bono Committee. Mr. Hoch is a member of the Oklahoma Bar Association, Oklahoma County Bar Association, and the American Bar Association. He is admitted to practice in Oklahoma, United States Supreme Court, 10th Circuit Court of Appeals, Western, Eastern, and Northern District of Oklahoma. He is a member of the Board of the City Rescue Mission (OKC), a local homeless shelter.

Become an Advocate

No profession is better trained to advocate. Learn about the causes of homelessness. Investigate what is going on in your community. Discover why homelessness is such a pervasive problem in America today (and still growing). Inquire as to why the fastest growing homeless population is comprised of *children*.

And then *advocate*. Challenge community leaders to do better. Write letters to the editor of your local newspaper. Tell other lawyers, judges, and anyone who will listen what your findings are and then have the courage to act. Have the courage to be the catalyst of change in your community. Why? Because as lawyers, we can.

Not because we should…that sounds too much like a moral or ethical obligation. Do it because you can—like no one else can—because you're a lawyer.

Touring Homeless Shelters in Los Angeles with Judge Harry Pregerson:

An Interview with a Man of Action

Kassandra Perez

With his brown Stetson, turquoise belt buckle, and leather jacket, Judge Harry Pregerson of the Ninth Circuit U.S. Court of Appeals is ready to take me on a personal tour of Los Angeles County. The tour will include Veterans' housing, shelters for homeless families, and a child daycare center. The Judge had a principal role in founding these facilities and continues to watch over them.

The success in public service that Judge Pregerson has achieved didn't come easily, especially when it involved helping the homeless. "You have to be persistent," he says. Reflecting on the NIMBYism he has had to overcome, he looks upon those who lack compassion for the homeless as his unwitting motivators. Born and raised in East Los Angeles, Judge Pregerson, who is 83-years-old, believes that this is where his compassion, understanding, and appreciation for diversity began. "I am comfortable with everyone," he states, and this is important because "just talking to people and understanding their concerns" is all that is needed to overcome their objections. When confronted with NIMBYism from a local homeowner's association or a local government entity, Judge Pregerson begins by asking, "What are you worried about?" He listens carefully to their concerns. He then discusses in detail how the project's programs are designed to help the homeless, particularly veterans and their families, get back on their feet and become productive members of the community. He also considers it important to tell local residents about the proposed project and its programs and how formerly homeless clients can be an asset to the community. If some are still concerned about how the programs will operate, he will lighten their concerns by inviting them to serve on the executive board of the facility.

While opposition may challenge him, Judge Pregerson has shown great courage, persistence, and dedication to his ideals in the face of adversity. While fighting as a Marine in World War II, he was severely wounded during the battle for Okinawa. After the war, he went on to receive his undergraduate degree from UCLA and his law degree from the University of California at Berkeley. Early in his legal career, he and law school classmate Bill Costley started a ground floor, neighborhood law office in Van Nuys, California, where they practiced together for 14 years. He and his partner prided themselves on never turning away a client—even if the client couldn't pay. They never kept track of "billable hours," but instead charged what they felt was reasonable. In 1965, during the Watts riots, Governor Pat Brown appointed Judge Pregerson to the Los Angeles Municipal Court. In 1966, Governor Brown appointed Judge Pregerson to the Los Angeles Superior Court. One year later in 1967, President Lyndon B. Johnson appointed him to the U.S. District Court. In 1979, President Jimmy Carter appointed Judge Pregerson to the Ninth Circuit Court of Appeals.

Throughout his career, Judge Pregerson has been a dedicated and passionate advocate for the dispossessed, the downtrodden, veterans, and, particularly, homeless men, women, and children. Judge Pregerson's desire to help others started when he was a youngster. For this he credits his parents, who believed in the importance of humanitarian values, and the Boy Scouts of America, which emphasized the importance of doing at least one good deed every day. He recalled the winter of 1987, when homeless men and women in Los Angeles without shelter were dying from hypothermia. To save lives, Mayor Tom Bradley opened the City Council

Judge Harry Pregerson of the Ninth Circuit U.S. Court of Appeals—a tireless advocate for people experiencing homelessness.

chambers and invited the homeless to spend the night there and be out of the freezing cold. Judge Pregerson tried to do the same at the foyer in the U.S. Courthouse, but was met with resistance. Unfortunately, this resistance was based on stereotypical thinking and negative feelings about homeless people. Judge Pregerson would continue to face such opposition for years to come.

That opposition motivated the creation of many facilities, such as the Salvation Army's Westwood Transitional Village and Bessie Pregerson Child Development Center, the Salvation Army's Homeless Veterans Haven Program, the U.S. Vets' Westside Residence Hall for Homeless Veterans, and the Salvation Army's Bell Shelter. These facilities and their unique programs were developed to meet the needs of thousands of homeless men, women, children, with an emphasis on homeless veterans and their families. These facilities represent just a sample of the public service work Judge Pregerson has done and continues to do, and they are the locations of his scheduled tour for the day.

The tour begins at 8:00 am at the Westwood Transitional Village. Its low-income housing consists of 41 air-conditioned units with two to four bedrooms. Fifteen units are set aside for formerly homeless veterans and their families. The facility offers many resources, such as a community center, a state-of-the-art computer lab, and a tutoring program. The facility also contains a dispensary where

UCLA medical and dental students, under the guidance of professors, provide free medical and dental services for the residents.

As he did with other projects, Judge Pregerson took the initiative to bring together the people who could plan, build, and operate the facility. He and Louise Oliver of the General Services Administration ("GSA"), recognized a need, located land, and began discussions with those whose support was necessary to build and operate the facility (including the Salvation Army, building trade unions, the Disabled American Veterans, and the federal governments GSA). To build the affordable housing complex and the day care center next door, the Salvation Army received a quitclaim deed of the surplus land from GSA. Judge Pregerson made a "wish list" of what needed to be done to secure and renovate the land and got the city and his friend, Mayor Tom Bradley, to help.

Next door, on the same property, is the Bessie Pregerson Child Development Center, off the busy Wilshire exit of the 405 freeway near UCLA. The Salvation Army dedicated the childcare center to the memory of Judge Pregerson's mother. In 1908, when she was sixteen years old, she fled Ukraine alone because of the suffering and prejudice inflicted on Jewish families in Czarist Russia. She worked for twelve hours a day, seven days a week, sewing in a sweatshop in Philadelphia to earn three dollars a week. Her 100-year-old sewing machine now sits encased in the lobby of the childcare center.

Priority at the day care center is given to children who live in the housing complex; however, children of local college students and the children of those who work in a neighboring federal office building and in an adjacent VA facility are also welcome. The center prides itself on its creative curriculum that pays particular attention to improving fine motor skills and socialization. An effort is also made to keep track of children leaving the center and to encourage college attendance in the years to come. Judge Pregerson enjoys visiting and interacting with these children who reflect the diversity of Los Angeles.

The next stop of the day is the Salvation Army's Veterans' Haven Program in Westwood, which opened in 2004. The Disabled

American Veterans and Jesse Brown, Secretary for Veteran's Affairs, dedicated this facility to the memory of Abraham Pregerson, Judge Pregerson's father. He, too, was an immigrant and in 1904, at the age of fourteen, he fled the persecution of Jewish people in Czarist Russia. During World War I, he fought in France as an American soldier. He was severely wounded during the Muse Argonne campaign and was awarded the Purple Heart.

The Haven Program has 250 beds and a five-phase program, including rehabilitation and job placement. There is also a separate women's program called "Naomi's House." The Salvation Army staff currently offers an outreach program to women veterans with substance abuse problems. Judge Pregerson reminds the director that he is working on getting equipment to build a gym and requests the dimensions of the available room to begin the process. He is confident of his ability to obtain equipment from his trainer, Bruce Gaims. He points out that when he was growing up, Joe Gold of Gold's Gym fame was his next door neighbor and that they used to work out together. To Judge Pregerson, it is not just about shelter and food for the night; he stresses a holistic approach because he believes that it is important to have a strong mind *and* a strong body. Even something like a gym is important for the residents to have access to, in Judge Pregerson's view.

At the time of his visit, residents were in the middle of one of their counseling sessions for homeless veterans, and Judge Pregerson decided to stop and listen. He was invited in and quickly introduced himself, reminding participants of his father's photo in the hallway. He expressed his pride in their progress, explaining, "I know it's not easy, most of life's problems don't just go away, you've got to work on them." The sincerity of his comments and his genuine interest in their lives is shown not just in words, but in action. After discussing various issues such as voting, completing the rehabilitation program, and the opportunity to get their outstanding warrants for minor infractions dismissed through the Los Angeles Homeless Court, the Judge welcomed questions. It was then that a resident quietly approached Judge Pregerson and explained a personal legal problem he was facing. After reviewing the paperwork, Judge Pregerson put the paper in his back pocket and promised to look into the matter. For another resident, he left his phone number on the inside cover of the resident's AA book with an offer to help. The Judge left the session promising the participants that he would be back.

The Westside Residence Hall in Inglewood, the next stop of the tour, was developed to take care of the special needs of homeless veterans. It began when a group of veterans, including Judge Pregerson, decided to do something about the thousands of homeless veterans living in encampments near freeway overpasses, under bridges, and on the streets and sidewalks of Los Angeles. The group formed a nonprofit corporation called U.S. Vets, led by Judge Pregerson, Louise Oliver, and David Ferrar, a retired Navy pilot, and located in an eight-story dormitory owned by Northrop. The dormitory, which was closing, had been used as housing for thousands of engineers and mechanics trained to work in the airline industry. With the help of a loan from the Century Freeway (I-105) Housing Program, U.S. Vets was able to acquire the property.

Westside Residence Hall is now home to 500 formerly homeless veterans. U.S. Vets operates similar nonprofit facilities for veterans in Los Angeles, Inglewood, Ventura, Long Beach, Riverside, Honolulu, Las Vegas, Prescott, Phoenix, Houston, and Washington, DC. Nationwide, U.S. Vets cares for approximately 10,000 veterans a year. Each facility is closely tied to the Department of Veterans' Affairs and local veterans groups. The Westside Residence Hall offers formerly homeless veterans affordable living quarters, a medical clinic, and recreational facilities. AmeriCorps, the national service program, works with U.S. Vets to help connect veterans to housing, needed services, and jobs.

While at the Westside Residence Hall, Judge Pregerson is reminded that it is past lunchtime; he hasn't noticed. He asks the cook, "What do we have for lunch?" The cook responds, "Peanut butter and jelly sandwiches." "Sounds good to me," is Judge Pregerson's response. He takes the time to have his peanut butter and jelly sandwich with Mr. Harold Young, a fellow World War II veteran and Tuskegee Airman now residing at the facility. Mr.

Young, an 89-year-old veteran, was forced to leave his apartment in Santa Monica after rent control was lifted. Judge Pregerson heard about his plight through the VA and immediately telephoned Mr. Young, who was on the verge of homelessness, and invited him to live at the Westside Residence Hall. Judge Pregerson dispatched a van to pick up Mr. Young's gear and move him into a private bedroom in a four bedroom suite with three other veterans. Judge Pregerson, a retired marine, and Mr. Young, a retired Army Air Force pilot, swap World War II stories. Mr. Young loves living at Westside Residence Hall; he is revered and respected by fellow veterans of more recent wars. As Mr. Young said with a big smile and his arms raised, "I am happy to be here with my new band of brothers."

The Salvation Army's Bell Shelter, the final stop in the tour, was established in 1988 when Judge Pregerson, with the help of U.S. Marshal Sam Cicchino, located 40,000 square feet of empty space at the Federal Supply Center in Bell, California. The Center was the former site of a World War II U.S. Army Air Force Depot. At Judge Pregerson's request, GSA made the space available for use as a shelter to house the homeless. The Bell Shelter has achieved amazing results. It started out with 18 Army cots. Today, the Bell Shelter encompasses an 80,000 square foot facility that cares for 500 men and women, and it employs a superb and well-trained staff of 80 people. It is a well-organized, modern facility with a wide variety of educational and rehabilitative programs. The Los Angeles Unified School District's Adult Education program operates four classrooms at the Bell Shelter. The classrooms are outfitted with new computers, and the residents can earn their high school diplomas, learn computer programming, and learn how to maintain and repair computers.

The Bell Shelter hosts a large, modern kitchen and dining room. Attached to the kitchen is a full-sized pizza oven donated by California Pizza Kitchen. There, residents are trained in the art of making delicious pizzas. The Shelter also boasts a beauty parlor, a barber shop, a Mayor Richard Riordan library, and a Joe Gold gym with state-of-the-art exercise equipment. The Bell Shelter has a highly skilled staff of psychologists, social workers, drug and alcohol counselors, and job development personnel, who provide a full range of programs (including parenting classes and anger management therapy) to assist the homeless to overcome their addictions and become productive members of society.

A lot of "blood, sweat and tears" went into the various projects, Judge Pregerson admits. He praises the Salvation Army, its executive directors, managers, and social workers for the Shelter's ongoing success over the past 18 years. While walking through each location, he remembers the names of each staff member. When speaking of him, most staff explain simply that this place wouldn't exist without him. They note that it is his persistence in making sure the projects stay on track that has been most important. "When he wants something done…it gets done," said Dr. Doug Loisel, Director of the Bell Shelter.

Throughout the day, residents of all ages, races, and backgrounds come to greet Judge Pregerson. Whether from previously meeting him or by recognizing him from photos adorning their residence

ABA © SARAH DAILEY

Kassandra Perez
Student
Pepperdine School of Law

Kassandra Perez is a third-year law student at Pepperdine School of Law. After her first year in law school she interned at the California Women's Law Center, working with incarcerated battered women in the California Habeas Project. Continuing to pursue domestic violence work, she worked for The Legal Aid Foundation of Los Angeles at the Santa Monica Domestic Violence Clinic. Kassandra is the President of the Latin American Law Student Association at Pepperdine School of Law and Chair for the annual Advocates for Public Interest Law Auction. She is currently the legal extern for the Los Angeles Homeless Court, working with both Public Counsel and the Los Angeles City Attorney's Office.

walls, they are grateful and show their appreciation. Judge Pregerson greets them, not just with a handshake, but with a hug. He says, "The best people I've ever met are at homeless shelters. Almost without exception, they are people who are kind, compassionate, and caring. As John Steinbeck said in *Cannery Row*, 'The things we admire in men, kindness and generosity, openness, honesty, understanding and feeling are the concomitants of failure in our system. And those traits we detest, sharpness, greed, acquisitiveness, meanness, egotism and self-interest are the traits of success. And while men admire the quality of the first they love the produce of the second.'"

As the day turns into night and his relentless nature persists, Judge Pregerson casually speaks of plans that he has in mind for a new shelter for homeless veterans' families in the San Fernando Valley, where he lives. Dr. Loisel compliments Judge Pregerson, saying, "He's such a joy, his heart is in the right place, and it's genuine. In all senses of the word, he's just a wonderful man, he's an American Patriot." Modestly, Judge Pregerson explains, "A lot of us went to law school because we thought it was a good way to help people and society." Judge Pregerson has unmistakably transformed this notion into reality.

Working to End the Homelessness of the Working:

A Lawyer-Organizer Partnership in Baltimore

J. Peter Sabonis

In 2004, Baltimore Magazine named the 50 most powerful people in the City and it ranked him first—ahead of the mayor, the governor, and even the media moguls. Having made a fortune as an attorney specializing in asbestos litigation, his law firm had become the first stop for anyone contemplating class action litigation. When Maryland joined the coalition of states that sued tobacco companies, it asked for his help. On top of that, he was the owner of a professional baseball franchise, the Baltimore Orioles.

And so it was with some trepidation that the small group of homeless men that was huddled on the upper floor of a converted firehouse picked him as their target. "He'll crush us," said one. "Let's start smaller," said another. Even as the lawyer who headed the Homeless Persons Representation Project, Inc. (HPRP), a non-profit legal service provider that liked to take risks, I wondered aloud about making the legal connection between Peter Angelos and the primarily homeless workers who cleaned the Orioles State-owned ballpark.

The Maryland Stadium Authority, not Angelos, operated the Camden Yards Sports Complex, home of the Orioles and football's Baltimore Ravens. And while the Authority collected a total of $12 million annually in rent and operating contributions from the two franchises, it, not Angelos, had contracted with a company to clean the two stadiums after events. And it was that company in turn, not Angelos, who out-sourced at least two-thirds of its 100-member clean-up crew to a national temporary staffing company and janitorial services agency. Most of the workers employed by the staffing company and janitorial services agency were homeless. Given the wages they received from their employers, they had little chance of changing that. According to the workers, they often were not paid for all the hours they worked on their six to ten-hour shifts (which frequently spanned the whole night); they were required to report to duty well before the ballgames ended and made to wait, without pay, until game completion and fan exit to begin work; breaks were not allowed; and workers were frequently harassed, some sexually.

HPRP created a special project to provide legal help to homeless workers trapped in the temporary worker industry—the "labor pools." But why should Angelos be held accountable for the plight of homeless workers at the stadium? Even most of the workers HPRP spoke with blamed themselves, their addictions, or their lack of initiative for their poor employment situation. Their own apathy made our initiative, which promised to reform a host of labor pool illegalities through litigation, look silly. "A suitcase, huh?" they'd ask, using the African-American Baltimore street vernacular for lawsuit, as we passed out coffee in the pre-dawn darkness along with fliers detailing unlawful labor pool practices. "You *really* think *that* would change things?" As lawyers, we really did. To us the pools were like shooting fish in a barrel. From discouraging worker compensation claims to reducing wages below the minimum through the collection of fees for transportation, gloves, boots, hats, etc., the pools seemed to be a litigator's delight.

The only problem was the lack of plaintiffs. Oh, we got great stories, including sordid tales of labor pool van accidents in which workers were given the option of getting immediate cash "advances" in lieu of being transported to get medical treatment. We heard about a medical waste facility, where permanent workers wore expensive hazard masks, long rubber gloves, and quilted jumpsuits while moving dead dogs, used needles, and body parts, but temporary workers got paper masks, thin paper suits, and cotton gloves. We heard about workers being transported to work sites, then being stranded by the pools and having to walk back to Baltimore through affluent, white neighborhoods with police cruisers as shadows.

Absent plaintiffs, we took the stories and made our complaints to the regulatory agencies and to the media. We received some attention, but little changed. That's when we decided to throw our traditional legal service model out the window. That's when we hired an organizer.

"Look," said Todd Cherkis, who had spent a number of years in Atlanta organizing labor pool workers against the pools themselves, "Angelos has a public image he cares about, the pools don't." We had to agree on that. "And he's considered a pro-labor lawyer," said Cherkis. Indeed, Angelos had begun his asbestos litigation career through a close partnership with the construction unions. But still, the legal responsibility for the treatment of workers rested with the labor pools, the companies that hired the temporary employees, and, perhaps, if we were creative, the Stadium Authority.

Diagramming these relationships on the wall of the shelter and watching the confusion and frustration replace the energy and agitation of my homeless audience, I remembered the tenant farmer in Steinbeck's *Grapes of Wrath* who threatens to kill the tractor driver who is going to knock down his house and plow over his farm. The driver responds:

"You're not killing the right guy."

"That's so," the tenant said. "Who gave you orders? I'll go after him. He's the one to kill."

"You're wrong. He got his orders from the bank. The bank told him, 'Clear those people out or it's your job.'

"Well, there's a president of the bank. There's a board of directors. I'll fill up the magazine of the rifle and go into the bank."

The Driver said, "Fellow was telling me the bank gets orders from the East. The orders were, 'Make the land show profit or we'll close you up.'"

"But where does it stop? Who can we shoot? I don't aim to starve to death before I kill the man that's starving me."

At least Todd was giving us a stopping point—and a sound one at that. For just as a combination of forces had pushed sharecroppers from the land during the Great Depression, there were many variables that had created the labor pool equation. Yet if Angelos and other high profile employers in Baltimore weren't directly responsible for the laborer's situation, they certainly reaped a specific benefit. The Orioles, after all, annually paid an amount to the Stadium Authority to cover ballpark operating expenses. Because of the vulnerability of homeless laborers, ballpark clean-up costs were deflated. Homeless laborers also reported being sent by labor pools to jobs across the State—cost cutting arrangements that, no doubt, assisted in keeping those institutions and businesses profitable. Perhaps contracting and sub-contracting arrangements allowed them a legitimate shield from legal responsibility, but moral responsibility was another matter—one that an organizer, not a lawyer, saw as an opportunity.

Of course, we did not arrive at this point overnight. When Todd first began the weekly meetings of homeless labor pool workers, turnout was light and workers often recounted substance abuse and bad luck as their rationale for pool participation. But gradually at these meetings they learned that an Atlanta Labor Pool Task Force noted that labor pools were growing at a 20 percent annual rate back in 1992, and that in 1999, the Bureau of Labor Statistics determined that the "personnel-supply-service" industry dominated by the pools was one of the fastest growing sectors of the labor market. Over time, the workers began to understand that the cost savings temporary labor companies offer (by assuming the cost of workers'-compensation, income and payroll tax withholdings, unemployment and health insurance) was increasingly attractive to many employers, not just those who utilized manual labor. During one homeless shelter meeting, workers took turns reading a newspaper article on Microsoft's use of temporary employees.

Over time, homeless workers began to see themselves as economic actors vulnerable to broad market forces. Over time, homeless workers began to understand that the terms and conditions of temporary employment would remain the same—even if every worker conquered his real or imagined personal demons. Over time, attendance at meetings increased, and workers with the courage to fight appeared.

An attorney was present at every meeting, ready to answer any legal question posed by the group. But unlike before, we didn't trumpet litigation as the solution. We offered it as strategic support, but humbled ourselves, admitting that lawyers could give the invisible a voice, not to be confused with power. Power, we repeated, using the mantra of Saul Alinsky's Industrial Areas Foundation, was the ability to organize money or people.

And so, by the time Cherkis suggested a picket at Orioles Park on the Opening Day of baseball season and a website page aimed at Angelos, the group had formed a mass and a consciousness critical enough to have its own name—the United Workers Association (UWA), hosted by HPRP. And with some anxiety, the UWA chose the most powerful man in Baltimore as its first target.

The break came four days before the Sunday night opener. A labor professor, who had come to support the UWA's effort, sent a message to a pro-labor listserv about the proposed action planned for Opening Day. Apparently an old-guard AFL-CIO confidant of Angelos saw the message and visited the UWA website. Within minutes, Angelos' inner circle was viewing the website and printing pages to bring to the Boss. Needless to say, the Man was angry. At least that's what his advisors called to say when they requested an immediate meeting with the UWA to discuss the proposed action. Three days before the Opener, an attorney and a labor advisor from Angelos' office came to meet three UWA members at the office of its counsel, HPRP. At the meeting, the representatives of the Oriole owner pledged to support our campaign if we would call off our picket and change our website. We modified each.

The following day, the front page of Baltimore's daily business periodical, *The Daily Record*, proclaimed boldly that Peter Angelos would support the laborers.[1] I have that front page hanging in my

1 The Daily Record, *April 5, 2004.*

office today. I will always have it hanging. While we had other good press and headlines during my 18 years fighting for the homeless in Baltimore, none approach the importance of that one. The richest man in Baltimore—a powerful businessman—professes his support for homeless workers who are exploited by business, in a business newspaper.

Within weeks of our meeting with Angelos' inner circle, we were called to a meeting with the Maryland Stadium Authority and then subsequently to a meeting with their contractor. The UWA presented its grievances and asked for higher wages and a code of conduct guaranteeing fair treatment of workers. Fair treatment was an easy promise for all to make. Higher wages was another matter entirely. Labor pool workers were earning $5.15 per hour. The UWA demanded the $8.85 an hour that was paid by city ordinance under all city service contracts. As a quasi-private state entity, the Stadium Authority was exempt from the ordinance.

Stymied by the differing cost estimates and concerns of the Authority and their contractor, we turned to Angelos in an attempt to cash in on his support and pressure the Stadium Authority. In a letter to the Orioles owner, we asked him to personally provide the $70,000 that we estimated was necessary to pay the workers $8.85 per hour for the remainder of the baseball season. Our hope was that the ploy would shame the Stadium Authority and contractor into increasing wages.

The stalemate was broken. In 2005, the Stadium Authority awarded its facilities management contract to Knight Facilities Management of Michigan, which promised to pay laborers $7.00 an hour and create a grievance system for employees.[2] These promises were kept. Additionally, Knight approved a UWA cooperative arrangement, in which a collective of UWA members will contract with Knight directly, eliminating the labor pool, to clean a portion of the stadium. The arrangement will net the members even higher wages.

2 The Daily Record, *March 8, 2005 [page number unknown]*

The UWA continues to grow, now attracting even non-homeless laborers. Wages at all labor pools in Baltimore have increased, and a number of pools have adopted or are adopting the UWA's code of conduct. The UWA and Casa de Maryland (a community organization that serves immigrants and day laborers) have engaged in discussions with the City of Baltimore to create a Workers' Center that will be shared by the organizations—a pioneering partnership of African-American and Latino day laborers.[3]

ABA © DANNY MILLS

J. Peter Sabonis *Staff Attorney*
KIDS Legal, Pinetree Legal Assistance
61 Main Street, Suite 41 Bangor, ME 04401-8300
207.942.8241 psabonis@ptla.org

J. Peter Sabonis is a staff attorney with KIDS Legal Aid of Maine, a project of Pine Tree Legal Assistance, in Bangor, Maine, and is a member of the United Workers Association's Board of Directors. He provided legal advocacy to homeless persons first as a staff attorney, and then as Executive Director, of the Homeless Persons Representation Project Inc., in Baltimore, from 1990 to 2004. Peter has also served as the Public Policy Director for Advocates for Children and Youth, Inc. in Baltimore, as well as a staff attorney with the Maryland Legal Aid Bureau, Inc. Peter began his public interest law career upon the receipt of his JD from Northeastern University in 1982. Since then, he has been a tireless advocate for homeless and impoverished people. Peter is well versed in the special legal problems of people experiencing homelessness. Peter has written extensively on criminalization issues, including ex-offenders and employment as well as the use of expungement as a tool to address access to employment and housing.

3 The Sun, *February 28, 2005 [page number unknown, editorial from that day—http:www.baltimoresun.com./news/opinion/bal-ed.laborer28feb28,1,1370873,print.story?coll=bal-opinion*

Today, I provide legal assistance to homeless youth in Maine. The UWA experience is ever present in my mind. While I throw myself into traditional legal advocacy, I understand that systemic change for any marginalized group can best be achieved through organization. And law can and always will provide a key support to this—if we attorneys are open and humble enough to recognize our role.

CHAPTER 2

Law Students and Professors Working to End Homelessness

SYLAW: Law Students Dedicated to Justice for Street Youth

Corey Fitzpatrick and Casey Trupin

In the 1990s, the number of homeless and at-risk youth ("street youth") in the greater Seattle area increased significantly. Today, on any given night, there are as many as 2,000 street youth, ranging from about 12 to 24 years of age, in the greater Seattle area. Keeping pace with this increase, service providers fought to expand and strengthen the services available to these youth. While they made phenomenal gains in providing youth with a wide variety of necessities, one aspect of the youth's needs remained unmet in Seattle.

The missing component was that of legal assistance. While most street youth have other basic needs met, there is often a legal issue which, if remedied, can expedite the transition to a positive and healthy adulthood. Legal needs for these youth vary, but generally fall into the following categories: abuse, neglect, and other family law issues; health, housing, and employment issues; educational barriers; and difficulty accessing state and federal entitlements. If these particular needs are not met, youth are often prevented from achieving other goals necessary for making progress toward stable housing, employment, and educational opportunities. These youth are then left with less constructive options for resolving their issues.

A group of law students, staff, and professors at the University of Washington took it upon themselves to fill this gap in services. Their efforts led to the creation of the Street Youth Legal Advocates of

Washington (SYLAW). SYLAW has helped hundreds of youth overcome the legal obstacles they face.

History

SYLAW fills the gap. In the spring of 1995, law students at the University of Washington School of Law began work on a street youth advocacy project. The project was intended to mirror an adult homeless advocacy project in which attorneys volunteered at a homeless shelter and provided information, referrals, and representation.

The program began with law students volunteering at a local youth drop-in center to supply legal information and referrals. Unfortunately, the program had difficulty getting off the ground and faded away. In the fall of 1996, several faculty, staff and students from the UW School of Law began to revive the dormant program. They hoped to include as one of the program's components a way to actually resolve the legal problems of the youth. The new program intended to use law students working under the guidance of a supervising attorney from the law school. In addition, each student was to have a community pro bono attorney at his or her disposal for advice on specific issues. This way, clients would not only receive education about their problems, but a resolution of them as well. Representation was to be limited to civil law, as youth are entitled to a free criminal defense by public defender agencies.

In the summer of 1997, the program successfully sought 501(c)(3) status and was incorporated as SYLAW, Street Youth Legal Advocates of Washington. Several students began intensive work on preparing SYLAW for its official launch, including researching issues on which the program was to educate and/or provide representation. To help better grasp what issues SYLAW might encounter, the program conducted a citywide survey of service providers and visited programs in the District of Columbia and New York. The students solicited community leaders for an Advisory Board, contacted care providers, applied for preliminary grants to get the project off the ground, and worked with care providers to better define how its educational and referral processes would work. In the fall of 1997, SYLAW began to provide comprehensive services.

SYLAW makes an impact through education. SYLAW partnered with innovative existing resources to provide outreach and legal education. Twice a month, students would ride along with Streetlinks, an outreach van that provided basic services to street youth in Seattle. The partnership produced multiple positive effects. Even when not offering legal information, the students were able to learn more about the youth and understand how and why they came to be on the streets. Students routinely described it as a life-changing experience. In addition, riding along in the van established SYLAW as a legitimate service in the eyes of the street youth community, a critical goal for any successful program, as the distrust of lawyers among this community runs high. Street youth rarely see lawyers as distinct from a system they feel helped put them on the streets. They often refer to public defenders as "public pretenders" and harbor even more disdain for prosecutors. The idea of a civil attorney, beyond someone who "sued people," was foreign to both youth and service providers. In fact, an early meeting with the director of a local health clinic ended with the frustrated director exclaiming, "I still don't get exactly what you're going to

SYLAW successfully represented Kayla, an at-risk youth who had been wrongfully expelled from a school because of a fight. The school district had implicated Kayla in the incident despite several witnesses who were willing to testify that she was not involved. Additionally, the school district had failed to properly notify Kayla's parents, who speak very little English, of their appeal rights. Following negotiations with SYLAW, the school district agreed to readmit Kayla to a school in the district and to expunge the incident from all of her records.

do, if not help these kids with their criminal cases." His frustration was understandable given that the creators of this program weren't exactly sure either. The early SYLAW volunteers knew only that there was a need, and the partnership further opened their eyes to the lack of legal information and the overabundance of legal barriers that existed for street youth.

To address this frustration and confusion, SYLAW began to offer community-based presentations on legal issues relevant to youth. SYLAW sent checklists with dozens of legal issues to service providers who could check the issues they wished to have covered in the presentations. Generally, two students, under the supervision of an attorney, would prepare the presentation using the outreach materials located in the growing SYLAW library. The students would attend the presentation, speak briefly about SYLAW and the referral process, and after presenting, would ask each participant to fill out an evaluation of the presentation. After a while, it became apparent that presenting to the providers was equally as important as presenting to the youth. While the low pay for service providers kept turnover high, it rarely approached the turnover in the youth population. Thus, training providers was critical to ensure that information was actually reaching new populations of street youth.

SYLAW's public education was not solely limited to teaching about specific legal tools. For a long period of time, SYLAW students taught a weekly class at an alternative school in a local drop-in center and modeled the curriculum on Street Law courses. Classes on topics as broad as the first amendment and legislative process were included, and the students were generally very engaged. SYLAW conducted classes for several different groups, including offender youth, Campfire Girls, and public school students.

Another method of reaching out was closer to traditional legal services. SYLAW began to offer weekly "hang out the shingle" information centers at local service provider sites, including alternative schools for street youth. Youth asked SYLAW volunteers questions and were provided with information and referral services.

SYLAW provides a voice for youth. Connecting with the youth and providing information soon became routine. But students expressed a recurring frustration with providing referrals: few legal providers were actually equipped to handle the issues of street youth. One problem was logistical: being able to meet youth where they were and when they were available. Another was being able to provide services in a holistic manner. While one attorney might be able to help a youth get federal benefits, he or she might not be equipped to handle the issues related to helping that youth escape an abusive parent. For most youth, having two attorneys is often overwhelming, and SYLAW quickly realized it was going to need to establish better services to represent these youth. At the same time, a statewide legal services provider, Columbia Legal Services, was again attempting to reach out to this population, but still was stymied by the fact that these youth didn't connect with the traditional style of providing legal services.

In 1999, Columbia Legal Services and SYLAW joined together and began to provide the full range of civil legal services and education for at-risk and homeless youth. Two to four students at a time interned at Columbia, each handling a number of cases. The student interns also helped with the outreach portion of the program, which was still largely performed by volunteer students.

Referrals to SYLAW were often made by caseworkers who had received written consent from their clients to contact a legal agency and to disclose any relevant information. In choosing whom to represent, SYLAW gave preference to youth who had been referred by a service agency. Walk-in clients were accepted on an availability basis.

SYLAW and Columbia invested significant resources in the law student interns. One goal of SYLAW was to create young attorneys who, wherever they practiced, would understand the legal needs of street youth. In order to make sure that law students got as much out of the program as possible, law student interns were required to commit at least 20 weeks to the program, but most stayed on for a year or longer. Interns were given substantial responsibilities: representing clients in court, working on briefs in state and federal court, and counseling clients on critical matters. It was not unusual for students to come in on weekends or work nights to accommodate clients—they did this not out of a sense of duty to SYLAW, but out of passion for the clients' cases. Former interns have gone on to work for State Supreme Court Justices, big and small law firms, the prosecution and the defense bar, and the state Attorney General's office, among other positions. They have often commented that their experience with SYLAW has helped positively shape how they approach issues involving youth. Former interns have taken on pro bono cases and worked with their firms to secure donations to keep SYLAW afloat.

In order to make legal information more accessible to youth and service providers, SYLAW launched a website (*www.sylaw.org*) and produced materials that informed at-risk youth and their service providers about relevant legal issues. Throughout the course of providing services, SYLAW interns discovered their clients often have better access to the Internet than to the mail or phone. Therefore, communication and information dissemination through the web became a useful tool.

SYLAW worked to involve private law firms as well, coordinating the law firm representation of 30 youth service agencies that were seeking to clarify the laws regarding services to at-risk and homeless youth. The results of the process were legal memoranda

SYLAW assisted David, a teen who had made it to his sophomore year of high school without earning any credits. David had severe learning disabilities, had begun to fail to show up for classes, and was facing possible time in youth detention as a result of a truancy contempt motion filed by the school district. SYLAW worked to get the truancy contempt motion dismissed, obtain special education services for the student, and work with the school and school psychologist to obtain full educational testing. David received additional help as a result and was on a path towards graduation.

which were circulated among all service providers to help them better serve young clients in need.

Braam v. State of Washington. Successes have come on systemic levels as well. The expertise gained through the SYLAW partnership greatly helped Columbia Legal Services in its role as co-counsel in *Braam v. Washington*,[1] a statewide class action lawsuit challenging the constitutionality of foster child treatment as it related to mental health assessments and care, placements, foster parent and caseworker training, and educational support. A major issue in the case became the number of youth who were poorly served and who, as a result, ended up on the streets both before they turned 18 and after legally becoming adults. In that case, the Washington Supreme Court held that foster children in Washington have a substantive due process right to be free from unreasonable risks of harm and a reasonable right to safety. The case was settled with the State, and among other things, it promised to reform the way it treated adolescents in its care, including improving its response to the problem of runaway foster youth.

SYLAW in Transition

SYLAW's major support came from AT&T Wireless through the Equal Justice Fellowship Program of NAPIL (formerly the National Association for Public Interest Law). AT&T Wireless provided funding for an attorney for two years. Additional funding was secured through local foundations, individual gifts, and general funding from Columbia Legal Services. For interns, SYLAW relied on fellowships, such as the ABA John J. Curtin, Jr. Justice Fund and the law schools' public interest fellowships. SYLAW interns also received work study and course credit.

In late 2004, Columbia Legal Services lost half of its staff as funding was shifted to another organization. With its reduced staff, Columbia began to take cases largely focused on systemic changes.

1 *For more information, see* www.braamkids.org.

A SYLAW-UW volunteer talks with a homeless youth at TeenFeed.

ABA © MAREN ANDERSON

As part of this change, the direct partnership with SYLAW was reduced to an advisory role, and SYLAW was no longer equipped to provide direct representation for youth. SYLAW is now focused on expanding its membership and applying for grant funding to allow SYLAW to again provide full-time staff attorneys to represent homeless youth. In the meantime, SYLAW's mission is being carried out through the efforts of its student chapter at the University of Washington School of Law (SYLAW-UW). SYLAW-UW continues to directly serve Seattle's homeless youth population by partnering with service providers in the University District to support existing programs and provide new legal services.

SYLAW's work within existing programs. SYLAW continues to provide significant services to the community, even without a direct legal services partnership.

Interactions between homeless youth and Seattle police officers are frequently characterized by feelings of hostility and mistrust. In hopes of easing this tension and cultivating greater understanding between police and youth, service providers have teamed up with the Seattle Police Department to create Donut Dialogues. Every year, SYLAW-UW provides much needed financial support for this event. The Donut Dialogues, created by and run in conjunction with Peace for the Streets by Kids from the Streets,[2] bring police officers and

2 *For more information, see* www.psks.org.

youth together in one room, and begin with an educational talk about basic laws regarding loitering, trespassing, and other areas where youth and police generally collide. This piece is then followed up by a question and answer period where police and youth break into small groups and try to reach a better understanding of each other. SYLAW-UW supports this program by providing financial support to pay for incentives for youth who participate as well as food. Incentives play a major part in many of the programs that SYLAW-UW facilitates. Youth have the opportunity to earn incentives (for example, bus tokens or small amounts of cash) for their participation. Incentives communicate to youth that we value their time, as well as allow them to get some of their needs met while attending one of our programs.

Natasha, an 18-year-old formerly homeless youth, had been involved in a two-year custody battle against the father of her child and her own mother when she got in touch with SYLAW. The father of the child was a multiply-convicted felon who had had little contact with the child because he had been in jail for much of the child's life. Natasha's mother had significantly abused and neglected Natasha when she was a child. After SYLAW became involved in the case, Natasha's mother voluntarily dismissed her petition for custody. The court entered a parenting plan that required the father to engage in substance abuse treatment, batterer's treatment, and other services before he has contact with the child. SYLAW also assisted Natasha in obtaining stable housing. With her housing and family law situations resolved, Natasha was able to obtain steady employment.

SYLAW breaks another barrier for youth. In 2004, SYLAW-UW partnered with the Washington Defender Association and other sponsors to start the Juvenile Records Sealing Clinic. A successful legislative reform effort headed by SYLAW, Columbia Legal Services, and a collaboration of youth services providers opened the door for thousands of young adults to seal their juvenile records. Young adults with juvenile criminal histories encounter many challenges when they apply for jobs, housing, financial aid, or take other steps necessary for adult independence. Many people incorrectly believe that juvenile conviction information is automatically destroyed upon a person's eighteenth birthday. In Washington, however, individuals must take proactive steps to ensure that their juvenile criminal history is sealed, and some offenses, such as sex offenses, may never be sealed. Prior to the legislative reform, Washington's laws in this area were the most severe in the United States.

Amanda, a 17-year-old youth, ran away from her physically and emotionally abusive parents. She sought emancipation in order to remain in the safe alternative living arrangement she had obtained. Prior to filing for emancipation Amanda had attempted to resolve issues through family counseling, but her parents refused to participate. Child Protective Services declined to intervene due to the client's age. The parents filed runaway reports and harassed Amanda at her place of work and her school, causing the A-student to miss school and to seek counseling. SYLAW prevailed in a contested emancipation proceeding which enabled Amanda to live away from home legally. As a result, she has resumed her excellent academic standing and refocused on planning for college. She also resumed efforts to engage her parents in family counseling.

The Sealing Clinic is held each month to help individuals who are eligible to seal their juvenile records navigate the court process. SYLAW-UW student volunteers meet with clients and assist them in determining their eligibility and completing the necessary paperwork. Since its inception, the Sealing Clinic has served over 100 clients and increased awareness of Washington's sealing laws. It is our hope that the clinic will improve awareness of the consequences of juvenile criminal history.

In order to increase our presence and build rapport with the homeless youth community, SYLAW-UW volunteers attend TeenFeed once a week. TeenFeed is a program run in Seattle's University District that provides an evening meal to homeless youth in the community. During TeenFeed, SYLAW-UW volunteers interact with homeless youth and engage them in conversation about their legal concerns and questions. Youth with specific legal needs are encouraged to visit the Street Youth Legal Drop-in Center (SYLD).

SYLD was launched in 2006. SYLAW hopes that SYLD will be a critical part of the mission to empower homeless and at-risk youth to address and eliminate the legal obstacles that may prevent them from reaching their goals. Staffed entirely by law students, SLYD is not able to provide legal representation to homeless youth. Instead, volunteers assist youth with identifying their specific legal needs and accessing pre-existing resources. SYLD volunteers help youth track down their public defender, ascertain the status of any pending criminal charges, and encourage them to quash outstanding warrants. SYLD volunteers also help youth access civil legal representation for matters related to housing, employment, and public entitlements.

Conclusion

SYLAW is a critical and innovative resource for the thousands of street youth in Washington State. While adapting to changing circumstances and funding issues, the program has consistently sought to provide legal services to youth in a meaningful way. The program has been popular among law students, restoring their faith in the connection between law and justice. It has also been popular among the youth themselves, creating new respect between the legal profession and young people who rarely see lawyers in a positive light. SYLAW has created bridges between private firms, providers and youth, opening lawyers' eyes to the possibilities that exist for positive partnerships. Throughout the decade that SYLAW has existed, while many things have changed, two constants have remained: the overwhelming need for legal services among street youth and the enduring commitment of an often untapped resource for serving this population—law students.

ABA © CASEY TRUPIN

Casey Trupin *Staff Attorney*
Columbia Legal Services
101 Yesler Way, Ste 300 Seattle, WA 98104
206.287.9665 casey.trupin@columbialegal.org

Casey Trupin is an attorney at Columbia Legal Services in Seattle, where he advocates for at-risk, homeless and foster youth as well as homeless adults. In 1997, Trupin co-founded Street Youth Legal Advocates of Washington (SYLAW), and went on to direct the program until 2005. He is also a member of the ABA's Commission on Homelessness and Poverty. Trupin has worked extensively with, lectured on, and written about troubled youth. In 1995-1996, he conducted a year-long study of resources for homeless youth throughout Latin America as a Thomas J. Watson Fellow. Trupin graduated with honors from the University of Washington School of Law in 1999 and was inducted into the school's Public Interest Law Association Hall of Fame in 2006. In 2005, Trupin was nominated by Senator Maria Cantwell and recognized by the Congressional Commission on Adoption Institute as an Angel in Adoption for his work on behalf of homeless and foster youth.

ABA © NEIL WOOD

Corey Fitzpatrick

Corey Fitzpatrick graduated from the University of Washington School of Law in June 2006. She is the current President of the SYLAW Governing Board and a former SYLAW intern. During her law school career, Ms. Fitzpatrick primarily focused on legal issues related to child welfare and juvenile justice. In 2004, she was a University of Michigan Bergstrom Child Welfare Law Fellow. As a third-year law student she participated in the Children and Youth Advocacy Clinic, where she represented youth in dependency proceedings. Ms. Fitzpatrick was recently awarded the 2006 Charles Z. Smith Public Interest Student of the Year Award in recognition of her commitment to public interest law.

All About Dignity:

A Collaboration in St. Louis to Defend the Rights of the Homeless

John J. Ammann

Introduction

"It was the best of times, it was the worst of times." This poetic line by Charles Dickens, which opened the epic *A Tale of Two Cities*, gained new life recently when a federal judge in St. Louis borrowed those words to open a 41-page decision that recognized the dignity of the homeless and chastised the police and city officials for depriving them of their rights.

The federal lawsuit known as *Chad Johnson, et al., v. Board of Police Commissioners*[1] and a related state court case hopefully will stand as a triumph for the dignity of the homeless. This article describes the basis for that hope and will also describe the collaboration of law school professors and students, legal aid attorneys, and other civil rights lawyers which led to the litigation and its successful results.

1 *Chad Johnson, et al., v. Board of Police Commissioners, 351 F.Supp.2d 929 (E.D. Mo. 2004).*

The Seeds of the Litigation

Twenty years ago in downtown St. Louis, there was little opportunity for a clash of cultures between middle income people and the homeless. Downtown was in a state of decline, and hardly anyone lived there. Vacant buildings were the rule. The homeless lived in the city, but went largely unnoticed because suburbanites came downtown only for work. The middle class might get panhandled over their lunch hour, but at 5 p.m. they were back in their cars headed for the suburbs. That changed in recent years, as developers renovated old warehouses into new lofts which attracted middle and upper class people, primarily young professionals, who had jobs downtown. As more and more people of means moved into the downtown area with their need for security and for space, the homeless were pushed off the streets by suspicions they would commit crimes, were pushed out of doorways where they once slept so the rich could get to their new homes, and were pushed out of the park where they rested so dogs of the new city dwellers had a place to play. Thus, the federal judge's reference to the best and worst of times was appropriate, as the revitalization efforts downtown ran headlong into the problem of homelessness.

Long before this new clash of cultures, the dedicated lawyers and social workers of Legal Services of Eastern Missouri (LSEM) had been representing the homeless. In fact, LSEM and Washington University Law School's Legal Clinic filed a class action lawsuit in the mid 1980s known as *Graham v. Schoemehl*, which resulted in a consent decree[2] requiring the City of St. Louis to provide a variety of services for the homeless and which led to the creation of a homeless service provider network still in operation today. Saint Louis University Law School's Legal Clinic has also represented the homeless in a variety of cases for many years. Lawyers from these institutions saw each other often in municipal court in the City of St. Louis where the homeless were frequently defendants in ordinance violation cases, and the attorneys began exchanging stories from the

2 *Pepper Graham et al. v. Vincent Schoemehl, No. 854-00035 (St. Louis, Mo. Circuit Court, Nov. 15, 1985). Consent decree available from author.*

homeless about how they were being pushed out of downtown, particularly during big events such as downtown loft tours and sporting events. Some were being arrested.

Meanwhile, the City and Police Department had entered into a contract with the Downtown St. Louis Partnership, the urban core's primary business organization, to create the Downtown Community Court. This court was funded by the Partnership, with a special assessment from a community improvement district sponsored by the Partnership paying for the salary of the judge, probation officer and prosecutor, and paying to reserve beds at the city jail for those arrested. The court was ostensibly designed for those committing "quality of life crimes," such as drinking in public, urinating in public, mass transit fare violations, trespassing and begging. Obviously, the homeless were prime targets of the new court.

So the accelerating revitalization of downtown, the influx of new residents, the simultaneous effort to remove the homeless from downtown through the use of police efforts and the Community Court, combined with a failure of the City to abide by all the terms of the consent decree, provided the backdrop for the litigation which would come next.

Forming the Legal Team

In 2003, lawyers at LSEM convened a meeting with faculty and students from the two St. Louis law schools and the legal director of the local office of the American Civil Liberties Union. The legal team, numbering 20 or more at times, was the first endeavor that combined the efforts of these four entities—the primary public interest legal institutions in St. Louis. As the members of the team compared stories from the many homeless clients they were representing, a clear pattern developed. St. Louis police officers were routinely telling the homeless and those appearing to be homeless that they were not welcome downtown and that they should stay out of the area. Many reported being told by police to stay "west of Jefferson," a reference to a main thoroughfare dividing downtown from the rest of the city.

Over the course of several meetings, a strategy developed that was the proverbial three-legged stool. The first leg involved consideration of a federal civil rights lawsuit to challenge the effort to remove the homeless from downtown and the arrest of the homeless without probable cause. The second leg was to challenge the creation of the Downtown Community Court as being an unconstitutional privately-funded court. Finally, the third leg was to ensure that proper services were available for the homeless, such as drop-in centers with meals and public toilets so that the homeless wouldn't have to loiter, beg, or urinate in public. The legal hook for this third leg was the 20-year-old consent decree in *Graham v. Schoemehl*, referenced above, which the City had not fully implemented.

The legal team sent a crucial letter to the Mayor and Police Chief on October 30, 2003, outlining a list of constitutional violations stemming from the way the homeless were being treated downtown. This letter proved to be crucial, as it was used in the litigation as evidence that the City was on notice about the claims of constitutional deprivation. While the Mayor and Police Chief decided they would not meet personally with the legal team, they did send their lawyers to a series of meetings with the representatives from the four institutions. However, there was little progress to resolve the concerns raised by the legal team. Meanwhile, the team continued to meet and collect evidence, waiting for some movement from the City.

While the "homeless lawyers" (as the team was often called) awaited action by the City, an event occurred that changed the complexion of the case and convinced the lawyers that they could wait no longer. During the Fourth of July holiday weekend in 2004, the City held its annual celebration known as Fair St. Louis. Hundreds of thousands of people come to the federal park grounds under the Gateway Arch each summer for the holiday weekend to enjoy food, rides, concerts, air shows, and fireworks. But in 2004, the City, the Police Department and the Downtown Partnership had a specific plan to remove the homeless from the streets during the Fair. In fact, several city officials used the word "sweep" to describe their own actions. Police arrested more than 70 people for quality of life crimes during the Fair, with almost all of those 70 people either being homeless or appearing to be homeless.

In many cases, the charges were evidence of a clear double standard that has always existed in the way the homeless were being treated in comparison to the middle class. For example, many of the homeless were charged with drinking in public, an activity that occurs hundreds of thousands of times at the Fair and in the fall at tailgate parties before the St. Louis Rams' football games, but which apparently was illegal when done by a homeless man a few blocks from the fairgrounds. The homeless were charged with begging, while middle class cheerleaders can stand in the middle of intersections collecting money for new uniforms.

In another particularly ironic aspect of the sweep, the homeless, who had gathered in a downtown park to enjoy the Fourth and the evening's fireworks display, missed the big show but had their own private fireworks display, courtesy of the police. The homeless were rousted from the park by police officers throwing firecrackers at them from unmarked vehicles. In addition, many of those arrested were forced to abandon their personal property or had it taken from then, including medication, food, and personal papers. One city

The primary attorneys and social workers involved on the legal team and their affiliations at the time of the litigation are as follows:

American Civil Liberties Union
Denise Lieberman
Steven Ryals

Legal Services of Eastern Missouri
Ann Lever
Daniel Glazier
Jennifer Heggemann
Susan Harris

Saint Louis University Legal Clinic
John Ammann
Susan McGraugh

Washington University, Civil Justice Clinic
Jane Aiken
Steven Gunn
Daniel Nagin

attorney explained to the Court that officers couldn't be expected to determine, when arresting a homeless person, "what was trash and what was personal belongings," since the homeless often carry their belongings in a trash bag.

The sweep was so well planned that a police precinct near downtown was set up to handle the high volume of arrestees, with long tables and lots of police forms ready to be filled out. Officers barked out random charges to lines of people, with no connection to any actual violation. Those arrested were then locked up in the City's jail for at least one night. One of the plaintiffs was stripped naked and held several hours in that condition. Many slept on the floor of the jail and had nothing to eat because it was so crowded.

The Court's decision in the federal court litigation summarized the evidence of the Plaintiffs in this matter:

> *It is clear to the Court that Plaintiffs have suffered harm and are likely to continue to suffer harm without judicial intervention at this stage of the proceedings. Among other things, Plaintiffs appear to have been subjected to arrests made in the absence of probable cause, inaccurate or fabricated charges, and intimidation tactics such as the throwing of firecrackers by police officers. They appear to have been subjected to forced labor in the form of community service work before being found guilty of any crime and to have had their property unlawfully taken. At least one was taken from Downtown and abandoned along the river front. Further, Plaintiffs have demonstrated that these harms do not appear to be isolated incidents of constitutional deprivations. Instead, they appear to be part of a larger effort to target homeless and homeless-appearing individuals to remove them from public areas. The evidence demonstrates that these violations have been occurring for at least a year and have persisted despite notice to city and police officials.*

Many of the instances of police misconduct alleged in the complaint occurred during the 2004 Fair, but others occurred at other times, thus establishing the policy required to prove a Section 1983 civil rights violation against government agencies.

The reference to forced labor in the opinion excerpt stems from a blanket order signed by the chief municipal judge of the City of St. Louis that essentially said anyone arrested for quality of life crimes over the Fourth of July weekend could get out of jail prior to the end of the holiday weekend if he or she completed eight hours of community service. To no one's surprise, the community service was cleaning up trash that middle class people had left in the downtown area. The clean-up crew was supervised by employees of the Downtown Partnership, with police officers actually turning custody of their prisoners over to the employees of this private entity. Not one of the arrestees had seen a judge for any purpose, much less conviction or sentence, before they did the community service.

After the Fourth of July events, the legal team began amending the draft complaint, which had been in process for months, to add the new allegations from the holiday weekend. The case was filed in September of 2004 in the United States District Court for the Eastern District of Missouri in St. Louis. It alleged violations of the Fourth Amendment prohibition on unreasonable searches and seizures and infringement of the right to travel, the right to be free from punishment without due process under the Fifth and Fourteenth Amendments, and the Thirteenth Amendment's prohibition on involuntary servitude for the forced community service. The suit was filed on behalf of 13 individuals and not as a class action.

Momentum Brings Victories in Two Cases

U.S. District Judge E. Richard Webber held a two-day hearing in September of 2004 on whether a preliminary injunction should be issued. Most of the original 13 plaintiffs attended the trial, and many of them testified. They were patient, respectful, and articulate. They told their individual stories of beatings, having police throw firecrackers at them, being arrested, being locked up in jail, sleeping on the floor, and having their property taken.

The local media covered the trial, and the *St. Louis Post Dispatch* ran front-page stories. At the height of this publicity, the state court judge hearing the challenge to the Downtown Community Court issued his decision. Prior to the filing of the federal lawsuit, the legal team had filed a state court case in Missouri Circuit Court in St. Louis for a writ of prohibition to have the Downtown Community Court declared invalid. With the front page stories about the forced labor and other constitutional violations from the Fourth of July weekend as a backdrop, the state court judge ruled that the entire Community Court was unconstitutional for being privately funded.[3]

Meanwhile the federal court, which had taken the Section 1983 case under advisement, issued a preliminary injunction on October 14, 2004. The Plaintiffs viewed the lengthy opinion supporting the injunction as a huge success, and not only as a legal victory. The Plaintiffs were visibly bolstered by the fact the federal judge listened to their stories attentively. In fact, at the end of the testimony, the judge acknowledged all the Plaintiffs, those who testified and those who didn't, thanked them for attending the trial, and thanked them for their respectful behavior in Court. When the decision was issued, the Plaintiffs and their lawyers were as thrilled that the judge believed their stories as they were to get the relief the Court entered. In fact, in its decision, the Court stated: "On Plaintiffs' side of the case, those who present themselves as Plaintiffs' witnesses appear to be very bright, articulate and believable." This sentence meant as much to the Plaintiffs as the rest of the decision.

The Settlement

While the parties prepared for trial, a mediation was scheduled in an effort to resolve the federal litigation. In the fall of 2005, after a full day of mediation, the parties settled the case with the City, the Police Department, and the Downtown St. Louis Partnership, which had been added as a party. The Police and the City agreed to certain

3 *State of Missouri ex rel. Derrick Bogan, Relator, v. Honorable Ruby Bonner, No. 044-250 (St. Louis, Mo. Circuit Court, Sept. 24, 2004). Opinion available from author.*

principles recognizing the rights of the homeless. The Police Department agreed to change many policies, with the primary change being an agreement to issue a summons for quality of life crimes instead of using an immediate arrest policy. The Defendants insisted that the settlement not be in the form of a consent decree, and while not ideal, the Plaintiffs agreed to allow for a settlement agreement that was not in the form of a judgment. Meanwhile the individual plaintiffs, who prior to the mediation had agreed to settle for the same amount for each man or woman regardless of the extent of damages, each received $1,200. An additional $20,000 was set aside for charities that serve the homeless, and a modest amount was agreed upon for attorney fees and costs. In addition to the important change in policies, the modest monetary settlement helped many of the plaintiffs obtain apartments or pay overdue rent at their SRO's.

Obstacles Overcome

Any major litigation has inherent obstacles. Suing a major city and its police department opens the door to worthy opponents whose clients want them to challenge every aspect of the plaintiffs' case. In addition, other factors made this litigation even more complicated. While the collaboration of four major public interest law institutions was a unique positive aspect, it also brought its challenges. The legal directors of each of these institutions had personal visions of the case, and there were many debates on issues of strategy. The legal team was also faced with internal administrative issues of four large institutions. Writing memoranda and briefs was a true challenge. As many lawyers in big organizations know, writing a brief "by committee" is most difficult due to varying writing styles.

In addition to the opposition of the defendants through the legal process with motions to dismiss and other filings, the political opposition by the City and Police Department proved powerful as well. The defendants had the support for their efforts to remove the homeless from downtown businesses, downtown loft developers, downtown residents, and in the case of the Downtown Community Court, the support of court personnel. The Mayor's personal blog had numerous postings by the Mayor criticizing the litigation and mentioning one of the plaintiffs' lawyers by name in his criticism of the case.

Perhaps the most significant difference of opinion was over the timing of the filing of the federal lawsuit. Some on the team would have filed the case earlier than it was filed, but taking a more deliberate approach allowed the team to be able to add the Fourth of July sweep to the complaint.

Student Opportunities

While the primary focus of this litigation was to reveal and fight the civil rights violations of police and government officials, in the process the case provided an opportunity for law students to learn many different aspects of civil rights litigation involving the homeless.

The primary benefit of the case was to expose law students to homeless men and women and their plight. Students joined lawyers going to shelters, meal programs, SRO's, hotels, parks, hospitals, abandoned buildings, and other places where the homeless can be found. They learned about the lives of the homeless, and many of the students realized how much their clients were just like them. The participation of the students hopefully also provided an opportunity for more positive race relations in the City. Since most of the clients were African American and most of the students were white, bringing them together in various aspects of the case educated everyone about the importance of acceptance.

Students gained some very real practical legal experience as well. Law students interviewed clients, drafted portions of the complaint, and researched and drafted motions and responses. They learned a significant amount of law, both procedural and substantive. They also participated in the strategy meetings and learned from several experienced attorneys. Several students were able to participate in taking the depositions of police officers.

Interestingly, the participation of students drew complaints from the attorneys for the defendants. City lawyers, upset that they had to use limited resources to fight the complaint, termed the litigation a "student project" and criticized the lawyers for providing bad examples for the students. The legal team took that criticism in stride, knowing that the litigation was an effort to end the abuse of the civil rights of the homeless and that the law students provided a valuable service to the plaintiffs.

ABA © JAMES VISSER

John J. Ammann *Professor of Law*
Director, Legal Clinic
Saint Louis University School of Law
321 North Spring St. Louis, MO 63108
314.977.2778 ammannjj@slu.edu

John J. Ammann is a Professor at Saint Louis University School of Law and is the Director of the Legal Clinic. He serves as a member of the Governing Committee of the ABA Forum on Affordable Housing and Community Development Law and is past editor of the Forum's Journal. He joined the faculty at Saint Louis University in 1994 after working for eight years at Land of Lincoln Legal Assistance in Alton, Illinois, where he specialized in housing and family law. He has also clerked for appellate court judges in Missouri and Illinois and is licensed in both states. At the Legal Clinic, Professor Ammann supervises students in representation of the homeless in minor criminal proceedings and in major civil rights litigation. He and his students also provide legal assistance to Habitat for Humanity and other nonprofit housing providers. In addition, Professor Ammann has served as co-counsel on successful litigation on behalf of Medicaid recipients, foster and adopted children, and children with disabilities. He has been voted Faculty Member of the Year twice by the students at the Law School and has received the Governor's Award for Teaching Excellence. He serves on several nonprofit boards, including Habitat for Humanity St. Louis and Legal Services of Eastern Missouri.

A Legacy of Dignity

The legacy of this effort is not yet clear. Many of the advocates know that great results in major litigation don't last forever, and that fighting for the rights of the poor and oppressed is a battle with no end.

On the day that the decision was issued, the local media were looking for a quote from one of the Plaintiffs' lawyers. In a brief phone call among some of the attorneys, an attorney from Legal Services summed up what we had been trying to do all along in one word: Dignity.

Homeless men and women were noticed and respected by middle class lawyers and law students who not only represented them, but ate with them, shared Christmas parties with them, and became friends with them. Homeless men and women were noticed and respected by a federal judge. Homeless men and women were noticed and respected by the local media who reported on the case and interviewed them about their circumstances. They had been able to get the City and Police Department to acknowledge in writing that new policies would be instituted protecting the rights of the homeless and for that matter, everyone, to be in public places and to be free from unreasonable searches and seizures of their person and property. Most importantly, the legal team hopes that the general public became a bit more sensitive to issues of homelessness from this effort.

The litigation has shown that by using our system of justice to recognize and enhance the dignity of the homeless, we have the opportunity to enhance the dignity of us all.

The John J. Curtin, Jr. Justice Fund:

Supporting Law Students Working to End Homelessness

Krista D. Kauper

With increases in the number of individuals who fall below the poverty line and a shortage of affordable housing over the last 20 years, homelessness has become a fact of life in the United States. Although by its nature it is difficult to measure, by some estimates, millions of Americans experience homelessness each year, and families with children are among the fastest growing segments of the homeless population. While they do not fit one general description, people who become homeless share common needs, including the need for legal assistance.

The American Bar Association is committed to serving the needs of those less fortunate and, through The John J. Curtin, Jr. Justice Fund, it provides legal assistance to the homeless. The Curtin Justice Fund, an endowed fund created and maintained within the ABA Fund for Justice and Education, aims to help homeless clients and to encourage careers in law which further the goals of social justice.

The Curtin Justice Fund provides stipends to law students who spend the summer months working for a bar association or legal services program designed to help the homeless. In the process, nonprofit organizations serving the underrepresented receive much-needed legal assistance, and the grants provide training and direct experience in public service law to the law student interns.

The ABA created The John J. Curtin, Jr. Justice Fund to honor Jack Curtin, ABA President from 1990-91. To acknowledge his outstanding achievements and the esteem in which he is held by ABA members and staff, his colleagues in the Association raised over $100,000 within a year of his leaving office to establish the Fund which they named in his honor. Jack Curtin's long-standing dedication to issues of social justice and civil rights led to approval by the ABA Board of Governors to use the income from the Justice Fund to place law students in legal organizations working to help homeless people.

Each summer, three law student interns receive stipends from The John J. Curtin, Jr. Justice Fund to work for a bar association or legal services program to provide legal assistance to homeless people. The Curtin Interns work to prevent homelessness and address the legal needs of people experiencing homelessness by providing supervised representation and/or policy-based advocacy. Through this program, the Curtin Interns receive an invaluable education in public interest law, and many go on to careers in the area of public service or take on pro bono work because of their internship experience.

The student interns provide legal support on a wide array of projects, including conducting intake at homeless shelters, researching issues related to public assistance, providing outreach and education concerning civil rights, providing legal assistance on mental health issues, and representing, under supervision, homeless and at-risk clients.

Jennifer Gehrig, Curtin Intern with the Legal Aid Society of Minneapolis, 1997

"The internship has been the most valuable part of my legal education thus far. Dialogue about the importance of poverty law is largely absent in law school. Therefore, this opportunity provided me with the reinforcement and affirmation I needed to continue pursuing a career as an attorney."

Lawyers nationally have mobilized to meet the legal needs of people experiencing homelessness through local bar services, law school clinics, and nonprofit organizations. In the past years, the Curtin Interns have worked with a number of organizations across the country, including:

- The Appalachia Research and Defense Fund in Jackson, Kentucky
- The Bar Association of San Francisco Homeless Advocacy Project
- The Bazelon Center for Mental Health Law in Washington, DC
- Coalition for the Homeless in New York City
- Columbia Legal Services in Seattle, Washington
- Covenant House in Anchorage, Alaska
- Lawyers for Affordable Housing in Dallas, Texas
- Lawyers Clearinghouse on Affordable Housing and Homelessness in Boston, Massachusetts
- National Law Center on Homelessness & Poverty
- San Diego's Homeless Court Program

Kristin Zimmerman, Utah Legal Services Project for Women, Justice, Economic Dignity and Independence

In 1998, Kristin Zimmerman, a student at the University of Utah College of Law, spent her summer months working for the Utah Legal Services Project for Women, Justice, Economic Dignity and Independence. The assistance Kristin provided was not only critical for one family she helped, but also had a profound impact on her career.

Through the outreach efforts of the Utah Legal Services Project, Kristin began working with a woman who had been denied reimbursement for child care by the Department of Workforce Services. The young woman was supporting four children and made just $7.00 an hour.

As Kristin explains, without assistance, the woman would not have made it. Kristin participated in an administrative law hearing and, by demonstrating that the case revolved around the simple fact of an incorrect form, was successful in obtaining child care reimbursement for her client. From this experience, Kristin learned how to deal with the welfare bureaucracy and the rewards of providing legal assistance to someone in need.

The internship was a tremendous experience for Kristin: "I am now a legal aid attorney—a domestic relations attorney. When I went to law school, I thought I wanted to go into legal aid when I graduated. The internship strongly reinforced that desire and taught me a great deal about the need for legal services. The experience still helps me today—through the internship I learned the skills I use every day."

Matt Schneider, Coalition for the Homeless

For Matt Schneider, the Curtin Internship was the first step in a career dedicated to public service. Matt interned at the Coalition for the Homeless in New York City during the summer of 1994. As Matt describes, "the Curtin Internship influenced my career immensely."

As a result of the rewarding experience at the Coalition for the Homeless, Matt pursued a fellowship from NAPIL/Legal Services Corporation to work in rural New York State, serving isolated rural people living on farms and in a patchwork of shelters. After graduation from law school, Matt was awarded a New York State IOLTA (Interest on Lawyers' Trust Accounts) fellowship for two years. Matt now works at New York Legal Assistance Group, where he continues to specialize in advocating for individuals involved in welfare-to-work programs.

The first step in this dedicated public service career was the Curtin Internship. Matt credits the Curtin Internship with profoundly influencing his career—a career dedicated to social justice.

Alicia Mandolini, The Bazelon Center

As a second-year law student at John Marshall Law School, Alicia Mandolini was awarded a Curtin Internship, and she spent her summer at the Bazelon Center in Washington, DC, a nonprofit legal advocacy organization for people with mental disabilities. During her internship, Alicia was immersed in mental health issues and legislation concerning fair housing. She conducted client interviews, composed a synopsis of cases for the Center's website, attended seminars and functions at the Senate building, and toured mental health facilities in the Washington area.

The Curtin Internship afforded Alicia the invaluable opportunity to spend the summer working with experts in the fields of mental health and fair housing law. These two subjects continue to play an important role in her life: Alicia works as a social worker at Thresholds, a group home for the mentally ill, and she is an advocate for fair housing issues in Chicago. As Alicia explains, "I never would have been exposed to these issues had it not been for the Curtin Internship."

Marissa Boyers, The Southern Arizona Peoples Law Center

For Marissa Boyers, the Curtin Internship was a life-changing opportunity. Marissa was a second-year student at Temple University School of Law in 1994 when she was awarded a Curtin Internship and spent her summer at The Southern Arizona Peoples Law Center in Tucson.

Marissa describes the Center at the time as a "one-man show," with one attorney/director. With the assistance of the Curtin

"The Curtin Internships create opportunities for law students that would otherwise be unavailable—opportunities that are life-changing and career defining. Without the Curtin Internship, I would not have been able to spend the summer serving the indigent in Arizona, and more importantly, the Law Center would not have been able to provide so many valuable services."

Marissa Boyers, Curtin Intern with the Southern Arizona Peoples Law Center, 1994

Internship, Marissa effectively doubled the amount of services the Center was able to provide to their indigent clients. Marissa participated in community organizing activities and provided supervised legal services to clients, often accompanying them to court. One of the highlights of the experience for Marissa was working with the director on a class action lawsuit for people receiving public assistance. Marissa notes that through the Curtin Internship, she participated in projects that she would never have been exposed to in law school.

Recently Marissa was honored by the Philadelphia Bar Association for her pro bono work with the Support Center for Child Advocates. She is an associate at Duane, Morris & Heckscher, LLP, where she continues to work in the public interest arena.

Lee Kaplan, Homeless Advocacy Project

Working with the Bar Association of San Francisco's Homeless Advocacy Project, Lee Kaplan spent the summer in 1993 conducting intake and providing supervised representation for homeless and at-risk clients.

Lee learned important lessons from her experience at the Homeless Advocacy Project, specifically, she notes, the importance of treating homeless clients with respect. Lee remembers one client in particular whose situation touched her. This client needed shelter for the night, but he had been told that all shelters were full. San Francisco's mayor had recently declared that homeless people were

For more information, visit the Commission's Web site at www.abanet.org/homeless/ or call (202) 662-1694.

The Curtin Justice Fund Internship Program is managed jointly by the ABA Commission on Homelessness and Poverty and the Standing Committee on Legal Aid and Indigent Defendants. The Program provides a $2,500 stipend to students in support of their internships designed to prevent homelessness or assist homeless clients.

not to sleep in the streets or in doorways. Frustrated, Lee went straight to the top and called the mayor's office to remind them of the mayor's promise and to demand that the mayor's staff find her client a bed. Suddenly, there was a bed available.

The Curtin Internship made it possible for Lee to make a difference for homeless and at-risk clients. She brought energy and compassion to her work at the Homeless Advocacy Project, and was able to see the impact of her work on behalf of those in need.

Joel Winful, Lawyers for Affordable Housing

In 1993, Joel Winful was one of the first three law students to receive a Curtin Internship. Joel, a second-year student at Southern Methodist University School of Law, interned at Lawyers for Affordable Housing (LAH) in Dallas. By helping provide legal services to low-income home-owners, Joel became involved in activities associated with public interest law and the provision of legal services to the poor.

Joel describes his experience at LAH as "very enriching," and he particularly remembers his experience assisting one low-income homeowner. "Mrs. S." was a 70-year-old woman whose home was badly in need of repair. In trying to make the repairs, Mrs. S had turned to a City of Dallas program that gives grants to low-income people to help them rehabilitate their homes. Working with LAH, a volunteer lawyer drafted the necessary paperwork. Although all

Each year, contributions to the Curtin Justice Fund increase the ABA's capacity to reach out to law students and homeless people nationwide.

To make a contribution to the The John J. Curtin, Jr. Justice Fund, please contact the ABA Office of the Fund for Justice and Education by telephone at (312) 988-5927.

that was needed to complete the process was for Mrs. S. to come to LAH and sign the document before a notary, Mrs. S. had no way to get to LAH. Joel took it upon himself to make a house call with a notary to enable Mrs. S. to sign the document properly. Joel explains that this experience taught him how the lack of money even for the bus or cab fare affects the lives of the poor every day. "The community at large thinks poor people who aren't in crisis situations don't need legal help. They often do," Joel notes.

Joel's experience as a Curtin Intern at LAH inspired him to continue his involvement with public service, and he remains committed to providing legal assistance to the poor and low-income members of the Dallas community. Joel now works for the Dallas County District Attorney's Office, and he commits his volunteer time to Legal Services of North Texas, which helps make access to the legal system a reality for all people, not just for those who can afford it.

ABA © KRISTA KAUPER

Krista D. Kauper *Director of Development*
ABA Fund for Justice and Education
321 N. Clark Street Chicago, IL 60610
312.988.5404 kauperk@staff.abanet.org

Krista D. Kauper is the Director of Development for the ABA Fund for Justice and Education, a charitable organization created to support the law-related public service and educational programs of the American Bar Association. Ms. Kauper oversees all fundraising activities for the FJE generally and assists ABA sections, divisions, and other entities in seeking outside funding to support their public service programs. Upon graduation from the University of Michigan Law School, Ms. Kauper joined Gibson, Dunn & Crutcher in Washington, DC and then served as Special Assistant to the General Counsel of the Resolution Trust Corporation. After practicing law for eight years, Ms. Kauper joined the University of Arizona College of Law as the Director of Development and Alumni Relations. In her eight years at the American Bar Association, Ms. Kauper has worked to increase awareness of the role of the FJE in the Association and to cultivate support for the Association's important public service work.

The John J. Curtin, Jr. Justice Fund continues to foster legal careers that further social justice. In the summer of 2006, the ABA Commission on Homelessness and Poverty and Standing Committee on Legal Aid and Indigent Defendants awarded fellowships to three law students with a demonstrated passion for public service. Hristiyaniya Atanasova of Boston University School of Law interned at Greater Boston Legal Services, where she assisted clients in securing housing, mediated landlord-tenant cases, and advocated for affordable housing in Boston. Ashley Fluhrer of University of Washington School of Law interned at Picture the Homeless in New York, providing direct legal services to homeless individuals and coordinating the organization's Constitutional Legal Rights Clinic. Jeffrey Yungman of Charleston School of Law interned at the Charleston County Public Defender's Office. Yungman's internship focused on reducing the number of homeless individuals who are incarcerated due to their homeless status and removing legal barriers for homeless people transitioning into the workforce. The American Bar Association is pleased to support the work of these law students and remains committed to providing fellowships to law students dedicated to championing the rights of people experiencing homelessness.

People Advocating Therapeutic Homes:

Law Schools Working to House the Homeless

Robert Whitman

Three years ago, I encountered a model of a home for helping individuals in need that struck me as especially workable and worthwhile. That model home is now referred to as a PATH-Type home. PATH-Type homes are individually owned therapeutic homes for mental health and addiction recovery. People Advocating Therapeutic Homes (PATH) was first organized in 2003 as an all volunteer, nonprofit Connecticut corporation. Through the efforts of volunteer law students, it has subsequently gained 501(c)(3) status. PATH's mission is to address the shortage of housing for people in recovery by promoting the creation and ongoing operation of affordable, self-supporting therapeutic homes. These homes provide a safe, structured, and supportive environment for up to one year for residents who have already received appropriate medical intervention. As a condition of occupancy, each resident must agree to follow the home's therapeutic rules, as well as meet financial obligations. In order to allow PATH to operate efficiently as an all volunteer organization and to avoid conflicts or insurmountable operational challenges, PATH was organized as an all volunteer "think tank." PATH does not own or operate any home, nor does it pay anyone a salary. Instead, it stands ready to help and support any would-be owner of a PATH-Type home.

Advantages Gained from PATH-Type Homes

PATH-Type homes are seen as effective long-term recovery units that provide stable and structured environments for recovery. While each owner of a PATH-Type home establishes the rules for the home, often home occupants are able to stay indefinitely until they are secure in their recoveries and able to make arrangements to move to other housing. Studies have shown that PATH-Type homes are a very effective means of giving homeless persons a chance to live in a supportive environment that fosters independence, self-esteem, and mental health or addiction recovery. PATH-Type homes have taken in many homeless people who have lived on the street and afforded them the opportunity of long-term successful rehabilitation.

Among the other unique attributes of PATH-Type homes are the following:

1. PATH-Type homes are privately owned homes open for mental health and addiction recovery to occupants who are able to work and pay rent to support the home.
2. Once established, a PATH-Type home requires no government subsidies.
3. Occupants are able to remain in a PATH-Type home for the extended periods of time that are needed to accomplish lasting recoveries.
4. PATH-Type homes provide basic clean and sober living arrangements, structure, and therapeutic group environments at an affordable price.
5. PATH-Type homes teach basic living skills (e.g. cooking, cleaning, and sharing responsibilities) to occupants who are then able to distance themselves from old and harmful environments, friends, and lifestyles.

Law Students Play a Leading Role

Perhaps the most interesting feature in the development of the PATH organization has been the opportunity for law students to be part of its creation, thus allowing the students to actively promote the idea of PATH-Type homes. The previously mentioned incorporation of PATH and its obtaining of 501(c)(3) status was largely engineered by law students. Through PATH, students are able to gain satisfaction in helping promote others' recoveries while simultaneously obtaining practical legal experience. Many occupants of PATH-Type homes require law student assistance in working out legal issues, and much of the research into legal issues concerning PATH is generated by law students.

At interested law schools, PATH, or some other worthwhile charity that could aid the homeless, might become the focus of a law school course or a school-wide effort. So often, law students are eager to serve the needs of the public. Organizing and operating a charitable organization can allow them to accomplish this goal while interviewing clients, researching legal issues, and drafting legislation.

Examples of Law Students' Contributions

In cooperation with the State of Connecticut Department of Mental Health and Addiction Services (DMHAS), the University of Connecticut Small Business Development Corporation, and Connecticut Community for Addiction Recovery (CCAR), PATH has been training future owners of PATH-Type homes. To help in this effort, PATH has also published a book entitled *Owning and Operating a PATH-Type Home for Mental Health and Addiction Recovery*. This book was largely a law student effort. PATH also encourages other departments at the University of Connecticut to participate in plans for research into mental health and addiction recovery. Hopefully, this will allow law students to act jointly with other university students.

Another example of law student work concerns the organization of PATH-Type homes. While PATH-Type homes had operated in Connecticut for some time, without a statewide accessible website, there was no easy way for those in need (or the professionals that helped them) to easily locate a home. In order to provide easy access to information, PATH now operates a statewide accessible website: *www.therapeutichomes.org*. The website shows the inventory of PATH-Type homes in Connecticut, contains links to other helpful websites, and carries law student papers dealing with zoning and other legal issues that impede the growth and development of these homes. A law student organization based at the University of Connecticut Law School called Law Students Supporting PATH has been networking with other law schools in the hopes of forming a nationwide linked group of websites to track PATH-Type homes available in each state. Law students have sought out PATH-Type homes in Connecticut and urged owners to list their homes on the PATH website. There is no charge for listing a PATH-Type home or for using the website to locate a home. Law students have also contacted fellow students at other law schools in an effort to encourage the creation of PATH websites in other states. PATH support groups are now forming in both New York City and Boston.

Robert Whitman *Professor of Law*
University of Connecticut School of Law
65 Elizabeth Street Hartford, CT 06105
860.570.5250 robert.whitman@law.uconn.edu

Robert (Bob) Whitman is a Professor of Law at the University of Connecticut School of Law. Bob is the founder and chair of People Advocating Therapeutic Homes (PATH), a 501(c)(3) charity that serves as a think tank in support of the model of a PATH-Type home for mental health and addiction recovery. Bob Whitman is a life member of the American Law Institute (ALI), a former commissioner (from Connecticut) to the National Conference of Commissioners on Uniform State Laws (NCCUSL), and an active member of the Senior Lawyers Division and the Real Property, Probate and Trust Law Section (RPPT) of the American Bar Association and the American College of Trust and Estates Counsel (ACTEC). Professor Whitman is the founder and co-planning chair of the Annual ALI-ABA Conference on Representing Estate and Trust Beneficiaries and Fiduciaries. He has authored many books and articles, including *How to Own and Operate a Therapeutic Home for Mental Health and Addiction Recovery* (with Terri O'Connell and published by the Graduate Group).

A final example of law student involvement relates to the establishment of the PATH-Type homes themselves. Homeowners needed a support organization to help them challenge restrictive local zoning practices that would prevent the establishment of PATH-Type homes in certain areas. While local residents occasionally would voice concerns about the creation of these homes in their neighborhoods, the reality is that PATH-Type homes cause absolutely no adverse consequences and are usually welcomed as good neighbors once they are established. PATH is now creating an annual law student writing contest to focus on existing legal issues and ways of removing obstacles to the development of PATH-Type homes. In Connecticut, PATH has helped homeowners challenge zoning restrictions and other legal issues that block PATH-Type home development. Law student research has been most important in understanding present law and the need for changes. Examples of law student work can be found on the PATH website.

Conclusion

PATH hopes that students at other law schools will join it in these efforts. For further information about PATH, please contact Virginia Lamb, President of PATH, at *valambwolf@aol.com*. Law students for PATH may be contacted at *robert.whitman@uconn.edu*. For information on the law student writing contest, please contact *lewis.kurlantzick@uconn.edu*. For further information on PATH's book, *How to Own and Operate a PATH-Type Home for Mental Health and Addiction Recovery*, please contact *toconnell@skelleyrottner.com.*

CHAPTER 3

Law Firms Working to End Homelessness

Private Firms Tackling a Public Problem:

How Law Firms Can Help Fight Homelessness

Jeffrey Alan Simes

The Plight of Homeless Children

Imagine you have just become homeless. You struggle to find shelter and ultimately find refuge in a homeless shelter far from your last place of permanent residence. You would like your children to continue to attend their public schools—the less disruption in their lives the better—but because you no longer reside in the school district, your children are not permitted by school district officials to attend school. "We are sorry," they say, "but this school is open only to residents of our school district. You don't live here any more. Goodbye."

Your protestations fall on deaf ears. Reluctantly, you go to the new school district where the shelter is located and try to enroll your children in the schools there. Better that they attend some school, you reason, than no school at all. But the new school district won't enroll your children without proof of residency—something you don't have. You don't have a lease, a utility bill, or any other piece of paper showing your permanent address because, quite simply, you have no permanent address. The school district also demands that you provide proof of immunization. You explain that you are homeless and have lost your records. You ask whether the school district can obtain the records from the last school district your child attended. The school district smugly explains that it is not in the business of tracking down students' documentation.

After much back and forth, you are told you can appeal the school district's decision directly to the state's Department of Education. You ask for the relevant form and are handed a lengthy, single-spaced document, requiring detailed, typewritten, notarized affidavits, along with a filing fee, all hand served on the relevant parties. The instructions as to how to fill out the form, you are told, are available on the Internet. You reflect that you have little more than the clothes on your back, much less a computer, access to notaries and process servers, or the other wherewithal necessary under the arcane appeals system to assert your rights.

Because your children's education is important to you, you persist. You finally find a way around this Catch-22 and manage to persuade a sympathetic administrator to enroll your children. Unfortunately, your troubles have only begun. You ask the district to send a school bus to pick up your children. They tell you that it is the problem of the Department of Social Services. Social Services agrees to send a bus, but days pass into weeks before a bus arrives.

Finally, the bus comes, and your children are off to school. Your patience has paid off! That evening, however, you receive a notice that the Social Services Department is moving your family to a dif-

Interested in learning more about the education rights of homeless children and youth?

Read *Educating Children Without Housing: A Primer on the Legal Requirements and Implementation Strategies for Educators, Advocates and Policymakers,* a guide published by the ABA Commission on Homelessness & Poverty and Steering Committee on the Unmet Legal Needs of Children. The book is available at **http://www.abanet.org/homeless/**. Also visit the National Association for the Education of Homeless Children and Youth at **http://www.naehcy.org/**.

ferent shelter in a different school district. A few days pass before the bus starts coming to the new shelter to take your children to school. Your children are becoming upset that they have spent so little time in recent weeks with their schoolfriends. Your oldest, a senior in high school, wonders if she will be able to graduate on time and with her friends.

With transportation re-established, you feel relief. But then the school district informs you that your children can no longer enroll in that district because—you suspected this was coming—they no longer live within the school district. You have now spent weeks seeking to enroll your children and get them transportation to school, and you are back at square one. The chances are great that your child will suffer academically and perhaps be left back a grade.

If, at this point, you have the presence of mind and patience to pursue the matter further, the cycle will simply repeat itself. No sooner will you work out the bureaucratic obstacles with the school district, then the Department of Social Services will move you to a new shelter, requiring a new round of frustration and pleading simply to secure the basic right for your children to attend the public schools. All the while, your children are falling further behind, risking failure, grade retention, and dropping out. What should be your children's best sources of stability and best avenue to break the cycle of poverty—the public schools—are simply unavailable.

Sadly, the scenario presented above is not a hypothetical—it was a reality faced by many homeless families throughout the country. It was the subject of a year of litigation against State, County and local authorities in the matter of *National Law Center on Homelessness and Poverty, et al. v. State of New York, et al.* brought in the United States District Court for the Eastern District of New York. That lawsuit exemplifies both the problems facing homeless families as well as the ways in which private law firms and nonprofit organizations can play a role in assisting homeless families and in breaking the bureaucratic cycles that help to perpetuate homelessness.

The Origins of a Lawsuit

The history of this case is an odd mix of serendipity and fate. Our law firm's growing New York office was looking for a significant pro bono matter that would enthuse and engage our personnel, but also that could help to integrate the New York office with the firm's other offices. In December 2003, that opportunity presented itself. Chance brought the National Law Center on Homelessness and Poverty to the pro bono administrator of our firm, who directed their call to me, because she knew I had been a teacher before becoming a lawyer. They had been tracking a large number of complaints in New York—particularly Suffolk County on Long Island—but they were having difficulty finding a firm with the resources and desire to take on this fight.

My first reaction was surprise that no other firm in New York—perhaps the most crowded legal market in the country—had expressed interest in taking on such a worthy and noble cause. Delving further into the matter, I began to sense why: fighting such a case could potentially involve a massive commitment by a firm at a time when many firms, ours included, were quite busy with existing client obligations. After discussions with our firm management, however, we decided to commit to this important cause, and we immediately began to investigate the claims, interview affected homeless families, and prepare our complaint.

The Nuts and Bolts of Taking on the Government

We concluded early on that the matter would be brought in federal court. First, a federal statute—the McKinney-Vento Act[1]—mandated (although the precedents were few) that states and school districts remove the bureaucratic obstacles of the sort that were preventing many children in Suffolk County from attending the public

1 *See 42 U.S.C. § 11431 et seq.*

schools. We were also concerned that State court judges—subject to election pressures—might be less inclined to vindicate the rights of the disenfranchised.

We concluded that a class action was the appropriate; because the population of homeless families is constantly changing and moving, seeking relief on behalf of a handful of specific homeless families might result in wasted efforts if the plaintiffs found permanent housing or obtained access once again to the public schools. We realized that the issues in this case were widespread and repetitive, and thus the broader relief available through a class action seemed most desirable.

Finding class representatives was no easy task. Because our complaint alleged a wide array of unlawful activities that were preventing homeless children from attending public school, we needed a comparably diverse array of representative plaintiffs. We had an institutional plaintiff—the National Law Center on Homelessness and Poverty—but we needed individual families whose stories were compelling and cried out for relief. We relied heavily on our friends in the local legal aid agencies and advocacy groups to direct to us potential plaintiffs who had been denied access to the public schools. Having been frustrated by many years of bureaucratic indifference at all levels, the legal aid attorneys and local homeless advocates were more than happy to help and proved to be a vital resource at all stages of the litigation.

We ultimately settled on approximately ten homeless families as our class representatives. While this was perhaps more than we needed, we faced a potentially long-lasting litigation, and we had to

Chris Garvey and Jeff Simes led the firm's team of advocates in the class action litigation seeking to improve homeless children's access to public schooling.

ABA © GOODWIN I PROCTER LLP.

be realistic about the prospects of our plaintiff's problems becoming resolved by the march of time, as well as the possibility that we might lose track of some of the homeless families over time. To ensure that we would have their stories preserved, even if they moved away, became permanently housed, or disappeared, we obtained detailed affidavits from each of the homeless families at the outset of the case. These proved indispensable later on, when we faced waves of motions from determined opponents.

Armed with our complaint and detailed affidavits from each plaintiff, we filed our lawsuit along with a motion for a preliminary injunction seeking immediate relief on behalf of S.P. (we fought hard throughout the case to protect the privacy of our plaintiffs), a fifteen-year-old with learning disabilities who had missed the better part of the school year due to bureaucratic inertia and resistance. When her family was evicted in December 2003, her mother pleaded with everyone who would listen to get her back into school. No one would help, and every government agency she spoke to insisted it was someone else's problem, resulting in months of school absences. So compelling were S.P. and her story that the Defendants agreed, the very day we filed the lawsuit and motion, to arrange immediate transportation for her to avoid an injunction and also agreed to expedite procedures for enrolling and transporting homeless children during the pendency of the lawsuit.

We had half-hoped for a speedy resolution to the case, prompted in part by signals from the Judge that he was surprised that the

State, County, and local governments were not eager to ensure that homeless children were getting a public education. Nonetheless, initial efforts to settle the case were unsuccessful. Although we sought no monetary damages in the lawsuit—and, in fact, we informed the Defendants that if a settlement could be reached expeditiously, we would waive any claim to the attorneys' fees to which the relevant statutes would entitle us—the Defendants were determined in their opposition. Not only did they insist that they were under no legal obligation to remove the obstacles that kept the public schools closed to homeless children, but they insisted that the homeless families themselves were solely to blame for their predicaments.

Waging War on All Fronts

We now hunkered down to contend with determined opposition by the State, County and local governments. Our Judge, sympathetic to the plight of homeless children, ordered that the case proceed at a blistering pace to avoid any more unnecessary absences. Within days of the Court's establishment of a demanding schedule for the lawsuit, we served hundreds of discovery demands on our opponents. Over the course of a single summer, we took and defended some 40 depositions in Albany, New York City, and Suffolk County, and reviewed thousands of documents from some 20 different defendants. With help from our client, the National Law Center on Homelessness and Poverty, we retained some of the best experts in the country to testify on our behalf.

While discovery was raging throughout New York State, we faced extensive motion practice from the Defendants. They moved to dismiss the Complaint, denying their legal obligations to the homeless children. Given the lack of precedents on this issue and the possibility that the matter would have nationwide ramifications for the rights of homeless children, we spared no effort in defeating this motion. The defendants also sought to oppose class certification, arguing that each homeless family's situation was unique and not capable of aggregate adjudication, a position that we vigorously contested.

To fight this war, we put together a small army of dedicated attorneys from both our New York and Boston offices.[2] This group worked furiously—often late into the night, and on virtually every weekend of an otherwise beautiful summer. Several of the attorneys opposing us literally quit their jobs. We soldiered on.

This dedication quickly yielded results. The depositions inexorably produced testimony much better than we had originally hoped. The problems ran deeper and broader than we had imagined, and we were able to document years of neglect and malfeasance in various levels of the government that had directly resulted in the denial of public schooling for homeless children. The defendants' own witnesses were forced to admit to serious, systemic problems in the education of homeless children in New York State and Suffolk County. Witness by witness, we were able to demonstrate a pattern of neglect that had resulted in widespread, and wholly unnecessary, school absences by homeless children.

Meanwhile, our plaintiffs did beautifully in their depositions. One plaintiff described in painful detail how hard her daughter cried out of frustration from missing school. Another described the cold indifference of governmental officials after she had fled domestic violence and sought to keep her child in the stable environment of a school. The defendants' efforts to portray the plaintiffs as troublemakers responsible for their own problems completely backfired; the poignant stories of the homeless families were unassailable.

The Defendants Throw in the Towel

The Judge ruled against the defendants' motions against our complaint and ordered a prompt trial.[3] This was a matter of major significance to our client, the National Law Center on Homelessness and Poverty, because it affirmed the right of homeless families to

2 *Our "core" trial team consisted of approximately a dozen attorneys. Over the course of the year or more than this litigation was prosecuted, some 42 professionals from our firm worked on the case.*

3 *See National Law Center on Homelessness and Poverty, et al., v. State of New York, et al., 224 F.R.D. 314 (E.D.N.Y. 2004).*

seek relief in federal court for the denial of access to a basic public school education.

We then prepared the case for trial. We prepped some 30 witnesses to testify and prepared cross examinations for the witnesses of our opponents. We drafted trial briefs, prepared exhibits, crafted demonstrative exhibits and slide shows, and prepared motions in limine and other evidentiary briefs. The hardest challenge was finding the right balance between the compelling details faced by individual homeless families and the "big picture" issues concerning systemic neglect.

The day before trial, the Court scheduled a final pretrial conference. We indicated our readiness for trial and presented to the Court a lengthy list of exhibits and witnesses. Outside the Judge's chambers, in the courtroom, our litigation technology staff was busily setting up computers and audio-visual equipment for the finely-honed multimedia presentations we had planned.

Our opponents, at this point, faced a difficult decision. With little or no evidence on their side, and with a prepared and well-armed opposition, the defendants faced the prospect of a public airing of serious problems in the education of homeless children. They also faced the possibility that a federal court would order sweeping changes in how they did business or even appoint a special master to supervise the day-to-day affairs of the bureaucrats. Late that evening, the defendants capitulated and agreed to substantial changes in the education of homeless children. Although we were eager to try the case, with the defendants offering us virtually everything we had sought in the lawsuit, we concluded the interests of the class were best served by accepting the eleventh-hour settlement. We entered into a consent order memorializing the rights of homeless children to unfettered access to the public schools.

Lessons Learned

Our experience in this lawsuit provides important lessons about the role of private law firms in advocating for people experiencing homelessness. First, on its most basic level, the case evidences the serious need for private law firms to contribute their resources and expertise to such causes. Large firms are well suited to fight protracted, hard-fought litigations of the sort that legal aid attorneys or nonprofit organizations might not be. Faced with the tight schedule in our case, we were able to put literally dozens of lawyers on the matter—a luxury available to few entities other than large law firms. We routinely work on large cases under difficult conditions, and thus the challenges presented by this case were merely our "bread and butter." Our scale, access to resources, and experience with complex litigation helped enormously. If large law firms are not willing to devote their efforts to such causes, it is entirely possible that serious injustices will go unremedied.

Second, the case shows the value of partnerships between the private sector and nonprofit organizations. Without the National Law Center on Homeless and Poverty, we would not have known of this case and would not have had the access to the expertise and national networks that were essential in litigating it. Conversely, the National Law Center did not have the staffing to litigate this matter and needed our help to act as lead litigation counsel. It was the mutual cooperation of for-profit and nonprofit entities that brought about the result in this case. It is our hope that the mutually beneficial relationship we have developed with the National Law Center on this matter will continue and extend to future matters of import to people experiencing homelessness.

Third, our firm received tremendous benefits from prosecuting this matter. Many of our younger attorneys received invaluable training experiences, including deposition work, expert discovery, motion practice, and court time. In addition, our senior attorneys felt great pride in fighting for such a just cause. The case also allowed our firm to integrate members of different offices in a single project, promoting unity and cooperation within the firm. The public recognition involved in this case was also a significant boon, particularly at a time when the "A lists" run by the major law journals were putting increasing attention on pro bono work. Despite the substantial devotion of firm resources that this case entailed, we learned that there are significant benefits that more than outweigh the costs of such important work.

Finally, the case affirms the enormous need for legal services for the homeless. That hundreds, or even thousands, of homeless children could be repeatedly missing school due to bureaucratic ineptitude is a matter so serious that no responsible person should permit it to continue. That the very same government officials responsible for educating homeless children would defend this situation is appalling and speaks volumes to the disconnect between the needs and rights of the homeless and the legal obligations of certain government agencies. Nonprofit groups and private law firms must continue to bridge this gap and correct such injustices.

Jeffrey Simes *Partner*
Goodwin Procter LLP
599 Lexington Avenue New York, NY 10022
212.813.8879 JSimes@goodwinprocter.com

Jeffrey Simes is a partner in the Litigation Department at Goodwin Procter in New York, where he has significant experience with complex business litigation, including securities and corporate governance, government and internal investigations, intellectual property, insurance, antitrust and products liability. With prior experience as a public school teacher in Brooklyn, New York, Mr. Simes has performed significant pro bono work in the area of education. In addition to the work highlighted in this article, Mr. Simes was also involved in litigation to improve public school funding for New York City schools and has successfully represented students with disabilities. In 2005, Mr. Simes was awarded the New York State Bar Association Pro Bono Award and the Pro Bono Publico Award of the American Bar Association in recognition of his pro bono efforts.

Gifts for the Homeless:

Law Firms Working Together to Help the Homeless

Laurel Glassman and Carol Weiser

This is the story of how a group of energetic lawyers in Washington, DC has been able to provide hundreds of thousands of items of essential new clothing and tens of thousands of bags of good quality used clothing to homeless men, women, and children in the DC metropolitan area. It is the story of how a small, simple idea for helping the homeless has grown into a large and successful operation that now supports more than 80 homeless shelters, soup kitchens, and transitional housing facilities with clothing and other essential items.

In 1986, a handful of young attorneys who were looking for a way in which the legal community could give back to the broader community in the nation's capital decided that they should do something to help the homeless survive the cold of winter. Initially, they collected money from their colleagues at three DC law firms as the December holiday season approached, used the funds to buy clothing at retail, and distributed that clothing to homeless men and women on the streets of DC and at holiday parties held by area homeless shelters. They called their group "Gifts for the Homeless" (GFTH).

In the intervening 20 years, GFTH has become more and more successful. Not long after that first effort, it was incorporated as a 501(c)(3) organization. The group began soliciting the participation of other DC law firms, buying new clothing at wholesale and taking all the clothing to shelters for more efficient distribution. In 1989, GFTH also organized a used clothing drive, recognizing that this effort would allow GFTH to reach even more people, and establishing the current practice of an annual campaign to collect used clothing and money to buy new clothing for area shelters.

An all-volunteer organization, GFTH has a 21-member board of directors, representing a broad cross-section of the legal community of the DC metropolitan area, including partners, associates, counsel, paralegals and administrators from law firms, in-house counsel, federal government attorneys, and service providers, such as a printing company that prints appellate court briefs. It accepts support from any person or organization, but focuses its efforts on soliciting donations of money and used clothing, as well as volunteers for the used clothing drive, from the local legal community. And when GFTH recently organized its first fundraising event, it was a "battle of the *law firm* bands"—with the requirement that every competing band have at least one member who was a lawyer!

GFTH Today

The used clothing drive, GFTH's biggest annual project, requires the participation of all members of the GFTH Board and many volunteers. During the December 2005 drive, 380 volunteers sorted nearly 4,000 bags of donated items and distributed them to almost 70 facilities that serve the homeless and needy in DC and the

Interested in learning how to replicate this program in your community?	Visit **www.gfth.org.**

Volunteers receive assignments from GFTH board member Erin Monaghan.

ABA © LAUREL W. GLASSMAN

Maryland and Virginia suburbs. The volunteers and the donations of clothing, shoes, sleeping bags, toiletries, and many other items came from over 70 law firms and other legal organizations.

To help with both the used clothing drive and its fundraising efforts, GFTH has established a group of "firm coordinators" at law firms and other legal organizations in town. In November of each year, GFTH sends out letters and e-mails to the firm coordinators announcing the annual campaign. (GFTH also posts this information on its website: *www.gfth.org*.) The firm coordinators are asked to send notices to staff at their firms requesting used clothing, volunteers, and donations. While the firm coordinators are collecting the clothing, sleeping bags, blankets, toiletries, and other items, the Board surveys each facility it serves, performing a "needs assessment" to determine what that facility needs in the way of used clothing. Since GFTH has no permanent location of its own, the Board must also locate vacant office or retail space in downtown DC that the owner is willing to donate as a sorting site for the weekend of the drive. On that weekend, the firm coordinators bring the donated items to the sorting site where the items are sorted, re-bagged, and distributed to the homeless facilities. Law firms cover the cost of pizzas and sodas to feed the hundreds of volunteers. Two Board members rent U-Haul trucks to haul the larger loads, and volunteers are enlisted to haul the smaller loads in their own cars or minivans.

During the December 2005 clothing drive, 380 volunteers sorted nearly 4,000 bags of donated items—which were distributed to 70 area service providers.

ABA © LAUREL W. GLASSMAN

The used clothing drive has grown exponentially over the years in terms of the number of volunteers, number of shelters served, and amount of clothing distributed, but the operation involves only a few basic requirements: finding empty office space for sorting by calling a few building management companies; putting out a call to the firm coordinators at legal organizations (often by e-mail) for used clothing and volunteers; contacting shelters to find out what their needs are; and sorting and delivering the clothes to the shelters. While GFTH runs its used clothing drive on a large scale, a similar drive could be run on a much smaller scale with only a handful of people—indeed, that is the way the GFTH used clothing drive was originally run.

The firm coordinators are also integral to GFTH's efforts to raise money for the purchase of essential new clothing for the homeless, such as thermal underwear, thermal gloves, thermal socks, knit caps, sweatshirts, sweatpants, and socks. With their help, GFTH has been able to raise over $100,000 each year in the past several years. The monetary donations come principally from individual lawyers and staff members. A few law firms have matching programs under which the firms match donations by individuals. Also, some firm coordinators raise money through fundraising activities, such as offering an ice cream party to the floor or practice group that contributes the most money, bake sales, and silent auctions at office Christmas parties.

GFTH is a unique charitable organization because law firms in DC and contributions from Board members cover all expenses. As a result, GFTH has no overhead and is therefore able to apply one hundred percent of the general purpose donations it receives to purchase and ship the new clothing items it buys. GFTH uses the funds it raises to purchase clothing at wholesale, in bulk, from manufacturers and have it shipped directly to a group of 20 to 30 shelters.

In 2004, the Board of GFTH decided to put on its first fundraiser for two reasons. First, the Board wanted to be more active in support of the homeless throughout the entire year. Second, the Board realized after surveying the shelters for which it buys new clothing that the money raised during the course of its annual fall campaign was meeting only a fraction of the new clothing needs of the homeless. After much debate, the Board settled on sponsoring "Banding Together 2004"—the "battle of the law firm bands"—as a summer associate event. Held in a Georgetown bar, the event featured seven firm bands (each including at least one lawyer) competing for the championship. The winner was determined by "Chicago-style voting," that is, by the audience stuffing money into the ballot box for its favorite band—of course, GFTH kept the money.

Banding Together 2004 was a modest success, raising $10,000 for the purchase of new clothing. Encouraged by these results, GFTH decided to host Banding Together 2005 at a well-known nightclub in the Adams Morgan area of DC and to make a greater effort to attract law firms and service providers as sponsors of the event. Hundreds of summer associates from law firms across town attended, and GFTH raised more than $30,000 from Banding Together 2005. The event was so successful, and so much fun, that GFTH will be presenting Banding Together 2006 at the same venue.

Lessons Learned

The GFTH Board has learned some useful lessons over the years. First, and foremost: even a small group of volunteers from the legal community can make a significant contribution to helping the need-

Banding Together 2005—a battle of the law firm bands—raised more than $30,000 to benefit area homeless service providers.

ABA © LAUREL W. GLASSMAN

iest citizens if the people are willing to put in just a few hours of work each month. Second: law firm support, and having individuals from law firms on the Board, has been essential to obtaining used clothing donations, enlisting volunteers, and raising money. The law firms that have worked with GFTH over the years take great pride in the work they do and the contributions they make to help our organization, and they believe that they benefit from the association with GFTH. Third: the willingness of so many people to help GFTH, just for the asking, has been phenomenal. Every year, GFTH has been able to obtain free use of office or retail space for the weekend of the used clothing drive, free use of recycling carts to move the donated items into and out of the sorting site, free food for the volunteers, free publicity from print and television media, free office supplies for mailings to firm coordinators, and so forth. Fourth, and finally: every member of the Board feels enriched by working with GFTH. GFTH hopes to keep growing and improving, so that eventually we can help every single homeless man, woman, and child in Washington, DC stay warm each winter.

ABA © LAUREL W. GLASSMAN

Laurel Glassman *Counsel*
Dewey Ballantine LLP
1775 Pennsylvania Avenue, NW Washington, DC 20006
202.429.2320 lglassman@deweyballantine.com

Laurel Glassman is a counsel in the Energy Markets and Regulatory Group at Dewey Ballantine LLP, resident in the firm's Washington, DC office. She has practiced in the energy area for nearly 30 years, representing large public utilities, major industrial enterprises, electricity marketers, and independent power producers in a broad range of federal and state energy regulatory proceedings, transactions, and litigation. She has actively served on the board of directors of Gifts for the Homeless since 1993 and is currently Vice President for Development.

Carol Weiser *Partner*
Sutherland Asbill & Brennan LLP
1275 Pennsylvania Avenue, NW Washington, DC 20004-2415
202.383.0728 carol.weiser@sablaw.com

Carol Weiser, a partner in the Washington Office of Sutherland Asbill & Brennan LLP, focuses her practice on employee benefits law. Her practice involves all areas of benefits laws, including qualified retirement plans, non-qualified deferred compensation and equity compensation arrangements as well as welfare and fringe benefit programs. Carol has been a member of the Board of Directors of Gifts for the Homeless, Inc. for a number of years and currently serves as the president and chairman. She is also active in the American Bar Association and was Chair of the Employee Benefits and Executive Compensation Committee of the ABA Section of Business Law from 1997 through 2001.

The Solo and Small Firm Practitioner's Guide to Helping the Homeless

Robert K. Downs

The connection of the homeless and the rest of society is, in many ways, the system of shelters, soup kitchens, free medical clinics, and other organized programs. These programs valiantly try to address the needs of those unfortunate enough, sick enough, or just poor enough to have nowhere to live. They have the goal of rehabilitating, healing, feeding, and providing a warm place to stay while trying to get the homeless on their feet and/or to become functional participants in ordinary living. But these programs, while wonderful, do not provide all the aid needed. Many of the homeless have legal problems of some sort, and most of these difficulties are relatively simple, including initial court representation on those issues that without representation are likely to be "inappropriately diverted, defaulted, or denied," or, as another example, the processing of Social Security or health care entitlements and getting those program entitlements that are their due. Many homeless also have untreated mental health problems, often leading to varying degrees of criminality—an area that "homeless courts" are now addressing. Most of these difficulties require only short-term help and can be solved relatively easily. The people that know the system and have the needed skills are a group that is almost as maligned as the homeless themselves—lawyers.

Until they need one, too many people have a low opinion of lawyers, often even quoting Shakespeare in *Henry VI* when he wrote "The first thing we do, let's kill all the lawyers." They ignore or do not know the context of the quote; that is, if the lawyers were gone, then the common people would have no one to stand up for them. Many, many lawyers provide pro bono legal help, most visibly through the large firms, which are able to take on key cases—or perhaps even dedicate two or three lawyers out of 300 to provide pro bono service. Similarly, solo practitioners and lawyers working at small firms routinely provide pro bono legal assistance.

Solo and small law firm attorneys tend to define pro bono work in a broader way than do those in large firms. For example, if a good relationship with the client has been established by the time the initial retainer runs out, many small firm lawyers will continue to work without additional funds or without the hope of being paid that which was appropriately anticipated. While we may view this as pro bono work, it is generally not so recognized.

How Many Pro Bono Hours Is "Enough?"

The American Bar Association's position is not just to recommend pro bono work; it is a responsibility. Model Rule 6.1 reads "Every lawyer has a professional responsibility to provide legal services to those unable to pay. A lawyer should aspire to render at least 50 hours of pro bono legal services per year."

The ABA's position is that a lawyer can fulfill this responsibility by providing a substantial majority of the 50 hours without fee or expectation of fee to:

> *(1) persons of limited means, or (2) charitable, religious, civic, community, governmental and educational organizations in matters that are designed primarily to address the needs of persons of limited means; and provide any additional services through delivery of legal services at no fee or substantially reduced fee to individuals, groups or organizations seeking to secure or protect civil rights, civil liberties,*

> *or public rights, or (3) participation in activities for improving the law, the legal system, or the legal profession. In addition, a lawyer should voluntarily contribute financial support to organizations that provide legal services to persons of limited means.*[1]

In a UCLA Law Review article entitled "The Politics of Pro Bono," Scott L. Cummings states that many solo and small firm practitioners view pro bono work differently than the ABA definition.

> *The world of small-scale practice is notoriously cut-throat, and solo and small-firm attorneys are forced to prioritize economic survival over professional altruism. Unlike their big-firm counterparts, they do not have the luxury of assigning pro bono work to a few highly leveraged associates. Moreover, there is a sense that many small-scale lawyers believe that their practice already encompasses significant pro bono to the extent that out of a feeling of responsibility, they work under contingency fee agreements and often reduce hourly rates or write off charges for clients who cannot afford to pay.*[2]

Many states have adopted variations of the ABA rule on pro bono service. Various jurisdictions of rules of professional responsibility, such as Washington, DC and Michigan, have adopted the ABA's 50 hour a year standard. Washington, DC extends this amount by also recommending that one percent of an attorney's income should be donated to legal services. Other states, such as California, do not make reference to pro bono work, but California Civil Code Section 6068(h) states "never to reject, for any consideration personal to himself or herself, the cause of the defenseless or the oppressed." In Illinois, a Supreme Court Rule requiring the reporting of a minimal amount of pro bono work or financial con-

1 *Model Rules of Professional Conduct Rule Rule 6.1 (2004).*

2 *Scott L. Cummings, The Politics of Pro Bono, 52 UCLA L. Rev. 1, 90-91 (2004).*

tribution, supported by both the Illinois and Chicago Bar Associations, is on the horizon.

There has been much discussion in the past as to whether to mandate pro bono work. This debate is actually centuries old; in fact, over 800 years ago St. Thomas Aquinas addressed the issue in Question 71 of the *Summa Theologica*, asking the question "Whether an advocate is bound to defend the suites of the poor?" His answer was a resounding "No!"[3] The conflict remains unresolved today.

Is Pro Bono Work Always the Most Effective Way to Help the Homeless?

It is important to not spend too much time defining what pro bono is and to actually spend time helping those in need. Often an attorney can be more effective providing other assistance than pro bono work.

In a 1992 Cornell Law Review article entitled "Mandatory Pro Bono: Comfort for the Poor or Welfare for the Rich?" John C. Macey stated that the low demand for lawyers' services by the poor and middle class provides strong evidence that most people regard legal services as an expendable luxury rather than as a necessity. Thus, if lawyers really wanted to improve the circumstance for poor clients, they could donate their money directly to them, letting their client decide for themselves how best to spend this largesse.

He may be overstating his case, but there is nonetheless truth in his argument. Sixty-three percent of the homeless population has at least one child.[4] These parents would most certainly place a higher value on food and education for their children than on seeking legal solutions for their problems, particularly if they were unsure of successfully obtaining such help in the first place.

---

3 *Jonathan R. Macey, Mandatory Pro Bono: Comfort for the Poor or Welfare for the Rich?, 77 Cornell L. Rev. 1115, 1116 (1992).*

4 *Michael G. MacLean, et.al., Homeless Adolescents' Paths to Separation from Family: Comparison of Family Characteristics, Psychological Adjustment, and Victimization, 27 J. Community Psychol. 179 (1999).*

Diana Faust, an attorney and the Assistant Executive Director at Franciscan Outreach Association in Chicago, said: "There are so many ways to help the homeless. Providing pro bono services is just one of them. The homeless also need someone who can refer them to appropriate social service organizations, advocates who will work for systemic change, and people who care enough to provide financial support to the organizations that meet their needs. The challenge is for a lawyer to think creatively and find the way to help that works best for a particular lawyer at a particular time." She also described specific ways in which solo and small law firm lawyers, who may not have an existing program for pro bono work within their firm, can provide assistance.

Solo Practitioners and Small Firm Attorneys Can Make a Difference

Solo and small firm attorneys tend to be, by the very nature of their business, general practitioners. Their broad-based knowledge can actually serve the needs of the homeless very well since clients experiencing homelessness often need an advocate with experience in many different areas of the law.

For example, I have provided legal services to homeless clients in need of assistance to modify child support obligations (without an income or home it is hard to pay support) or to enforce visitation orders (often as a result of failure or inability to pay support). I have helped get criminal records expunged in an effort to resurrect a life. I have also helped to secure the government benefits, usually disability based upon a deceased parent's Social Security entitlement, to which they were entitled. These few cases illustrate how the legal needs of the homeless don't fit into any niche, and thus how a solo practitioner or small firm attorney is well equipped to truly help a client who is experiencing homelessness. The following discussion highlights other ways that lawyers can make a difference.

Refer Clients to Appropriate Social Service Organizations

Attorneys are often the first point of contact when someone in the community has a problem. Sometimes the best way a lawyer can help is by referring the person to the best social service. An attorney should have a list of community nonprofits, as well as a list of local legal assistance resources. Simply referring someone to the correct agency is sometimes all that is needed.

Conducting a simple Google™ search with "homeless" and the name of your town or county will provide the names of many service organizations, such as shelters, food pantries, domestic violence organizations, medical clinics, substance abuse centers, and mental health resources. Refining such a search is equally uncomplicated, requiring only the names of these groups added to the original topic. Some communities even offer case managers, sometimes called client advocates, who work one-on-one with homeless individuals to help them set goals, identify services they need, find providers, and follow up with any difficulties that arise. Finally, because many homeless shelters require photo identification for admittance, it is a good idea to know the most effective way for a person to obtain or re-obtain a state ID.

Learn How to Identify Domestic Violence Issues

One leading cause of homelessness is domestic violence. The 2004 Annual Report of the National Law Center on Homelessness & Poverty (available at *http://www.nlchp.org/About/index.cfm/*) indicated that "44% of cities surveyed reported that domestic violence was a primary cause of homelessness in their cities in 2004." Many victims of domestic violence contact attorneys in order to get protection orders or for information concerning custody issues. As attorneys, we must learn about domestic violence and constantly be aware of the need for confidentiality. These issues, while, always important, are even more important in domestic violence situations. The

National Domestic Violence Hotline at *www.ndvh.org* and the National Coalition Against Domestic Violence at *www.ncadv.org* are just two sources of information on this topic.

Homeless Children Have a Right to Schooling

The federal *McKinney-Vento Homeless Assistance Act* (42 USC 11431 et seq.) requires schools to educate homeless children. While school administrators are most likely aware of this law, local school personnel are probably more concerned with filling out documents that are unnecessary to the registration of a child in school. The very lack of an address can cause administrators to improperly bar the schoolhouse door. Additional information on this Act can be found at *www.ed.gov/programs/homeless/guidance.pdf*.

Make a Donation for the Homeless in the Name of Lawyers

Although lawyers can provide much-needed aid by the pro bono practice of law, in donating money to homeless shelters and other nonprofits, the money allows those agencies to do what they do best—namely, help the homeless. Most homeless service organizations lack sufficient funding, and any infusions of cash are likely to directly impact program services.

For example, in Chicago, one attorney started a project called "Lawyers United for the Homeless" that pools donations from lawyers and supports the 250 bed shelter, soup kitchens, and case management services operated by the Franciscan Outreach Association. (See *www.franoutreach.org/LawyersUnited.htm*). Just recently, when Franciscan Outreach received public funding for two case managers to work in Chicago's downtown area but did not have funds to buy computers for them, Lawyers United pitched in to procure computers and necessary equipment. The next goal of Lawyers United is to network in the legal community for new members so that it can fund a third case manager to work with the homeless on the streets. The lawyers' donations will mean the difference between life and death for at least some of the homeless. New York City has a similar organization, viewable at *www.coalitionforthehomeless.org/donate/donate.html.*

Volunteer Directly at Service Organizations

In our busy lives, we sometimes forget how much fun it is to volunteer. It is easy to volunteer at a soup kitchen, a homeless shelter, or teach homeless children how to read. Directly volunteering grants the instant reward of making a difference without the time commitment that pro bono work entails. Organizing groups of coworkers or friends and family to volunteer can be a way to

ABA © FAITH BENNETT

Robert K. Downs *Partner*
Downs Law Offices, P.C.
150 North Wacker Drive Chicago, IL 60606
312.781.1963 bob@downslaw.com

Bob Downs is a founding partner of Downs Law Offices, P.C. in Chicago, Illinois. His practice focuses solely on Family Law. He was the 2005–2006 president of the Illinois State Bar Association (ISBA). Bob served in the Illinois House of Representatives, where he received the Ethel Parker and Best Legislator awards. He was honored with the American Bar Association (ABA) Family Law Section "Pro Bono" service award in 1995. Mr. Downs was an Incorporator of the Chicago Volunteer Legal Services, Inc. (previously known as Legal Advice Clinics of the Church Federation of Greater Chicago) and has received numerous recognitions, including from the Legal Assistance Foundation of Chicago, the National Center for Missing and Exploited Children, and the Circuit Court of Cook County, Domestic Relations Division. In 1992 he completed the New York Marathon in 4 hours, 43 minutes (something only a runner would appreciate).

encourage others, costing less time than pro bono, but being equally necessary—there are never enough volunteers. Finding a place to volunteer requires nothing more difficult than a simple Google™ search with the name of your hometown; another option is to contact a local church, synagogue, or mosque and explain the type of volunteer work you wish to do. Almost universally, they will be grateful and pleased to point you in the right direction. These hands-on volunteer activities are also great opportunities to network with other volunteers both socially and professionally.

Our Obligation to Help

We, as attorneys, have far more resources to help the homeless than do most people. We know and understand the system; we operate in the world of government bureaucracy every day. We have the ability to help even those who do not know exactly what kind of assistance they need. We can truly be a mouthpiece for those who lack a voice, and what is a lawyer but one who speaks for others?[5]

5 *Special thanks for assistance provided by: Margaret C. Benson, Executive Director, Chicago Volunteer Legal Services; John C. Wroblewski, Associate, Downs Law Offices, P.C.; and Christopher K. Downs, Writer-in-Residence, Downs Law Offices, P.C.*

The National Law Center on Homelessness & Poverty:

Partnering with Law Firms to Help End Homelessness

Maria Foscarinis

Since its inception in 1989, the National Law Center on Homelessness & Poverty has been fortunate to have benefited from the pro bono help of many dedicated lawyers and law firms. In fact, these pro bono relationships were instrumental in establishing the organization. Having been on the other side of the pro bono equation as a litigation associate at Sullivan & Cromwell in New York—and having gotten involved in advocacy on behalf of homeless people through a pro bono case I handled while at the firm—I acquired an early appreciation of the importance of pro bono relationships.

When I left the firm to become a full-time advocate on behalf of homeless people in Washington, reaching out to pro bono lawyers and law firms was one of my first priorities. And when I started NLCHP, I turned to one of those firms—Hogan & Hartson—to help us draft bylaws, incorporate the organization, and apply for tax-exempt status.

Over the years since then, NLCHP has been honored to work in partnership with many pro bono law firms. The partnerships have vastly increased our capacity to carry out our mission and helped us achieve successes that have made a difference in the lives of homeless and poor people. To list just a few examples:

- With Covington & Burling, we worked to achieve major federal legislation—including the *Stewart B. McKinney Homeless Assistance Act*, the major federal law aiding homeless people.
- We also worked with Covington on litigation to enforce Title V of that law, which requires federal agencies to make vacant property available to service providers to help homeless people. To date, over $85 million worth of property has been made available as a result of our joint efforts.
- With King & Spalding, we filed litigation to enforce the right of homeless children to go to school—under Title VII of the McKinney Act. After being initially dismissed, we achieved victory on appeal. The result was a precedent setting decision that has helped the nation's 1.35 million homeless children receive the education they need for a better future.
- With Goodwin Procter, we have just successfully concluded litigation to enforce homeless children's education rights—under the recently amended McKinney-Vento Act, as well as the *Individuals with Disabilities Education Act*.
- With Schulte Roth & Zabel, and in collaboration with the Lawyers Committee for Civil Rights, we are litigating to ensure that Katrina evacuees who have become homeless are able to secure the housing assistance they are entitled to from the Federal Emergency Management Agency.

Our partnerships with law firms encompass a wide range of work. Our mission is to serve as the legal arm of the national movement to prevent and end homelessness, and we construe our role as lawyers broadly. Our work includes law reform litigation, legislative and administrative advocacy, as well as legal education and out-

Interested in learning more about how your firm can provide pro bono legal assistance?

Contact the ABA Center for Pro Bono at (312) 988-5759 or visit **http://www.abanet.org/legalservices/probono/.** Or, contact the National Law Center on Homelessness & Poverty at (202) 638-2535 or visit **http://www.nlchp.org/**.

reach. We also provide support to local-level partners, and this can involve transactional assistance. Our pro bono partnerships have covered all aspects of this work. For example:

- Hogan & Hartson has provided legal research on a range of topics, from the rights of homeless toddlers to early childhood services to the rights of homeless adults to vote, allowing us to provide up-to-date legal advice to thousands of local-level lawyers and groups across the country and to advocate for legislative change on the federal and state levels.

In a currently active project, the firm is helping us implement a federal law under which providers of services to homeless people may acquire property on military bases that are being converted to civilian use; the property may be used for housing and/or services for homeless people. The firm is conducting research to help us create model agreements that we can use in assisting providers to negotiate property acquisition.

- Howrey Simon conducted legal research on cases involving laws "criminalizing" homelessness—helping NLCHP to write a report on the topic that is a resource to lawyers and advocates nationally.
- With Sidley Austin, we filed an *amicus* brief in the U.S. Supreme Court, arguing that homeless people should not be subjected to state laws that require them to produce identification—on pain of criminal punishment—when they are often legally prevented from obtaining such identification.

Nor is pro bono limited to U.S. law firm offices. The London office of Covington & Burling organized an unusual multi-country effort to research laws relating to housing and homelessness in the E.U.—helping us to write a report on homelessness and the human right to housing and thus breaking new ground in our advocacy.

How NLCHP Works with Pro Bono Partners

NLCHP works with firms in a variety of ways. In general, we do not "farm out" matters to firms; we remain active partners. For example, we co-counsel litigation matters with our pro bono partners, reviewing or writing portions of briefs, providing legal expertise, developing facts, and discussing strategy. The extent of our involvement varies depending on the firm's capacity as well as our own resources.

The exception is when we are asked for help by a local group on a matter involving individual representation. Because we do not typically get involved in such cases (unless they have systemic implications that fall within our priority areas) we may refer such cases to law firm partners and simply provide advice as needed.

Recently we have initiated an effort to strengthen our relationships with pro bono firms and lawyers through a new program: Lawyers Executive Advisory Partners (LEAP). LEAP is a unique program whereby law firms support NLCHP financially through an annual contribution and also provide pro bono support on a voluntary basis. Firms that join LEAP receive priority consideration for pro bono work as well as invitations to special events. Most important, LEAP deepens our relationship with our pro bono partners, formalizing their integral role in our organization.

Looking to the future, NLCHP hopes to expand further our relationships with law firm offices so that they are truly national. Most, if not all, of our law firm partners have multiple U.S. offices, and NLCHP works in communities across the country. We see great potential for building more partnerships and also offering opportunities for pro bono work beyond the more traditional big-city offices.

In addition, we see potential for expanding pro bono partnerships beyond law firms to include in-house corporate legal departments. Some corporations already have pro bono programs or are in the process of developing them, and we are eager to develop these relationships.

Crucial Partners

Pro bono lawyers and law firm partnership are key to our success as an organization. NLCHP has an impact far beyond our small size by leveraging the time, resources, and dedication of the private bar. This makes a crucial difference in our own work. But just as importantly, it also helps build support for our efforts. Lawyers are important participants in the political life of their communities, and their involvement can make a difference. By working with the private bar, we educate and involve important opinion makers on issues of homelessness and poverty.

The involvement of the ABA, through the Commission on Homelessness & Poverty and other committees, is also critically important. As a premier professional organization for lawyers, the ABA's leadership signals the importance of these issues to the profession. Moreover, as a practical matter, the ABA's involvement can

Maria Foscarinis *Executive Director*
National Law Center on Homelessness & Poverty
1411 K Street, NW Washington, DC 20005
202.638.2535 mfoscarinis@nlchp.org

Maria Foscarinis is founder and executive director of the National Law Center on Homelessness & Poverty, a not-for-profit organization established in 1989 as the legal arm of the nationwide effort to end homelessness. Ms. Foscarinis has advocated for solutions to homelessness and poverty at the national level since 1985. She is a primary architect of the *Stewart B. McKinney Homeless Assistance Act*, the first major federal legislation addressing homelessness, and she has litigated to secure the legal rights of homeless and poor persons. Ms. Foscarinis writes regularly about legal and policy issues affecting homeless and poor persons, and her work has appeared in legal journals, general audience publications, and books. Ms. Foscarinis is a 1977 graduate of Barnard College and 1981 graduate of Columbia Law School, where she was an editor of the Law Review; she also holds a Masters of Arts degree in Philosophy. After clerking for the Honorable Amalya L. Kearse of the U.S. Court of Appeals for the Second Circuit, she was a litigation associate at Sullivan & Cromwell. In 1985, she led the establishment of the Washington office of the National Coalition for the Homeless until she founded the National Law Center on Homelessness & Poverty.

help influence national policy by harnessing the lobbying power of that institution and providing leadership to state and local bar associations to make a difference in their communities.

Pro bono involvement can have far ranging consequences for individual lawyers also, as I can attest. When I volunteered to take a case representing homeless families on Long Island as an associate in Sullivan & Cromwell's New York office, visiting my clients gave me a view into extreme poverty in the midst of suburban plenty that I'd never before seen. It also gave me a glimpse into the truly important difference I could make as a lawyer for people whose voices might otherwise not be heard. The impact was profound, and I chose to translate my experience into a fulltime career.

But law firm lawyers can make a major impact without making such a radical shift in career, through pro bono service. It really does make a big difference in the lives of people whose voices might otherwise go unheard.

Public Counsel and Law Firms:

Collaborating to Prevent Homelessness and Poverty

Paul L. Freese, Jr.

This year Public Counsel celebrates its 35th anniversary as the nation's largest provider of pro bono legal services to impoverished and low income individuals, as well as to nonprofits that provide vital services to such individuals. Public Counsel is the public interest law office of the Los Angeles County and Beverly Hills Bar Associations and the Southern California Affiliate of Lawyers for Human Rights. Each year, our staff of 50 recruits, trains, and supervises the advocacy efforts of more than 3,500 volunteers and delivers free legal services to more than 25,000 individuals and nonprofit organizations.

Public Counsel strives to provide a holistic range of pro bono opportunities geared to address the emerging needs of the poor and afflicted. For example, we recently worked with major law firms, local bar associations, and other public interest law offices to marshal support for the unmet legal needs of victims of the 9/11 and Katrina catastrophes. We mobilized an intensive outreach effort focused on homeless families that were ending up on skid row to enable them to secure housing away from the dangers and insidious influences of that unhealthful environment. With the growing recognition of the high prevalence of youth who experience poor outcomes after an experience in our foster care system, we tailored projects designed to help these youth access improved educational and employment opportunities, independent living program benefits, community based supports, and mentoring and tutoring options. We developed adoptions and guardianship programs designed to help youth who are at risk of ending up in foster care or impoverished households obtain permanent, loving homes. We are also launching projects focused on improved access to mental health assistance and supportive housing in light of the growing specter of severely mentally ill individuals living on the streets.

Public Counsel is incubating projects that focus upon the affordable housing crisis, which is especially acute in Los Angeles County. When welfare reform made it imperative for single mothers to enter the work force, our childcare law project worked strenuously in impoverished communities to help increase the availability of affordable child care facilities, recruiting volunteer attorneys to litigate on their behalf and helping them fend off NIMBY (Not In My Back Yard) driven zoning restrictions that do not comport with state law. When lending con artists preyed upon elderly retirees, our volunteer attorneys went after such predators to protect our vulnerable clients from losing their homes.

When given individuals from Third World countries who had fled the torture or salvaging extra-judicial executions of repressive regimes, Public Counsel responded by founding a project to enable these individuals to secure protection under federal laws protecting persons seeking political asylum. We have more recently expanded our work on behalf of immigrants to include projects specializing in Violence Against Women Act cases and Special Immigrant Juvenile Status cases—the latter being the foremost of its kind in the country because it invokes a federal law that enables the naturalization of undocumented youth who are abused, abandoned by their parents, or at risk of long-term involvement within our foster care system.

Noting studies that indicate the poor outcomes that haunt former foster youth—especially those who cross over into the delinquency system—we launched a program that regularly takes our volunteers into probation camps and juvenile halls. There, they advocate to ensure for more humane treatment, improved access to education, and special education services, as well as transition services for when the youth returns to the community.

These are but a few of the ways in which we strive to tailor our internal resources and expertise. Coupled with considerable resources, we can effectively tap partnerships with local law firms to address the needs of those striving to evade poverty and despair.

We have solidified six primary projects over the course of our history that provide viable vehicles for pro bono volunteers to use their legal talents to help the less fortunate and give back to their communities. These include our Childcare Law Project, Children's Rights Project, Community Development Project, Consumer Law Project, Homelessness Prevention Law Project, and Immigrants Rights Project. (See our website, *www.publiccounsel.org*, for more information on each of these projects and for the contact information of staff involved with these projects).

Public Counsel employs a variety of means to recruit pro bono volunteers. We developed an extremely strong and active Board of Directors that is comprised largely of managing or senior partners from L.A.'s largest law firms. These individuals are extremely proactive not only in generating material support to sustain our organization, but also in recruiting volunteers from their respective firms. Many of our Board members themselves have taken on significant pro bono cases. Our Board members also facilitate presentations by Public Counsel staff to the attorneys at their firms so that we can inform them of the pro bono opportunities that are readily available.

We have adapted our recruitment techniques to respond to the reality that attorneys are extremely busy. Thus, early on in our history, we began conducting regular legal clinics in the evening at our office. We would have prospective clients come to meet volunteer attorneys who would provide consultation and advice and, assuming no conflict, would take on the matter for full representation. Young associates at major firms found that involvement with our legal clinics not only provided exciting opportunities to give much appreciated help to individuals in need, but also enabled them to obtain invaluable court experience.

In the past decade, we have developed a very special "Adoptions Saturday" project along with a fellow public interest law office, The Alliance For Children's Rights. This project utilizes volunteer attorneys to finalize adoptions of children in foster care and thereby enable them to have permanent, loving homes. Being connected with a loving family dramatically improves outcomes for these vulnerable children (by contrast, if a foster youth does not receive help while becoming adopted or have a legal guardianship put in place to help provide for his or her care, the likelihood of that youth experiencing homelessness or long-term exposure to correctional and rehabilitative institutions is inordinately high). We are proud to note that Public Counsel finalized its 5,000th adoption this past year, thanks to the generous assistance and diligent efforts of literally hundreds of volunteer attorneys, paralegals, and law students.

We have also worked closely with the local Superior Court to make our services more accessible to the poor and to create a wider array of opportunities for pro bono volunteers to be engaged with the needy in our community. For example, we regularly receive referrals from the Dependency Court to set up Guardian Ad Litems for foster children with tort claims arising from abusive treatment, requests to help foster children with unmet immigration needs, and requests for advocacy support to help foster children access special education or regional center services.

Public Counsel has a dynamic staff that excels at leading pro bono volunteers to where they can witness the reality afflicting the poorest in our community. Specifically, we regularly lead volunteers on street outreaches to the homeless, and we have established numerous evening and weekend legal clinics on site at community centers, homeless shelters, and youth services centers.

Each summer, Public Counsel draws upon literally hundreds of summer associates from major law firms. After a training session in the morning, we lead them out to public social services offices on skid row and in other areas where poverty is especially acute so that they witness first hand the life-shattering effects of dispossession and homelessness. During the summer of 2005, 54 of Los Angeles' most prestigious law firms provided us with close to 500 summer associates for a full day of advocacy. The evaluations that these summer clerks left with us attest to the profound effect this project had in awakening their consciousness to the stark need in our community, as well as enabling the associates to appreciate the enormous power their advocacy skills can play in helping those in need. (Sometimes the experience plays out in humorous ways, as one of our volunteers shared the following story: "I was standing in line to go into a popular nightclub with my friends, when I noticed a homeless man looking at me. I thought he looked familiar and then he came up to me with a big smile and said—'Hey, you were my lawyer at the social services office the other day!'")

With the encouragement and support of Ninth Circuit Judge Harry Pregerson—California's preeminent champion of homeless veterans—Public Counsel launched an "adopt-a-homeless-veteran-shelter" in 2003. In this effort, three major law firms provided a reg-

ABA © TED ZEPEDA

Paul L. Freese, Jr. *Director of Litigation & Advocacy*
Public Counsel
P.O. Box 76900 Los Angeles, CA 90076
213.637.3809 pfreese@publiccounsel.org

Paul L. Freese, Jr., is the Director of Litigation & Advocacy for Public Counsel, the public interest law office of the Los Angeles County and Beverly Hills Bar Associations and the largest provider of pro bono legal services in the United States. He has been a member of the California State Bar since 1988. From 1988 to 1994, he worked as a litigation associate with the law firm of Perkins Coie. He joined Public Counsel in March, 1994, and acted as Directing Attorney of the Homelessness Prevention Law Project for more than six years before being promoted in January 2001 to his current position in which he supervises more than 20 attorneys and their staff. He serves on a vast array of working groups and task forces that address the needs of the poor and marginalized, particularly those of emancipating foster and probation youth and the homeless.

ular stream of volunteer attorneys to staff legal clinics offered on site at major homeless veteran shelters, rehabilitative centers, and transitional living programs.

Public Counsel worked with the Superior Court to establish a Homeless Court program (which drew upon the model that Steve Binder with the San Diego Public Defender's Office developed). We recruit and train volunteer attorneys to appear as *amicus curiae* on behalf of the participants in Homeless Court, where they convey the deeply moving stories of how the participants managed to pick up the pieces of their shattered lives and find the courage to press forward in a positive direction without giving up hope. Now in its sixth year, the Los Angeles Homeless Court has established its effectiveness as a vehicle to help transform lives, resulting in county supervisors approving additional funding to allow it to dramatically expand its services to the community. Public Counsel is presently working closely with the Superior Court and the County Department of Mental Health to support an innovative "Prototype Court" that will focus upon the most chronically homeless who have co-occurring mental heath and substance abuse disorders.

The staff and pro bono attorneys at Public Counsel remain inspired by a sentiment once expressed by Albert Camus, that "perhaps we cannot create a world in which children will never suffer, but we can reduce the number of suffering children, and if you don't help, who will?" By working together, we are confident that our efforts will be instrumental in preventing homelessness and poverty.

CHAPTER 4

Bar Associations Working to End Homelessness

The American Bar Association Commission on Homelessness & Poverty

Amy E. Horton-Newell

In 1991, The Commission on Homelessness and Poverty was established by the Board of Governors of the American Bar Association (ABA). The Commission is charged with the following tasks: (1) Educating members of the bar and the public about legal and other problems of poor and homeless people and ways in which lawyers can assist in solving or ameliorating them; (2) training lawyers in areas needed to provide pro bono legal assistance to homeless people and those at risk of becoming homeless; (3) working with all ABA entities on issues arising in their jurisdiction that affect poor and homeless people; and (4) engaging in such further activities as may be necessary and proper for the fulfillment of these responsibilities, including working with state and federal executive branches and legislative bodies concerning matters relating to the poor and homeless. These tasks are carried out by one staff attorney and 13 volunteer members appointed by the ABA President.

In 1986, the ABA passed a resolution expressing the ABA's support of legislation and programs that protected the rights of homeless people, created housing and other programs to aid homeless people in their battle for self-sufficiency, and urged pro bono legal representation of homeless clients. To implement this resolution, the ABA Section of Individual Rights and Responsibilities created the Representation of the Homeless Project, which in turn provided technical assistance to bar association pro bono homeless programs, educated the profession about homelessness and the needs of homeless people, and drafted policy for the ABA House of Delegates (the ABA's legislative body). Building on the work of the Project, in 1991, the ABA created the Commission on Homelessness and Poverty to demonstrate the Association's commitment to addressing the legal needs of homeless and impoverished people.

In carrying out its mission, the Commission provides policy-based advocacy on behalf of homeless and impoverished people. The Commission, through the ABA Governmental Affairs Office, works with Congress to develop and fund programs that will address the causes of homelessness and poverty in the United States, as well as to enact laws that will protect and provide for those in desperate need of assistance.

The ABA presently has numerous policies on issues related to homeless and impoverished people, including the following:

- affordable housing and public housing
- the "digital divide"
- the education rights of children and youth who are homeless
- funding for federal programs serving people who are homeless and impoverished
- health care
- homeless courts
- legal services for people who are homeless and impoverished
- postal services for people experiencing homelessness
- predatory lending
- public benefits
- voting rights for people who are homeless and impoverished

The Commission is committed to educating the bar and the public about homelessness and poverty and the ways in which the legal community and advocates can assist those in need.

To achieve this goal, the Commission drafts publications and conducts training sessions across the country to equip the legal community to advocate on behalf of people who are homeless or poor. The Commission also coordinates with national, state, and local advocates and organizations to facilitate the exchange of information and resources.

One of the Commission's current priorities is to facilitate the creation of homeless courts throughout the country (see article in Chapter 6). Why the need for homeless courts? People who are homeless are routinely issued citations for such minor offenses as illegal lodging, jaywalking, and drinking in public. Caught up in the daily struggle for food, clothing, and shelter, a person who is homeless has few resources to draw upon in order to respond properly to the criminal justice system. Consequently, misdemeanor citations and infractions are often not dealt with, compounding the problem as warrants are issued and additional fines are assessed, which often preclude the homeless from accessing desperately needed services such as public benefits and mental health and/or substance abuse treatment—not to mention employment and housing.

In October 2004, the Commission hosted a national conference on homeless courts in San Diego—home of the nation's first home-

Publications prepared by the Commission on Homelessness & Poverty include:

- *The Homeless Court Program: Taking the Court to the Streets*
- *Educating Children without Housing: A Primer on Legal Requirements and Implementation Strategies for Educators, Advocates and Policymakers*
- *Representing the Poor and Homeless: Innovations in Advocacy*
- *NIMBY: A Primer for Lawyers and Advocates*

less court established in 1989 at Stand Down. Since the conference—and under the leadership of its current chair, Steve Binder—the Commission has provided technical assistance to several jurisdictions that have established homeless courts or are in the process of establishing homeless courts. The Commission is proud to be the leader in fostering replication of this innovative program that expands access to justice, reduces court costs, and helps homeless people move towards self-sufficiency.

In addition to its work related to homeless courts, the Commission focuses on an often overlooked segment of the homeless population: homeless youth. In 2002, the Commission published *Educating Children without Housing: A Primer on Legal Requirements and Implementation Strategies for Educators, Advocates and Policymakers*, a resource that has been used at Department of

ABA © CRAIG NEWELL

Amy E. Horton-Newell *Director*
American Bar Association Commission on Homelessness & Poverty
740 15th Street, NW Washington, DC 20005
202.662.1693 hortona@staff.abanet.org

Amy E. Horton-Newell has served as the Director of the Commission on Homelessness & Poverty at the American Bar Association since 2001. Amy is also the Director of the ABA Standing Committee on the Law Library of Congress. She coordinates ABA policy development and programming related to the special legal needs of people experiencing homelessness and poverty. On behalf of the Association, Amy collaborates with national, state, and local advocacy groups, associations, and government agencies to address issues related to homelessness and poverty. Amy also serves on the Board of Directors for the Montgomery County Coalition for the Homeless in Maryland. Amy received a Bachelor of Arts in Spanish from the University of Maryland, College Park, where she was elected to Phi Beta Kappa. She graduated from the University of Maryland School of Law and was admitted to the Maryland Bar in 2000.

Education trainings across the country. The Commission also routinely hosts educational programs on the special legal issues faced by homeless youth, including access to shelter, education, and medical care.

The Commission also administers the John J. Curtin, Jr. Justice Fund Legal Internship Program (see article in Chapter 2). Named for the former ABA President, the program awards stipends to law students who spend the summer months working for a bar association or legal services program designed to prevent homelessness or assist homeless or indigent clients or their advocates. The program provides much-needed legal assistance to organizations serving the underrepresented and gives students direct experience in a public interest forum. Through this, it aims to help homeless clients and to encourage careers in the law that further the goals of social justice.

As the Commission celebrates its 15th Anniversary in August 2006, its members—both past and present—reflect on the achievements the Commission has accomplished as well as the work that remains to be done. The Commission will continue its advocacy on behalf of people experiencing homelessness and those living in poverty by rallying lawyers across the country to take action and supporting their efforts. We invite you to join us.

Interested in learning more about the Commission on Homelessness & Poverty?

Visit **http://www.abanet.org/homeless** or call (202) 662-1694.

Bringing in the Bar:

Creating a Bar Committee on Homelessness

Jane Hunter Shaeffer

With its white sandy beaches and its warm, beckoning climate, Florida naturally attracts a mix of people from all strata of the social ladder. Besides the retirees, the young and the restless, the fun seekers and the jet setters, the international moneymakers and the persons who follow the work force quest, the Sunshine State is a haven for 83,391 homeless persons. That number is as great as a small city, so it naturally follows that this large group of vulnerable citizens presents a multitude of challenges for the people of Florida.

It seemed fitting, then, that some of the most influential persons in the state—the lawyers—should be called upon to help with this growing phenomenon and to take responsibility for some repair work on behalf of the homeless. Following past successful examples, it became evident that the most appropriate vehicle would be the very powerful and capable Florida Bar.

Having worked with the Public Interest Law Section (PILS) on behalf of abused and neglected children in the state, it was obvious to me that the coming together of justice-oriented lawyers could certainly help to resolve the dilemmas of the homeless. This section's work with the legal needs of children has been outstanding. Once the Bar became involved in working with this most vulnerable group of people, legislation followed guaranteeing protections for children that had never been thought of before. Lawyers from all over the state logged thousands of hours of pro bono work on behalf of these children. Why, then could not something similar be done for the second most vulnerable group, the homeless?

As in other states, Florida officials have mixed attitudes toward the homeless—many are helpful and concerned, others hostile and vindictive. For instance, Florida has the dubious distinction of having the "meanest city in the U.S.," (Sarasota), as determined by the National Coalition for the Homeless and the National Law Center on Homelessness & Poverty (*A Dream Denied: The Criminalization of Homelessness in U.S. Cities*, 2006). Yet, at the same time, the state has set up an Office of Homelessness in the Department of Children and Families and does fund some helpful programs throughout the state.

Getting a committee started was only easy because of the leadership of the PILS organization. Gerald Glynn, an Orlando attorney, professor at Barry Law School, and a top advocate for children, was serving as Chair of the Section, and the Chair-Elect was Carolyn Salisbury, Professor and Director, Children's Law Clinic at the University of Miami. Glynn immediately welcomed the idea and after formal approval by the section executive council, an Ad Hoc Committee on Homelessness was formed. A very unique feature of this section is that it is not limited only to lawyers, making the membership interdisciplinary.

Finding and recruiting lawyers and advocates to join was the next step. From time to time, newspaper articles noted lawyers working in the field, and it was well known that legal services and public defenders were representing the homeless. In addition, the homeless coalitions attracted advocates from a multitude of professional fields. The *Bar News*, a twice-monthly publication of our association, assisted the effort by writing and circulating an excellent article on our goals and objectives. Although there was not an overwhelming response, enough persons (about 30) agreed to come together and form a nucleus that became an active and viable group.

It is the structure of the Bar Association that in-person meetings are held three times a year, but as the state spans such a broad territory (from Pensacola to Key West is 792 miles), it is difficult for members to get to all meetings. For many in the practice areas dealing with the homeless, there are limited resources of time and money for travel. Upon the advice of Bar staff, we use conference calls for meetings. I had previously felt that this method would be unworkable, but it has turned out to be extremely successful—there are persons working alongside me whom I have never met face to face, but work we do.

Our activities, so far, have been to "educate, activate and advocate." We have found that we are able to bring together persons of various talents who have expertise in the many facets of law involving the homeless, and that has resulted in a sharing of ideas and an enthusiasm to get involved. We have sponsored three statewide seminars in the past three years, which have attracted over 200 lawyers and non-lawyers. In addition to individual advocacy on behalf of the homeless, committee members have lobbied in support of, or in opposition to, legislative measures that affect the homeless with the goal of helping this at-risk population.

We found a wealth of help from the American Bar Association Commission on Homelessness and Poverty, the National Coalition for the Homeless, and the National Law Center on Homelessness & Poverty. All sent information and materials, gave advice and support, and came to Florida to lecture at and participate in the seminars.

As to publicity for our seminar events, we have used flyers by e-mail to groups such as public defenders, legal aid offices, and the local and statewide coalitions. Our *Bar News* will do brief stories, which is publicity to every lawyer in the state. Our section has its own newsletter which is published both on e-mail and on paper as well as distributed to the membership.

Does your state or local bar association have a Committee on Homelessness?

Interested in starting one? Contact the ABA Commission on Homelessness and Poverty to learn how. Visit **www.abanet.org/homeless** or call (202) 662-1694 for more information.

One attraction of our seminars is the offering of Continuing Legal Education credits. By making certain that our topics are educational, the Bar will accredit our offerings in advance. The other attraction for our attendees is that we do not charge for attending the seminars, and we keep costs low by donations and sponsorships. We try to accommodate our attendees by arranging for low-cost hotels near the site of the event. We all know that people in this business are not "well-heeled."

A plan is in the making to offer tapes of our seminars to prospective members, whereby if we send them a DVD for viewing they can earn CLE credits. Their payment to us is to join the committee.

Sources of membership are varied. We are attempting to bring in law students and engage law schools to help with events. Our last seminar was co-hosted by the Florida A&M Law School Homelessness Clinic in Orlando, and the preceding one was held at Stetson Law School in Tampa. Our first seminar was co-hosted by the Ninth Circuit Public Defender's Office in Orlando.

Being creative in attracting membership is the key to organizing a statewide committee. There is no "doing lunch," as distances prohibit that type of effort, but there is a very effective and old fash-

ABA © JANE SHAEFFER

Jane Hunter Shaeffer
2600 Bantry Bay Drive Tallahassee, Florida 32309
jrshaeffer@aol.com

Jane Hunter Shaeffer holds a BSJ and MA from the University of Florida and a Juris Doctor from Vanderbilt University. Shaeffer is licensed to practice in Florida, the District of Columbia and Tennessee. Although most of Shaeffer's professional life focused on Dependency Law having served as the state Director of the Florida Guardian Ad Litem Program, her volunteer work has centered on working with the homeless. Shaeffer was one of the founders of The Shelter, an emergency shelter in Tallahassee established in 1987, and she presently serves on its board. Shaeffer also founded the Committee on Homelessness of the Public Interest Law Section of The Florida Bar.

ioned method of recruiting called word of mouth. It is amazing how much can be accomplished just by talking to other lawyers and advocates who "know somebody who knows somebody."

A further goal of the committee is to write about homelessness, particularly for the *Florida Bar Journal,* in the hope of educating our 75,000 members. Once our "big Bar" takes on helping the homeless, real statewide changes will take place.

Working on the premise that there is strength in numbers, it is felt that a committee recognized as a part of the Bar gives advocates for the homeless credibility not obtainable any other way. By working together, we develop a structure and direction for this advocacy, as well as the comfort of knowing we are not out there all alone.

Homeless Experience Legal Protection (HELP):

Attorneys' Outreach Program for the Homeless

Judge Jay C. Zainey

In New Orleans, as in most major cities throughout the United States, the Pro Bono Project and other legal service organizations provide excellent legal representation to the poor and disadvantaged. However, the homeless population, many of whom are mentally impaired, do not know how to access these services. As a result, the Homeless Experience Legal Protection (HELP) Program was formed in New Orleans in May 2004.

The purpose of the program is for attorneys to reach out to the homeless population by providing legal consultation services at the homeless shelters and centers. There are more than 350 New Orleans area attorneys and notaries who are active volunteers in the program. Legal consultation services are provided in-house at various homeless centers five times a week by three different law firms. "Office hours" at the centers are generally from 7:45 AM - 8:45 AM so that there is no interference with the attorney's court schedule. Each law firm is scheduled for a month.

Many basic questions are answered by the volunteers. Even though the answers are simple in the eyes of the attorneys, they can be extremely important to a person who has never had previous access to legal counsel. Similar to a situation in which a person learns from his physician that he has no medical issues, a person who learns from his attorney that he has no legal problems is given a strong sense of security. For a homeless person, this strong sense of security is possibly the only sense of security he or she will experience.

For those people who have been faced with "real" legal issues, the legal triage provided by attorneys in the various firms has been credited with helping a number of them escape the bonds of homelessness and has enabled our less fortunate brothers and sisters to rebound as productive members of society. The time and attention an attorney gives to his client has, in many instances, been a source of restoring dignity to the client.

There are many success stories for both the client and the attorney providing legal advice. As one of our volunteer attorneys explained: "When the person came in to see me, his face was downcast. After he and I discussed his legal issues, and came up with solutions, he looked up to me and thanked me for treating him as a human being—and with dignity and respect…He walked out the door...I felt like I won the biggest case of my career. I would like to see this person again to thank him for giving me the opportunity to really make a difference in his life." And by the way, this particular client was a former attorney who was down on his luck.

Helping Clients Secure Identification Cards

A major problem facing the homeless occurs when they lose their identification cards. As we know, our identification cards are very important possessions. To people who have no place to call home, an identification card is their lifeline. Without identification, a homeless person is unable to spend the night in a homeless shelter, or cash his Social Security or Veterans Benefit check, and, in some cases, is even subject to arrest.

Consider one example of how a HELP volunteer assisted "Jerry," a mentally ill Vietnam veteran living in New Orleans. Jerry lost his identification card. Because homeless shelters require identification, he would have to spend the night on the streets. And without identification, Jerry would remain penniless because he could not get a job, could not receive his social security or veterans benefits, and could even be subject to arrest. Fortunately, a HELP volunteer attorney at one of the local homeless shelters had previously made a certified copy of Jerry's identification card and had retained it on file at the shelter. Instead of trying to locate substantiating documentation to obtain a replacement identification card—a process that takes 30 days on average—Jerry was able to pick up the certified copy of his identification card from the shelter and bring it to the Office of Motor Vehicles, which then provided Jerry with a replacement.

In Louisiana, the Department of Motor Vehicles, charged with the responsibility of issuing identification cards, allows a person to use a certified copy of his identification card as sufficient documentation to obtain a replacement identification card. As a result, besides those law firms and individuals who provide legal consultation services at the homeless centers five times a week, attorneys and notaries provide notarial services at four homeless shelters and centers thirteen other times during the week. After the certified copies of the identification cards are made, they are kept on file at the homeless center. If a person loses his or her identification card, instead of having to wait (with no roof over his or her head) for 30 days to obtain the necessary substantiating documentation, the person merely returns to the homeless center where the certified copy was made and brings it to the Office of Motor Vehicles, where a duplicate identification card will be made immediately.

During the first year of operation, approximately 700 certified copies of identification cards were made. Of those people, more than 150 (25 %) lost their identification card, returned to the center and obtained their certified copy, and immediately were able to obtain a duplicate identification card. Otherwise, each of these people would have lived on the streets for at least 30 days.

Of course, before a person can obtain an identification card, he or she has to have a birth certificate. The number of our homeless brothers and sisters who do not have birth certificates is astonishing. Ironically, a person cannot obtain an identification card without a birth certificate, yet he is unable to obtain a birth certificate without an identification card. As one can imagine, as long as this vicious circle exists, it is literally impossible for a person to combat homelessness.

We do not realize it, but our ticket to practice law gives us incredible power—the power in certain instances to put a roof over someone's head. Under Louisiana law (Revised Statute 40:41, as amended), an attorney can request a birth certificate for a person even when a person cannot obtain one on his own. Because of the great need in this area, attorney volunteers are scheduled at two homeless centers every Monday to assist the homeless to obtain their birth certificates.

Helping Clients Secure Social Security Benefits

Studies have shown that more than half of the homeless population suffers from some form of mental illness. Anyone who practices Social Security law knows how tedious, time consuming, and slow the process is for a person applying for SSI benefits. If you add to that the fact that a person is more likely than not to be mentally ill, the process could be unbearable.

Another issue being addressed by HELP volunteers is the creation of a process which would make it easier for homeless people who are qualified to obtain Social Security benefits. Here is how it works: An attorney volunteer meets with the applicant and obtains all medical records on behalf of the person, instead of relying on an agent for Social Security to do so. In many cases, the attorney, with proper medical authorization from his client, can expedite the process by going to the physician's office to obtain the records. In certain cases, when it is obvious that a homeless person has a very low IQ, arrangements are made with volunteer psychologists to evaluate the person at the homeless center and immediately issue a report. The attorney would then take his client (with medical records already in hand) to the Social Security Office and would assist the client by providing his or her medical and psychological reports to the Social Security representative completing the application process. Under Federal law, a person might be eligible for immediate emergency Social Security benefits upon presentation of his complete set of medical documentation.

The HELP Program Post-Katrina

Since the devastation wrought by Hurricane Katrina on August 29, 2005, the number of people and families who are either homeless or displaced in the greater New Orleans area has been staggering. As the floodwaters from Hurricane Katrina slowly receded and the electricity was partially restored, the legal profession, like the cavalry, returned to the hurricane ravaged city of New Orleans. Even though many lawyers suffered incredible personal tragedies such as losing their homes and their law practices, they returned to New Orleans to pick up the pieces of their lives and to resume their roles of protecting the legal rights of their clients.

Since the hurricane destroyed the homeless centers and shelters in New Orleans, the New Orleans area HELP volunteers have shifted gears and are offering legal consultation and notary services to the thousands who make up the new homeless community. HELP volunteers are now providing these services at the Disaster Relief Centers that have been opened to address the needs of the victims of the hurricane. These attorneys, and countless others, put aside their personal tragedies to care for others. The New Orleans area lawyers (and lawyers throughout Louisiana and the country who assisted them in their time of need) truly make our profession an honorable one.

The typical homeless shelters were destroyed, and thousands of the "new homeless" were knocking on the doors of the newly created Disaster Relief Centers and crying out for help. Yet even the devastation caused by Hurricane Katrina could not stop the New Orleans area attorneys from coming to the aid of their fellow citizens. One lawyer wrote in September 2005, a short time after Hurricane Katrina left her homeless: "I would like to volunteer to help at the disaster centers for a few hours each week…I have

Contact Judge Jay Zainey at Jay_Zainey@laed.uscourts.gov to receive a copy of the HELP manual.

Interested in creating a HELP Program in your community?

limited transportation resources at this point. I would gladly help with bankruptcies, if I can get access to DSL. (I have internet access, now, because a neighbor lets me use her land line. I cannot get a land line...until February 1, 2006). Because I actually believed that I would be back the next day, I left…in the wee hours of August 29 with only my pets, my toothbrush and the clothing on my back. I finally got back down there last week, and there is nothing left. Consequently, I need office space…and either a suit and dress shoes or info on any nearby clothing stores that might be open. I know it will do me a lot of good to get back into the swing of things by working at the relief centers."

The legal profession—our profession—is truly an honorable profession. Bar associations and attorneys across the nation came to the aid of their fellow attorneys. Donations in excess of $500,000 were made by total strangers to New Orleans area lawyers in need, their only bond being the legal profession and the public we serve. Staff members from bar associations in neighboring states assisted the staff of the Louisiana State Bar Association, who were displaced approximately 150 miles from their headquarters in New Orleans.

Chief Judge Ginger Berrigan of the Eastern District of Louisiana coordinated efforts with the Federal Courts in the Middle District and Western District of Louisiana and the Southern District of Texas. The judges in these districts generously shared their chambers and their courtrooms with the judges of the Eastern District of Louisiana so that the Federal Court system in New Orleans would function in an efficient manner. Eastern District of Louisiana Clerk of Court Loretta Whyte, who lost her home in the hurricane, and her entire staff, many of whom became homeless because of the devastation caused by the storm, put aside their personal tragedies and opened offices in Federal Courts throughout Louisiana so that attorneys and their clients would have access to the Eastern District Federal Court. Soon after public officials announced that the mandatory evacuation was terminated and that people could return to their battered homes, the legal profession returned. The Federal Courthouse reopened, offering space for State Civil and Criminal District Courts to make a temporary headquarters, since both of those courts were unable to reopen.

Upon their return, many of the attorneys had no homes, no offices, and no clients. The Louisiana State Bar Association, under the outstanding and tireless leadership of Frank X. Neuner, Jr., established Disaster Relief Centers throughout the state, as well as call centers so that volunteer attorneys could assist in addressing the legal needs of the thousands of people who were adversely affected by Hurricanes Katrina and Rita (the latter of which struck the state within a few weeks of Katrina).

The HELP Program immediately sprung into action, its attorney volunteers providing pro bono legal consultation and notary services at the major Disaster Relief Center in New Orleans for two to four hours a day during the months of December and January. At the time of this writing, volunteer attorneys continue to provide pro bono legal services for two hours a day at the major Disaster Relief Center in New Orleans.

The Louisiana State Bar Association, in conjunction with the Louisiana Bar Foundation, established a relief fund with the hundreds of thousands of dollars generously donated by fellow lawyers and bar associations. This relief fund assisted hundreds of attorneys whose lives and practices were destroyed by the catastrophic hurricane.

The HELP Program volunteers, with the assistance of the approximately 1,900 volunteer attorneys who belong to the Louisiana State Bar Association SOLACE (Support of Lawyers/Legal Personnel—All Concern Encouraged) Program and attorneys throughout the state of Louisiana opened their homes and offices (and their hearts) to displaced and homeless fellow attorneys who had lost everything. Attorneys throughout the country donated office furniture in an effort to assist New Orleans area attorneys who needed to completely rebuild their law practices. Over 6,000 attorneys (approximately one third of the attorneys in the state of Louisiana) were displaced as a result of the mandatory evacuation of the metropolitan New Orleans area.

Lawyers have historically been the leaders in their communities. All too often the news media reports on the "bad apples" of the legal profession. Overlooked, and not reported as "newsworthy," are the thousands of lawyers who serve the homeless—and each other—in their times of need. Many of these lawyers, who now have no home or office, and who are literally "homeless," have passed acts of sale so that others will have a place to live. They have fought for the freedom of those prisoners who were incarcerated and who, because of the evacuation of the prisons, remained in jail beyond their release dates. They have protected the rights of landlords as well as those of tenants who were displaced as a result of the deadly hurricane. And finally, they have worked—and continue to work—at disaster relief centers giving pro bono legal advice and notarizing FEMA documents so that citizens can begin rebuilding their lives.

The following are just a few quotes which sum up all that is right about our legal profession:

A HELP volunteer attorney who lost her home and who was displaced, stated: "I have temporarily re-located from Lakeview to the Prairieville area and can volunteer. Because of child care issues I am limited in availability to weekends, but would like to do whatever I can if there is a center near me."

And another HELP volunteer attorney stated: "I will be able to volunteer. Perhaps, you can have someone contact me as my telephone and such do not work well. My entire home, on Treasure Isle in Slidell, was blown down. I have finally recovered somewhat and have clothes and zest to move forward again."

Still another HELP volunteer, returning to New Orleans after having been evacuated for three months asked:

"Are there any Disaster Relief Centers in the New Orleans area? I'm back at work, and would be happy to volunteer."

Hurricane Katrina has taught us that no one is safe from tragedy.

Creating a HELP Program in Your Community

The HELP Program has proven to be a simple—yet effective—way to assist the "poorest of the poor." HELP volunteer attorneys and notaries have been instrumental not only in protecting the legal rights of the homeless, but also have been credited with assisting many individuals in escaping homelessness. HELP Programs are currently operating in New Orleans, Lafayette, Shreveport, and

Baton Rouge, Louisiana. Plans are underway to create HELP programs in New York City, Washington, DC, and Memphis, Tennessee. Starting a HELP Program is quite simple:

1) Responsible directors of homeless shelters and centers are identified in a particular city. The program is explained to them, and their needs are determined.
2) Contact people from each major law firm are identified (usually with the help of the local pro bono organization) and local bar associations are asked to announce the program to its members. Everyone is invited to attend a lunchtime get-together so that the program can be explained to the potential volunteer attorneys.

ABA © STEVEN MUNSTER

Judge Jay C. Zainey *U.S. District Court*
Eastern District of Louisiana
500 Poydras Street Room C455
New Orleans, LA 70130
504.589.7590 Jay_Zainey@laed.uscourts.gov

Honorable Jay C. Zainey was appointed by President George W. Bush to the United States District Court for the Eastern District of Louisiana on February 19, 2002. In May 2004, Judge Zainey organized the Homeless Experience Legal Protection (HELP) Program. Prior to Hurricane Katrina, approximately 400 attorneys provided legal consultation services and notary services at four homeless centers in New Orleans. Since the hurricane, the HELP volunteers have been providing legal services at the major Disaster Relief Center in New Orleans to assist the "new" homeless. While currently carrying a full docket in the Eastern District of Louisiana, Judge Zainey also assists his colleagues by presiding over cases in both the Southern District of Texas and the Southern District of Mississippi. Zainey is past president of the Louisiana State Bar Association and the Jefferson Bar Association, is currently on the Board of Directors of the Pro Bono Project, the New Orleans Chapter of the Federal Bar Association, Magnolia Special School, and is President of the Judge John C. Boutall American Inn of Court. Judge Zainey is a past member of the President's Mental Retardation Task Force.

3) The schedule of dates and times are listed, and interested attorneys are asked to sign up for a specific date and time to volunteer.
4) Usually the executive director of the local bar association will take over the scheduling duties once the program is off and running.

By participating in HELP Programs around the country and with a little effort, attorneys and notaries can use their God-given talents to assist those who are less fortunate to escape homelessness, rebuild their lives, and restore their dignity. Isn't that what the legal profession is all about?

Lawyers Clearinghouse on Affordable Housing and Homelessness

Josephine McNeil and Maribeth Perry

The role of individual attorneys engaged in pro bono activities, with the support of their local and state bar associations, has been and continues to be central to address the legal problems of individuals and organizations facing homelessness and poverty. This article depicts the efforts and achievements of an organization born 18 years ago from the coming together of concerned attorneys. Highlighted in this article are the three primary pro bono programs operated by the organization:

- Community Legal Referral Program
- Massachusetts Legal Clinic for the Homeless
- Boston Bar Association Business Law Project

History

The Lawyers Clearinghouse on Affordable Housing and Homelessness (the "Clearinghouse") began to take shape in 1987 in response to the growing crisis of homelessness in the city of Boston. Several different groups of lawyers, including those from the Boston Bar Association and the Massachusetts Bar Association, had begun to examine various ways in which legal resources could be applied to combat homelessness. Once these disparate groups realized that they were all working towards a common goal, they came together and formed the Clearinghouse. The goal of the Clearinghouse was to mobilize attorneys willing to provide pro bono legal services to affordable housing developers, tenants' groups, advocacy groups for the homeless, and other organizations involved in addressing the issue of homelessness.

In 1990, after only three years of operating as a bar sponsored pro bono program, the Clearinghouse received the American Bar Association's Pro Bono Partnership Award and has served as the model used by bar associations seeking to establish similar pro bono programs throughout the country.

Programs

The first program of the Clearinghouse, the Community Legal Referral Program, matches volunteer lawyers with nonprofit groups that develop or sponsor affordable housing, promote economic development, or operate as homeless shelters, tenant organizations, and housing and homeless advocacy groups. In order to qualify for the Clearinghouse's services, the group must operate or intend to operate as a nonprofit organization in Massachusetts; engage in activities related to affordable housing, economic development, prevention of homelessness, or shelter services; and be unable to afford legal services or demonstrate that the cost of obtaining legal assistance would adversely affect their ability to fulfill their mission.

Once a request is received, it is screened by our legal referral director for its eligibility, and the opportunity to provide the requested legal service is offered to our panel of volunteer attorneys, usually through the pro bono coordinator at the collaborating law firms. It is not unusual to receive one or more responses from potential pro bono attorneys within a day of sending the request. The types of legal services needed and provided through the program are varied in scope and complexity, resulting in a wide range of pro bono opportunities and hourly commitments. For example:

- An organization that provides food, clothing, furniture, and other necessities to the poor had been operating since 1983 as a program of a national church. In order to facilitate a more effective fundraising mechanism for its mission, the organization sought help to file for its own tax-exempt status separate from that of the sponsoring church. In addition, the organization sought a volunteer lawyer to serve on its board, and the Clearinghouse was also able to assist the group with both requests.
- A group of tenants living in single room occupancies in a local YMCA were concerned that upcoming changes at the YMCA would leave them homeless. They sought assistance to clarify their rights as tenants under HUD's Uniform Relocation Act. They also sought help to join with a local nonprofit group to form a legal entity to address the issue of homelessness in their community.
- A local highly-regarded homeless shelter with an innovative and cost-effective supportive housing model offering transitional housing to homeless families along with on-site skill programs and support services contacted the Clearinghouse. The organization planned to renovate their 12-unit apartment building and required legal assistance to restructure their debt and review contracts with architects and general contractors.
- An organization that provides women with the resources and support they need to emerge from conditions of domestic violence, sexual abuse, poverty, discrimination, social isolation, and degradation sought help to close a loan that was critical to the organization's financial stability.

By 1993, the Clearinghouse found itself in the enviable position of having more attorneys interested in providing pro bono services than nonprofit clients to refer. After much discussion by the board of directors and research by the staff to determine if the organization should expand its focus to individuals, the Clearinghouse initiated a new program—the Massachusetts Legal Clinic for the Homeless. The program was based upon similar programs operating at the time in Washington, DC and Cape Cod.

At its inception, the program was a joint project with Greater Boston Legal Services and the Volunteer Lawyers Project, and it now utilizes the expertise of staff from the Boston University Law School Clinical Program and the Hale and Dorr Legal Services Center of Harvard Law School. Currently, it is a collaborative enterprise of seven of the State's largest law firms. Groups of attorneys from these firms provide monthly on-site legal services to the residents of three of the area's larger shelters: the Pine Street Inn, Friends of the Shattuck Shelter, and St. Francis House in Boston.

Examples of the types of issues and legal services provided through the program are as follows:

- A client had applied to the Boston Housing Authority (BHA) for Section 8 housing and had been denied. The denial was based on his criminal record. A pro bono attorney took on the appeal and helped the client submit documentation to the BHA regarding his rehabilitation efforts since his last legal problems. The client had completed a program related to drugs and alcohol, was sober, and was enrolled in a work-related training program. Soon after submitting the documents, the client was notified that due to mitigating circumstances the prior determination was reversed, and he received his Section 8 voucher.
- A client came to the clinic seeking assistance with his claim for Social Security Disability Insurance (SSDI) benefits. The client, who was in his mid-40s, had worked various manual labor and kitchen jobs until May 2001, when an injury prevented him from working. Since the injury, he had been in constant pain and became depressed. Volunteer attorneys first met with the client after his application for SSDI benefits had been denied. He had filed a Request for Reconsideration on his own that had not yet been decided. Despite additional medical evidence and the written legal argument the advocates presented to the SSA, his request for reconsideration was denied. The decision was immediately appealed, and a hearing before an Administrative Law Judge was requested. Soon after the hearing, a "fully-favorable" decision was received and the client received his benefits.

In 2002, the Clearinghouse was approached by the BBA Business Law Section Pro Bono Committee to discuss the lack of pro bono opportunities for business lawyers and how the Clearinghouse might help that committee better meet the pro bono needs of its members. The result was the creation of the BBA Business Law Project, which operates like our Community Legal Referral Program but offers legal services to all nonprofit organizations in need of assistance with corporate or business related legal needs other than those related to housing and homelessness.

The Clearinghouse legal referral staff has been able to provide business attorneys with a wide range of business related legal cases. The needs of the nonprofit organizations are varied and examples of the types of legal services provided through the program include:

- A nonprofit organization with a mission to train service dogs to provide safer, more stable and rewarding lives for those who suffer from Type I brittle diabetes and/or epilepsy requested and obtained assistance to file for a trademark.
- An organization that promotes teen leadership and employment opportunities sought assistance with a lease review, a fiscal agreement, and analysis of government regulations to facilitate their plans to add a storefront operation to their existing Internet bookselling business employing youth in state custody. They intend to develop the storefront bookstore into an art gallery for youth as well as an incubator for youth entrepreneurs who will receive seed money to fund selected proposals for small business ventures.
- A group seeking to provide a community-based alternative to the Massachusetts CHINS (Children in Need of Services) program for families with high risk children sought assistance to incorporate and file for tax-exempt status. The program offered by the group will include full-time case workers, a hotline to help runaway children and their families, and an investigation arm to locate missing children.

In addition to the previously mentioned programs, the Clearinghouse also partners with Volunteer Lawyers for the Arts (VLA) on a bi-monthly seminar geared towards representatives of organizations considering incorporating in Massachusetts and/or filing for federal tax-exempt status. The goal of the nonprofit seminar is to provide education to such organizations so that they are well informed about the process and to ensure that our volunteer attorneys are working with prepared clients on the road to success. The Clearinghouse also provides a panel of attorneys who collaborate with the VLA panel to lead the classes.

ABA © PHILIP B. HERR

Josephine McNeil *Executive Director*
Citizens for Affordable Housing in Newton Development Organization
1075 Washington Street West Newton, MA 02465
617.964.3527 jam_cando@msn.com

Josephine McNeil is the Executive Director of Citizens for Affordable Housing in Newton Development Organization, Inc. d/b/a CAN-DO. CAN-DO is a community-based nonprofit housing development organization with a mission to create affordable housing in the City of Newton. Her tenure with CAN-DO has spanned 11 years. Prior to her appointment as Executive Director, she ran her own affordable housing and economic development firm. Her background includes employment as a real estate attorney for the Boston law firm Brown Rudnick Freed and Gesmer and a position as Senior Project Manager for a real estate developer whose focus was on affordable housing. She received the Human Rights Award from the Newton Human Rights Commission in 2001; was highlighted by the Newton Women's Commission in the 2002 Portrait Project; and received the Robert Swett Award in recognition of her efforts to develop affordable housing in the City of Newton. She was appointed by the Mayor to serve on the Comprehensive Planning Advisory Committee and chairs the sub-committee charged with developing the Housing Element. Josephine also serves on the board of several regional and national organizations including the Citizens Housing and Planning Association, the Individual Rights and Responsibilities Section Council of the Massachusetts Bar Association, the Lawyers Clearinghouse for Affordable Housing and Homelessness, and the Standing Committee for Pro Bono and Public Service of the American Bar Association. Finally, she has chaired and served as a member of the ABA Commission on Homelessness and Poverty.

Other Clearinghouse Activities

Over the years, the Clearinghouse has participated in and collaborated with other groups on specific targeted programs that benefit low income individuals and/or organizations with missions to improve low income and distressed communities. The Eviction Defense Project, Lawyer for the Day Program (Housing Court), Homebase First-Time Homebuyer Program, and Second Mortgage/Foreclosure Defense Coalition are examples of programs in which the Clearinghouse recruited lawyers and contributed their time and expertise. Furthermore, Clearinghouse committees, such as the Loan Simplification Committee and Legislative Committee, have worked on issues affecting affordable housing and homelessness in the community.

The vitality of the Clearinghouse can be attributed to the numerous Massachusetts attorneys who have served on the Board of Directors over its 18-year history. They have continued to seek ways to make sure the organization remains relevant to the attorneys and community it serves. Currently, the Clearinghouse's Strategic Planning Committee is in the process of writing a plan that will set

Maribeth Perry *Executive Director*
Lawyers Clearinghouse on Affordable Housing and Homelessness
16 Beacon Street Boston, MA 02108
617.778.1980 mperry@lawyersclearinghouse.org

Maribeth Perry joined the Clearinghouse as its Executive Director in 1996. She is responsible for the overall administration of the organization. Maribeth is the former Co-Executive Director of the Central Massachusetts Housing Alliance, Inc., and she is Executive Director of the Housing Information Center, Inc., housing agencies, providing services to landlords, tenants, homeless people seeking shelter, elder homeowners, and first time homebuyers. Maribeth graduated from Hofstra University School of Law in New York and the University of Utah. She is the author of *The Successful Landlord*, a guide to the rights and responsibilities of owning and managing rental property in Massachusetts.

the direction for the organization for the next several years. In addition to the continuation of our core programs, some of our future goals include the following:

- Increasing participation in advocacy/policy/legislative initiatives by lending our legal expertise in support of such efforts.
- Conducting and coordinating legal educational programs for lawyers, nonprofits, and community groups.
- Expanding marketing efforts to clients, attorneys, and others to raise the profile and awareness of our organization and our services.

Conclusion

The Clearinghouse has been engaging the private bar in pro bono activities since its inception in 1988. At that time, there was recognition that real estate lawyers had unique skills and abilities that were needed to address the issues of the lack of affordable housing and homelessness. During the intervening years, the Clearinghouse has sought to provide an increasing number of Massachusetts attorneys with pro bono opportunities that utilize their specific skills and expertise to create and preserve affordable housing, reduce the incidence of homelessness, provide assistance to the homeless, and provide assistance to organizations that benefit the low income communities in Massachusetts.

CHAPTER

Nonprofit Legal Organizations Working to End Homelessness

Equal Justice:

Working for the Rights of the Homeless

Shelbi D. Day

As a small child, I became concerned about the plight of the homeless when, at age four, I stood in the back yard of my home and watched a man rummage through a nearby garbage bin. At that age, I did not understand why anyone would search for food in such a place, and I was devastated by my mother's explanation that the man did not have money to buy food and did not have a place to live. As an adult, I have come to better understand the issues surrounding homelessness, but I am no less bothered by the fact that there are citizens among us who lack food, shelter, and other basic life necessities.

For me, this was the first of many exposures to social injustice within society that motivated me to pursue a career in civil and human rights. Ironically, more than twenty years after that experience, my career in civil rights began with an opportunity to work to protect and defend the civil rights of homeless individuals. I am currently an Equal Justice Works Fellow at Southern Legal Counsel, Inc. (SLC), where I am working on a two-year fellowship project that aims to address the civil rights abuses that homeless people face as a result of state and local efforts to make criminal the life sustaining activities of homeless individuals and the status of being homeless. My project attempts to address such abuses through litigation, public policy advocacy, education, and outreach.

The "criminalization of homelessness" does nothing to address the root causes of homelessness and serves only to decrease visibility of homeless individuals by driving them out of, or removing them from, public spaces. This approach, which is pervasive throughout Florida and across the United States, simply recycles homeless people through the criminal justice system for offenses related to their homelessness and oftentimes results in civil rights abuses.

In September of 2004, I began my Equal Justice Works Fellowship at SLC, a nonprofit public interest law firm located in Gainesville, Florida, that has advocated the causes and interests of un-represented and under-represented groups throughout Florida since 1977. The Equal Justice Works Fellowships Program creates partnerships among public interest lawyers, nonprofit organizations, law firm/corporate sponsors, and other donors in order to afford under-represented populations effective access to the justice system through fellowship projects. Equal Justice Works is currently the national leader in creating public interest opportunities for law school graduates, and it funds approximately fifty two-year Equal Justice Works fellowships each year. My project is funded by Equal Justice Works and the Florida Bar Foundation.

The idea for my project was born out of SLC's investigations into complaints by homeless advocates, which revealed systemic civil rights abuses of homeless individuals in North Central Florida. Seeing a need for a full time attorney to further investigate and address these issues, SLC and I developed the fellowship project. SLC has significant experience in developing and litigating systemic reform cases involving a diverse range of civil rights issues. SLC's primary funding is through grants from the Florida Bar Foundation, and it does not receive any government or LSC funding. With few restrictions and its focus on systemic reform, SLC is an ideal host for my project, which seeks to challenge unconstitutional state and local laws and police practices.

During the first year of my fellowship, I conducted extensive public records requests and interviewed homeless individuals and their advocates in various locations throughout Florida in an effort to identify systemic issues related to civil rights abuses of homeless individuals. I also conducted education and outreach, which included working with fellow members of the Florida Bar Public Interest Law Section Committee on Homelessness to design continuing legal education seminars about legal issues related to homelessness; giving presentations on the existence and consequences of criminalization of homelessness; and creating pocket size street information cards and "Know Your Rights" information that aimed to educate homeless individuals.

In February of 2005, I wrote an *amicus curiae* brief in support of a public defender, Chris Cosden, who challenged an anti-sleeping ordinance in Sarasota, Florida. The ordinance prohibited homeless individuals from sleeping in public places between the hours of sunset and sunrise. Despite the lack of available shelter beds for Sarasota's homeless population, several homeless individuals were arrested under the ordinance. The First District Court of Appeals denied the City's application for certiorari review of the lower court's decision finding the ordinance unconstitutional. Since that time, I have reviewed ordinances, laws, and law enforcement policies and practices being used against homeless individuals in other municipalities in North Central Florida, in an attempt to identify systemic civil rights abuses. Currently, I am assessing potential legal action to address such abuses. In the course of my project, I have come to realize that injustice against homeless individuals is pervasive and easy to identify, but it is increasingly difficult to bring legal action to challenge such issues. Many times, civil rights abuses at the hands of police and governments must be challenged at the local level, which is time consuming and costly.

The biggest accomplishment of my fellowship occurred in March of 2006, when I filed a lawsuit in the United States District Court for the Northern District of Florida on behalf of three homeless individuals against the City of Gainesville and Sheriff Stephen Oelrich in his official capacity as Sheriff of Alachua County, Florida. The Plaintiffs had been harassed, threatened, and arrested by local law enforcement officers for standing on public sidewalks, holding small cardboard signs that solicit alms.

The 42 U.S.C. § 1983 lawsuit challenges the constitutionality of two state statutes and a local ordinance that prohibit soliciting on public streets and right-of-ways without a permit. The laws and enforcement thereof violate the First and Fourteenth Amendments to the United States Constitution, on their face and as applied to Plaintiffs and other homeless individuals by Defendants. The statutes themselves do not provide permit schemes or any standards for such, and they leave enforcement and creation of applicable permit schemes to local governments. Although the City of Gainesville has adopted the statutes into its Code of Ordinances and Gainesville Police Officers actively enforce the laws to prohibit homeless individuals from standing on public sidewalks holding signs soliciting alms, the City has not adopted a permit scheme that applies to such activity. Instead, the City enacted an ordinance similar to the statutes, which prohibits charitable solicitation on public streets and rights-of-way without a permit, but allows such permits only to tax-exempt charitable organizations. Alachua County Sheriff's Deputies also use the laws to prohibit homeless individuals from soliciting alms on traditional public fora in the County, but there is no permit scheme in Alachua County that applies to such activity. Despite the lack of an applicable permit, both Gainesville Police Officers and Alachua County Sheriff's Deputies regularly tell homeless individuals that they cannot solicit alms on public sidewalks and streets without a permit. Plaintiffs' Motion for Preliminary Injunction, seeking to enjoin enforcement of the laws and the unconstitutional enforcement thereof, is currently pending before the court.

I am one of six Equal Justice Works Fellows currently working on issues related to homelessness. Each of the other Fellows could have written this article and shed light on other aspects of fighting homelessness and the injustices that homeless people face. As I have been inspired by these fellows' projects and stories, I share a little about each of their projects below.

Since September 2004, Elisa Della-Piana, who is at the Lawyers' Committee for Civil Rights in San Francisco, has been working to advance the self-sufficiency of homeless persons by advocating against the criminalization of life-sustaining activities. Elisa identifies policies that criminalize homeless people and challenges those policies through legislative advocacy, impact litigation, and individual representation. During the first year of her program, she successfully created a program in San Francisco, through which private practitioners provide pro bono representation to homeless individuals charged with quality of life offenses. A vast majority of the time, the lawyers that Elisa recruits and trains are able to get the charges dropped. Elisa also engages homeless persons through outreach and education, and she connects them with resources that may provide an exit to homelessness. Her fellowship is sponsored by Bingham McCutchen, LLP.

Amy Zaremba, a 2005 Fellow at the Georgia Justice Project, is working on a project sponsored by Greenberg Traurig, LLP that aims to decriminalize homelessness. Amy, who has twelve years experience working with and for homeless people, works to reduce the number of homeless individuals who are arrested in Atlanta, Georgia for offenses related to their being homeless. She does so by providing legal representation to homeless people who are arrested for quality of life offenses such as sleeping in public; educating homeless individuals on their rights; educating others about the special needs of people who are homeless; and advocating for changes in laws and regulations in Atlanta.

Zenaida Alonzo has been at the Chicago Coalition for the Homeless since 2004, working to dispel negative images about homeless youth through legal advocacy. Zenaida, whose project is sponsored by The Chicago Bar Foundation, aims to meet the unique legal needs of homeless youth who are at risk of homelessness through a mobile "kid-friendly" legal clinic. She travels to locations where homeless youth can be found and provides convenient and accessible legal services. During the first year of her fellowship, she served over 100 clients. This year, Zenaida is working with other attorneys at The Law Project of the Chicago Coalition for the Homeless on a class action lawsuit against the Chicago Public Schools regarding its Renaissance 2010 Plan, a plan to close 60-90 schools by 2010, thereby depriving hundreds of homeless students of their "school of origin" guaranteed by a Consent Decree, the *McKinney-Vento Homeless Education Act*, and the *Illinois Education for Homeless Children and Youth Act*. Zenaida has a special interest in advocating for homeless youth because she was homeless herself during her senior year of high school. Because of that experience, Zenaida understands "what these kids are going through and their needs" and knows "how vital it is to have caring people and support to make the transition into a successful adult."

Emily Benfer, at the Washington Legal Clinic for the Homeless, began her project concerning homeless children in 2005. Emily's project, DC HEART, is sponsored by Arnold & Porter LLP and aims to defeat child homelessness through education, legal advocacy, creative resources, and community teamwork. Her project helps break the cycle of homelessness for children and future generations by providing legal assistance in the areas of education, healthcare, and public benefits; conducting workshops at shelters; collaborating with community groups and education providers; and providing outreach programs to parents. Emily's dedication to the needs of homeless children and families was first inspired when she discovered the dangerous and threatening family shelter conditions during an internship at the Washington Legal Clinic for the Homeless. "In that setting of despair, I realized that my most valuable contribution as an advocate is to strive for a system that recognizes the strengths of individuals in need, lifts them above their struggles and helps them to achieve their full potential," Emily stated. "Human beings deserve no less."

Since 2005, Bernadette Segura has been at Texas Rio Grande Legal Aid providing legal representation, advocacy, and outreach to San Antonio's homeless population. Her project seeks to help homeless individuals in San Antonio find safe, affordable housing and to narrow the gap between the San Antonio homeless residents eligible for mainstream benefits and those actually receiving them. Bernadette provides clients with legal advice and representation, helps them prepare legal documents, and performs outreach activities to encourage the homeless population to apply for mainstream benefits and to assist them in securing affordable housing. She is

Shelbi D. Day *Southern Legal Counsel, Inc.*
1229 NW 12th Avenue Gainesville, Florida 32601
352.271.8890 shelbi.day@southernlegal.org

Shelbi Day is an attorney at Southern Legal Counsel, Inc. (SLC) in Gainesville, Florida. She joined SLC in 2004 through a Fellowship sponsored by Equal Justice Works and the Florida Bar Foundation. During her two year fellowship, Ms. Day is focusing on the civil rights violations that result when local governments criminalize the life-sustaining activities of homeless individuals and/or the status of being homeless. Prior to joining SLC, Ms. Day served as a law clerk to the Honorable Charles R. Wilson of the United States Court of Appeals for the Eleventh Circuit. She became a member of The Florida Bar in October 2002, and is admitted to practice before the United States Court of Appeals for the Eleventh Circuit, the United States District Court for the Middle District of Florida, and the United States District Court for the Northern District of Florida. She is a member of the Young Lawyers Division, the Executive Council of the Public Interest Law Section of The Florida Bar, and the Ad Hoc Committee on Homelessness. She received her J.D. with high honors from the University of Florida Levin College of Law in 2002, her M.A. *Phi Kappa Phi* from the University of Florida, and her B.A., *magna cum laude*, from Missouri State University.

the only attorney at her program who works with homeless individuals. Bernadette's project is sponsored by Texas Equal Access to Justice Foundation.

My fellowship, and the stories shared with me by other Equal Justice Works fellows working with homeless individuals, has had an impact on my career and person. I am inspired by the courage and perseverance of individuals who struggle daily to survive life circumstances that most of us could not even imagine. I have been touched by individual stories of survival and perseverance of the human spirit through even the worst adversity. Over the past year and a half, I have constantly run up against the cruel stereotypes people have of homeless individuals and have been taken aback by the way that homeless people are treated by fellow citizens, police officers, and governments. Plainly, homeless individuals are treated in inhumane and unfair ways that no human being should have to endure. The biggest lessons that I have learned are that a little respect and empathy go a long way; even the smallest gesture of kindness is met with gratitude and appreciation; and everyone has a story worth listening to. I am regularly humbled and reminded how fortunate I am.

Traditional and Non-Traditional Homelessness Prevention

Edward Hoort

Introduction

The best way to address homelessness is to prevent it. It is not enough to open the front door of a shelter if people go out the back door and are on the streets once again. We must prevent people from becoming homeless in the first place and provide opportunities for people to obtain stable and affordable housing in the future.

However, as illustrated by a recent survey in the city of Flint, Michigan, preventing homelessness involves meeting needs that go beyond mere housing. Flint social agencies offered free dinners for the homeless in different parts of town in exchange for the completion of a five question survey. To no one's surprise, the homeless respondents identified the following issues as the most important to them: housing, jobs, income assistance, and transportation. Or, to state it even more simply, they needed housing, income, and transportation. Of course, to some extent, housing and transportation both require income.

Legal Services of Eastern Michigan (LSEM) has undertaken a number of efforts regarding homelessness prevention. Some of these efforts involve legal strategies that are traditional for a legal services program. Others are non-traditional and involve numerous collaborative partnerships. While we will briefly review the traditional efforts, most of this analysis will examine the non-traditional efforts in which the legal services office acts as a catalyst and advisor within a broader community effort that involves major contributions by numerous private and governmental partners.

We will examine both types of strategies used by LSEM in Flint, Michigan, a city which has undergone significant demographic changes. In 1970, Flint had a population of 250,000. In 2000, the City's population had dropped to 124,000. Over 60% of the City of Flint qualifies for legal services, that is, they are under 125% of the federal poverty guideline. As a result of the economic and related population decline, Flint has numerous empty buildings and homes. They are decrepit, abandoned, and have become home for drug dens and gangs. According to the 2000 PURA Study conducted by the University of Michigan-Flint in concert with the Charles Stewart Mott Foundation, over 50% of the housing is in a state of disrepair.

Traditional Homelessness Prevention

As part of its traditional efforts to prevent homelessness, LSEM advises and represents persons in eviction proceedings and defends land contract forfeitures. LSEM intervenes in mortgage foreclosures and files Chapter 13 bankruptcies where appropriate. This is traditional housing work for a legal services program.

Similarly, in order to stabilize income and prevent homelessness, LSEM visits shelters and represents claimants seeking disability benefits through the Supplemental Security Income (SSI) and Social Security Disability (SSD) programs, as well as the state's interim disability assistance program. LSEM helps homeless and potentially homeless people obtain additional sources of income through income maintenance and supplementary programs such as food stamps, TANF, Medicaid, child care assistance, unemployment insurance, and other programs. Again, this is traditional income maintenance work for a legal services program.

Non-Traditional Homelessness Prevention

Improving the Tax Reversion Process

In 1993, LSEM was approached by a group of nonprofit housing providers working in Genesee County, where Flint is located. These organizations were able to obtain tax reverted residential property from the State at little cost. However, the tax reversion process was so complicated that it was seldom followed correctly, and title insurance companies refused to give title insurance on any property that came from the State tax reversion process. As a result, the nonprofit providers were unable to obtain mortgages on any of the properties, making it impossible for them to rehabilitate the properties for, and sell the properties to, low income consumers. The existing reversion process took five to seven years, during which time the property condition declined. Due to the lengthy and frustrating process, most tax-reverted properties were recycled to speculators and slum landlords who let the property decline even further.

LSEM worked with the Genesee County Treasurer to draft proposed legislation that would streamline the tax reversion process. A version of this legislation was enacted in 1999, PUBLIC ACT 123. This new legislation had a number of positive effects. First, it shortened the tax reversion process from five to seven years to no more than two. The shorter time frame reduced the amount of time property stands empty and reduced blight. Second, the new law passed title to the Treasurer through a *quiet* title action. This granted clear title. If property then went to nonprofit entities, they could obtain mortgages for rehabilitation or sale. Third, by clearing up title questions as a matter of law, it enabled owners to obtain mortgages on the reverted properties that could finance rehabilitation of the properties. Fourth, it took the properties out of the hands of speculators by transferring homes to the Treasurer. The Treasurer could then protect the property from speculators. (See explanation of bundling below.)

Protecting Homeowners from Losing Their Homes

After the new reversion legislation was enacted, LSEM began work with the Genesee County Treasurer to design a tax foreclosure prevention program. Under the Genesee County program, the Treasurer identifies all homeowners who are subject to losing their homes due to tax reversion and shares this list with LSEM. The law requires the County to visit each home threatened with reversion, and Genesee County contracts with LSEM to perform this service. LSEM uses trained teams of two to visit each home personally. During their discussion with the homeowner(s), the teams identify alternative sources of ongoing income, special programs to help with property taxes, potential problems with the property titles, and inform the homeowners how they can obtain an additional one year extension to repay back taxes. LSEM also helps identify homeowners who can obtain poverty exemptions from future taxes based on indigency and helps those homeowners seek this relief. In 2001, LSEM visited over 1,400 homeowners. Only four of those persons lost their homes. In 2002 LSEM visited over 1,600 homes and fewer then 10 persons lost their home. In 2003, over 800 homes were visited and again, fewer then 10 persons lost their home. In 2005, none of the 880 homes threatened with tax foreclosure were lost. LSEM adapted this program for replication in rural areas, and it is now assisting the Sanilac County Treasurer implement a version of the program there. In addition, Genesee County's approach is being considered or implemented in areas in Michigan outside LSEM's service area, including the Counties of Washtenaw, Saginaw, Ingham, Jackson, Wayne, and Calhoun.

Traditional and Non-Traditional Efforts to Prevent Homelessness:

As part of its traditional efforts to prevent homelessness, LSEM advises and represents persons in eviction proceedings, defends land contract forfeitures, and intervenes in mortgage foreclosures. Non-traditional homelessness prevention mechanisms employed by LSEM include improving the tax reversion process, preserving the existing housing stock, and stabilizing housing by increasing homeownership.

Helping Tenants Remain in Tax-Reverted Property

Many homes that are subject to property tax foreclosure are occupied by tenants, as opposed to owners. LSEM helped to create a separate program to maintain these tenants in their homes even after the property had been taken over by the County Treasurer. LSEM invited a number of nonprofit housing providers to a meeting with the Genesee County Treasurer. Tenant occupied properties that were taken by the Treasurer were divided among the nonprofits. The nonprofits were given a management fee for acting as managers of the property. Rents were set uniformly at $300 per month, keeping with the ability of low-income people to pay. A procedure for paying for repairs was developed.

Preserving Existing Housing Stock

LSEM has also worked on a variety of strategies for preserving housing through its participation in the Genesee County Treasurer's Tax Reversion Policy Council. That Council drafted legislation that has enabled Genesee County to preserve and maintain affordable residential housing stock.

1. Land Bank Tax Increment Financing

The policy council drafted legislation Public Act 340 of 2005, establishing a land bank to receive tax reverted properties. The Land Bank can then use the reverted properties to encourage local development and infill housing. Infill housing is new construction on vacant land. All lands sold by the Land Bank are subject to tax increment financing. For fifteen years after the property is sold by the Land Bank, 50% of all tax revenues from the property are returned to the Land Bank, which uses these funds to pay for housing development, demolition, and rehabilitation in the County.

2. Side Lot Acquisition

The Policy Council sought to improve the value of the Land Bank properties and to reduce blight. It began a program in which vacant lots were made available to adjoining property owners. Under this program, the land remaining from a demolished structure could be sold to an adjoining property owner for as little as $1. This increases lot size and reduces blight. The vacant land is thus returned to the tax rolls and 50% of the revenue generated from these properties in taxes for the next 15 years is used to fund the Land Bank.

3. Bundled Properties

Under the tax reversion statute, tax reverted properties must be placed up for public auction. This process, however, increases the likelihood of speculators purchasing the properties for rental property. The Policy Council developed a program in which reverted properties are "bundled" before they are placed up for auction, which requires speculators to bid on the entire bundle. The bundles include enough unusable properties to make it economically unfeasible to purchase the group. This prevents unscrupulous speculators from obtaining the property and allows the Land Bank to return the property to useful service or to demolish the property for side lot or infill acquisition.

Property that is not bundled is placed up for auction. All funds generated by the auction above the amount of back taxes, including interest, fees, and penalties are used to fund the Land Bank. The Land Bank is now the largest property owner in the County.

Protecting Tenants from Homelessness

The ongoing relationship between the County Treasurer, housing agencies, and LSEM is a continuing resource which can be mobilized to prevent homelessness. Recently, for example, a development group approached LSEM regarding their plans to purchase a local SRO (sleeping room only or flop house) and convert it to condominiums. This plan would involve dislocating numerous persons. However, by using the resources of the Land Bank, relocations can occur at a very reasonable cost because residents are transferred to Land Bank properties managed by local housing nonprofits.

The rent of $300 a month in Land Bank property plus utilities is less than was charged by the SRO. Similarly, the Land Bank resources were used to house families relocated because of Hurricane Katrina. This program assures that hundreds of families are not made homeless. It reduces future tax burdens and places persons in homes at $300 per month.

Stabilizing Housing by Increasing Homeownership—GAIN$

Another housing-related innovation that LSEM has helped to implement in the County is a program called GAIN$. This project enables low income persons to establish Individual Development Accounts, which are a special type of bank savings account for low-income persons. The IDA funds can then be used to help low-income persons purchase a home. A client saves a little money in the account each month. Local banks have agreed to waive all fees on these accounts. While saving, each IDA holder attends a series of classes on financial literacy. Upon reaching $1,000 in savings, the IDA holder's savings are matched with an additional $3,000 in funds. This is a three for one match. These funds are provided by a combination of the Charles Stewart Mott Foundation, the Ruth Mott Foundation, The Community Foundation of Greater Flint, and the United Way of Genesee County. Funds were also obtained from the U.S. Department of Health and Human Services (HHS). The funds can only be used for four purposes. They can be used for small business startup or development, higher education, home purchase, or transportation. (HHS funds cannot be used for transportation, so the match for these funds is provided locally.)

LSEM designed the structure of the GAIN$ project and raised the match funds. LSEM also provides all financial oversight of the project. The actual day-to-day operation of the program is undertaken by Metro Housing Partnership, a nonprofit organization that LSEM works with on a variety of other issues regarding homelessness and housing. Each GAIN$ participant is assigned to a separate local social agency or church that sponsors the client and provides case management. For example, Habitat for Humanity sponsors a number of clients.

GAIN$ participants also undergo asset specific training, in either home repair, business planning, career planning, or car purchases and maintenance. Each of these programs assists persons in either housing, income maintenance, or transportation.

The GAIN$ program works with the Land Bank to help program participants purchase homes from the Land Bank for the cost of back taxes. LSEM is currently working with a Local Bank and Fannie Mae to provide $20,000 to $30,000 mortgages on the property for rehabilitation. The Land Bank has agreed to provide the rehabilitation and oversee the process. Metro Housing Partnership also administers a down payment assistance program that can add between $5,000 and $10,000 to the clients' down payment. In addition, Metro holds Section 8 Family Self Sufficiency funds that can add dollars to the equation.

Community Benefits from Non-Traditional Homelessness Prevention Strategies

Education Stability

According to "Poverty in Genesee County: A Social Crisis," published in 2004 by the Social Systems Research Institute, there are six elementary schools in the Flint area that have over a 100% turnover of children in a single year. This lack of housing stability adversely affects students and schools. Evictions from substandard rental property and condemnation of aging homes contribute to this problem. The GAIN$ program will work in conjunction with the Land Bank to increase neighborhood stability. The Land Bank is using GIS technology to map all homes eligible for rehabilitation in specific elementary school districts. The GAIN$ program will then tie in the $4,000 savings and match from GAIN$ the $5,000 to $10,000 in down payment assistance with the $20,000 - $30,000 from Fannie Mae. These funds will then be used to purchase and rehabilitate the home. This work will be done under the auspices of the Land Bank. The end result is that IDA participants will be placed in totally rehabilitated homes, secured by a very affordable first mortgage of no greater than $30,000. This program will target properties in school districts that have especially high mobility rates. By increasing the number of homeowners in the neighborhood, the project will bring stability to both the neighborhood and the school district. The goal is to place 150 new homeowners in each targeted school district.

Reduction of Blight

LSEM met with the Genesee County Treasurer, the C. S. Mott Foundation,[1] and Fannie Mae to obtain a GEO Express loan of $5 million dollars. (GEO Express is a General Obligation loan secured by county funds.) These funds are used to demolish abandoned homes. Over 200 structures per year are being demolished. (When LSEM teams visit homes, they also inventory structures to identify those buildings which should be torn down immediately.) Funds from this source are also being used to rehabilitate suitable structures.

Community Lawyering

The efforts of LSEM in the above efforts illustrate a number of principles for this innovative work. First, much of the work is transactional. As such, it is an area where pro bono efforts can be of great use. Secondly, it is clear that much of the work that is done is not accomplished by lawyers, but by other agencies in the community. Lawyers can, however, provide important expertise when it comes to drafting and implementing legislation, and in designing the corporate and financing structure needed to undertake housing projects. These collaborative efforts, together with support from key local funders, are very necessary for the success of the projects. Third, in order to take advantage of the opportunities for inter-relationships, it is important for advocates to be involved in the community on an ongoing basis. Building relationships through regular participation in groups concerned about homelessness, such as the local Continuum of Care (CoC) required by HUD and MSHDA, the Committee Concerned with Housing, the Community Housing Resource Board, and other local entities is essential. LSEM's work

1 *The C. S. Mott Foundation has generously supported much of the early activity of the land bank and tax reversion programs in Flint.*

with the local CoC includes assisting in the drafting of Consortium Homelessness Prevention Grants. These Challenge grants were awarded by MSHDA and the Michigan Council of Foundations. At a local level, the Community Foundation of Greater Flint was an active participant in these efforts. After the grants were awarded, all Consortium members worked together to raise the matching funds. The first grant made first month's rent and deposit available for low-income people so that they could access available housing and not become homeless. The current grant will provide the near homeless with two types of assistance. Funding can be used for those people who have delinquent taxes to help pay their arrearages and retain their homes. The Challenge grant moneys can also be used to assist those people who are on a public housing waiting list to pay back utility and water bills so that when they reach a point on the list where housing is available, they will not be denied by these outstanding bills. This too prevents homelessness. The moneys for these programs are held in a Homeless Prevention Endowment Fund at the Community Foundation. Local homeless service providers work to keep adding dollars to this fund so that the benefits to be derived from it can be ongoing. Fourth, in order for legal services advocates to have the time needed to undertake this work, it is necessary for their program to authorize staff to spend time on activities that do not generate case numbers, but rather generate long-term positive impact on the community they serve.

Edward Hoort *Executive Director*
Legal Services of Eastern Michigan
436 S. Saginaw Street Flint, MI 48502
810.234.2621 ehoort@lsem-mi.org

Edward Hoort is the Executive Director of Legal Services of Eastern Michigan (LSEM). LSEM provides legal services to low-income clients in the following areas in Michigan: Arenac, Bay, Clare, Genesee, Gladwin, Gratiot, Isabella, Lapeer, Midland, and Saginaw counties. LSEM assists clients through community legal education, brief service, counsel, and advice, as well as representation that can take the form of negotiated settlements or litigation.

Reaching Out to Hawaii's Homeless

Emiko L.T. Ryan

Kauai, or the "Garden Isle," is a picture perfect paradise known for its impressive cliffs, blue skies, and breathtaking beaches. It is lesser known for its homeless problem. Every night at many of the beaches and parking lots on Kauai, individuals and families set up camp under tarps, in tents, or in cars. Even more people are forced to share accommodations with family members and friends, many of whom do not have homes of their own either. This common situation is due in large part to the tight housing market that forces many local residents to be priced out of their homes, leaving them unable to find affordable housing. Additionally, the island of Kauai is the only county in the State of Hawaii without a shelter for the homeless.

Sensing a need in the community for directed legal services for the homeless community, Greg Meyers, the managing attorney for the Kauai Office of the Legal Aid Society of Hawaii, applied for two grants to fund Holistic Legal Services for the Homeless (HLSH). Once the grant monies had been secured, I was informed that I was going to be heading the project. I was floored. I did not feel qualified to start a project that had such potential. I had no specialized knowledge of the homeless and no experience developing a project. All I had to go on was the general concept of the project. The grant application described in basic terms what the project would entail: outreach and legal representation for anyone who is homeless.[1] It was simple enough as a concept, but not so simple to execute.

Developing Holistic Legal Services for the Homeless

Step One: Who Are We Helping?

The first step in developing our project was to define what "homeless" meant. We chose to include not only those living in their vehicles or at the beach, but also those in the women's shelter, in transitional housing, and those living on the couches and floors of friends and family (the "hidden homeless"). Our goal was to bring as many people under the grant's umbrella as possible. In addition to defining homelessness, we needed to get a rough estimate of how many people would be categorically eligible for our services under HLSH. We talked to the local agencies familiar with the homeless population and concluded that there were approximately 550-600 homeless people living unsheltered on Kauai. We had no way of ascertaining the number of hidden homeless.

Step Two: Who Are Our Partners?

Once we had defined homelessness and ascertained how many potential clients we had, our next step was determining which agencies would be willing to assist us. To that end, we scheduled meetings with potential partners who already worked with the homeless. The purpose of these meetings was two-fold. First, it was to get the word out about HLSH. In order for us to receive referrals from these agencies, we needed to explain the project so they knew when and how to make referrals on behalf of their clients. The second purpose of these meetings was to determine what potential legal issues the homeless might have.

It was imperative to collaborate with Kauai Economic Opportunity, Inc. (KEO). They were the agency with the most inter-

1 *HLSH was funded by grants from G.N. Wilcox Foundation and the Atherton Foundation.*

action with, and outreach to, Kauai's homeless population. In our meeting with them, we discussed various ways through which we could reach the homeless, as well as which services we could provide. Perhaps the biggest assistance we received from KEO was the opportunity to ride along with their Care-A-Van. We knew this would help us reach a larger percentage of the homeless population than we would have been able to on our own. From this initial discussion with KEO, we drafted a Memorandum of Understanding between Legal Aid and KEO. KEO agreed to allow us to ride along with the Care-A-Van, and we agreed to be available to give advice and counsel to the clients that they referred to us.

Furthermore, we joined the local Continuum of Care (COC), a county-wide organization comprised of representatives from agencies that work with the homeless. COC facilitates networking opportunities as well as plans for Homelessness Awareness Week every November.

Step Three: What to Teach?

It was our opinion that education needed to be a strong component of this project in order to ensure its success. For that reason, we developed a two-pronged educational concept: Legal Aid Society of Hawaii's Homeless Training Series.

The first prong involved four trainings designed specifically for service providers. The topics of the trainings were public benefits, public housing, consumer law, and temporary restraining orders. In addition to explaining the general law in these areas, we focused on how these rules and laws affected the homeless. The trainings were conducted by either an attorney from Legal Aid or a service provider from a local agency. For instance, representatives from local public housing agencies came to speak about the current crisis involving the lack of affordable housing and the ins and outs of obtaining and maintaining public housing. In addition, we provided each attendee with printed materials that offered more in-depth information on the topics covered in the training.

The second prong involved teaching the homeless population about their rights under the law. Two weeks after training was conducted for service providers, a corresponding training and dinner were held for the homeless. Many of the attendees learned of the trainings from their service providers who had attended our trainings. The same topics were covered, but the emphasis was on what the participants could do. Some options included applying for benefits even after they had been denied, appealing a denial of a HUD voucher, and stopping harassment from creditors. The purpose was to empower the homeless so that they could advocate for their own rights.

Implementing Holistic Legal Services for the Homeless

As one may guess, designing a program is much easier than implementing it. It was time to learn whether or not we had developed a program that would meet the needs of the homeless community.

Outreach to the Homeless

How do you find homeless clients? Where do they congregate? What are their demographics? Once you have homeless clients, how do you maintain contact with them? What information could I offer? These were just some of the questions I contemplated before going on my first ride along with the Care-A-Van. Prior to my first outreach experience, I compiled a number of forms (retainers, consent to release, paper intake) in a plastic file. I received words of wisdom from my Honolulu Legal Aid office counterpart, Janet Kelly, on how to be prepared to meet a homeless client. She told me to treat each encounter with a homeless client as though I might never see them again. By that, she meant that I should give clients as many brochures and informational documents as possible so that at the very least, they had some reference material to review.

Another resource I relied heavily upon was "Trink," the Care-A-Van driver and homeless outreach worker for KEO. She explained to me that the homeless on Kauai moved from beach park to beach park. This was in part because of the weather changes with the seasons on each side of the island and in part because of camping rules for the beaches that limited the number of days a person could spend in one place.

The first couple of times I rode along with the Care-A-Van, I simply observed. I watched Trink's interactions with those who approached the van. I observed the people at the various sites where the Care-A-Van stopped to provide services. I noted how the people living on the beach or in their cars were comprised of a large number of single Caucasian men from the mainland, in addition to local families with small children and the elderly and disabled. I started

Adam[2] was a 42-year-old single male with mental and physical disabilities who lived out of his station wagon at the beach park. Due to his disabilities and substantial work history, Adam received nearly $900 per month in SSDI benefits. Unfortunately, Adam was only receiving about $570 per month, as the rest was being levied by the federal government for unpaid taxes from 1992 and 1993. Adam's girlfriend was pregnant, and he wanted to find an alternative living arrangement. Because his money was being intercepted by the government, he was unable to do so. During one of Legal Aid's HLSH Project visits to the beach, Adam sought help from the Project. After nearly 9 months of investigation, countless phone calls to IRS, and the priceless assistance of the Taxpayer Advocate, Legal Aid was able to help Adam receive a $1,800 refund from the IRS and stop SSA from intercepting his benefits. Adam was both appreciative and thankful for our efforts, and is moving in the right direction with his life.

2 *Name changed to protect confidentiality*

having conversations with them to begin to get a better idea of what issues many of them faced. The issues they had primarily revolved around public benefits. Many were attempting to get state disability benefits, General Assistance, or had recently been denied or terminated from these benefits. A number of them were in the process of applying for Supplemental Security Income (SSI). I also heard stories about living on the beach and the conditions the people faced. Some reported that the Park Rangers were harassing them or that the rules for the parks were not being enforced consistently.

These concerns were the impetus for the creation of our brochure, "Homeless on Kauai." In this brochure, we included

Matt[3] was referred to Legal Aid by word of mouth at the beach where he was living in his car. He was homeless but awaiting a Section 8 Voucher. He came to us because he had received a telephone call from Section 8 that indicated he was being removed from the list for failure to turn in all requested documents. Matt claimed that he had been in the Section 8 office the week before the letter was sent and had attempted to turn in documents for both himself and his partner. He was told that his partner's documents were not needed because she had been a HUD participant years before in the state of Washington. We called the HUD Section 8 Voucher Administrator and discussed Matt's situation. During the conversation, we were told that Matt was a liar and had failed to comply with their request, so nothing could be done about it. We requested that they send a denial letter with his appeal rights stated. Matt came back to our office once he received the denial letter. The letter stated that he had 10 days from postmark to

3 *Name changed to protect confidentiality*

campsites, fees, and rules for all County and State run beach parks. Additionally, we listed local agencies that provide services to the homeless as well as suggestions from the American Civil Liberties Union on how to interact with the police.

Representation

Through our outreach efforts at both the beaches and the social service agencies, we were able to increase the number of homeless clients we served. Their legal issues involved everything under the sun, from public benefit denials to tax set-off problems to child custody concerns. As I tried to develop cases and compile docu-

submit his written request for an informal hearing. However, a quick check of the County Administrative Plan showed that the time for appeal was actually 15 days from the date of receipt. We sent a letter requesting an informal meeting and attached a copy of the County Administrative Plan. During a phone call from the Administrator, we were informed that they had changed the policy. After we questioned whether or not this change had been made public, we were told first that it was not, and second that doing so was not necessary. As a last resort, we contacted the County Agency's Executive on Housing. He agreed to discuss the matter with the Administrator. A week later, we received a call from the newly appointed Interim-Administrator granting us an informal meeting. At the meeting, Matt explained that he and his partner had separated, and he was now a household of one. The Interim-Administrator agreed to allow Matt to be placed back on the waiting list in his original place. Matt was very happy to have this problem resolved and to be assured a Section 8 Voucher sometime in the future.

ments, it became increasingly clear that representing the homeless was much different than representing someone with a permanent place to store important documents. Many times my homeless clients would report that because they had to move suddenly, some belongings were often overlooked or lost. Others would return to their campsites to find that their site had been ransacked and things had been stolen. Additionally, many of these clients did not keep very good track of their previous locations, doctors they had seen, or contact information of previous treatment providers and family members.

Besides the problems with gathering evidence and documentation, it was difficult to keep in touch with many of our homeless clients. The transient nature of homelessness often made it hard to locate clients when they were needed. The stressors that the homeless deal with such as medical emergencies, family strife, and the daily struggle to find food and shelter made it difficult for clients to remember to keep me updated as to their whereabouts. Some clients disappeared and never reappeared. Others disappeared for a couple of months and resurfaced later, wanting to know if I have heard anything about their case. And then there were those clients who showed up for appointments and followed through with tasks that I had assigned. What was useful in maintaining contact with my homeless clients was collaboration with outreach workers from other agencies. Often if I was unable to locate a client, I contacted a service provider that I knew was working with the client to see if he or she knew where the client might be staying. More often than not, I was successful in locating my client through this process.

Lessons Learned

Outreach

When we began this project, we believed that outreach at the beaches and other locations where the homeless congregated would provide us with most of our HSLH clients. We quickly learned that this would not be the case. The most important aspect of going out to the beaches and riding along with the Care-A-Van was to get the name "Legal Aid," and more specifically my name and face, out among the homeless community. That is not to say that I never got a client from outreach, but the majority of those that I met at the beach never followed through with their case. Nevertheless, this outreach is crucial to a successful program. The homeless trust and respect people who are willing to meet with them in their environment. The outreach also provided me with an opportunity to talk to the homeless about being homeless on Kauai. In doing so, I gained a better understanding of the problems facing the homeless.

Through outreach, Legal Aid made a name for itself with the homeless on Kauai. This is evidenced by the number of homeless people who called our office and asked for me by name, or who walked in and asked for me. These were all the result of word-of-mouth referrals.

Collaboration

The issues we had with outreach highlight the necessity of collaborating with other agencies that are already out in the field. We did not have the staff, time, or resources to spend on extensive outreach efforts. Therefore, it was vital to develop good working relationships with other agencies. One of the ways through which we accomplished this was allowing people who were homeless to bypass our centralized intake system in Honolulu. Instead, homeless clients were allowed to call me directly or through one of their social service providers, and I would do the intake personally. This ensured that clients did not fall through the cracks during the delays often associated with centralized intake, and the service provider would be assured that their client received immediate attention.

The clients who were the most successful with their legal issues were those who also had service providers assisting them. The social workers provided necessary support and encouraged their clients to follow through with appointments and gathering of evidentiary documents. These services complemented and enhanced my ability to provide the best legal services possible for their case.

Delivery of Services

I learned that delivery of services had to be drastically changed when the client was homeless. It was not enough to give clients my business card and expect them to call me when they had questions or wanted to make an appointment. I had to drive out to the beach where the client was living to get papers signed or just to have a meeting. I also had to accept that the homeless clients were much more likely to just drop in at the office without an appointment. Their limited access to phones and transportation made it unrealistic to expect them to call ahead, make an appointment, or come back at a later time. As a result, I needed to drop what I was doing when they walked in to address their questions or concerns.

The most important lesson that I learned in working with the homeless concerned the art of listening. As members of our society, the homeless are often overlooked, ignored, and treated with disdain. Many become accustomed to being snubbed and pushed around from agency to agency. Few people take the time to listen to their concerns and stories. I can spend ten minutes listening to a homeless person tell me of their woes and ascertain that they do not have a legal problem. While they may be disappointed that they are unable to find relief in the law, having had the benefit of a sympathetic ear at least provides them with some modest satisfaction. Listening also allows me to perhaps pick up on other legal issues they may be unaware of, such as a denial of disability benefits or an illegal eviction.

Onward!

After a year of HLSH, we felt there was room to expand our project. Expansion also necessitated a need to secure new sources of funding for this project. We reviewed the legal services that we had provided and talked with agencies about other services we could provide. In addition, we took ideas that were already in place in our larger Honolulu Legal Aid office and adapted them to fit our small rural island.

Homeless Legal Advocacy and Prevention Project (HLAPP)

HLSH was a year-long project. Toward the end of our year, we started thinking about how we could secure money to continue this work and add more services to expand the project. What we arrived at is now HLAPP. The seeds for this particular project were sown with a discussion we had with an Administrator at County Housing during a Homeless Awareness Week candlelight vigil. She explained to us that she had many residents in her units that were near eviction. While she understood very clearly the ramifications of eviction and wanted to avoid evicting her tenants where at all possible, her close work with many of her residents meant that they did not take her threats and admonitions seriously. She wondered whether Legal Aid would be able or willing to provide advice or counsel and, where needed, representation for clients who were skating on thin ice. She perceived that hearing the dire consequences of eviction (such as the life-time ban on County Housing) from an attorney would carry more significance. This discussion produced the "Prevention" prong of HLAPP.

Now, in addition to doing outreach and generally representing those who are already without homes, we will aid those who are at risk of becoming homeless. We are designing a referral system whereby the State Housing Authority has the resident sign a release and referral which will be faxed to the Legal Aid office. We will set

Homelessness in the News

Recently, the issue of homelessness has been on the front page of the local newspapers. In May of 2006, Maui County and the City of Honolulu conducted sweeps of parks where the homeless have lived for years. Hundreds of homeless people were displaced, and area shelters and faith-based organizations scrambled to piece together temporary emergency shelter. Governor Linda Lingle acknowledged the need for additional shelters and services and pledged additional funding for programs committed to ending homelessness in Hawaii.

up an appointment to meet with the resident in their home to ascertain what level of assistance we can provide. Conducting the meeting in their residence, we feel, is a key component to this project. It allows the client the convenience of not traveling to our office, which increases the likelihood of follow through.

With the dire lack of affordable housing and the overpriced rental market, keeping existing housing is of utmost importance because often the only alternative is living on the beach or in a car. There are approximately 150 individuals and families with Section 8 vouchers currently trying to find housing. The waiting lists for low-income and subsidized housing grows longer and longer as vacancies become rarer. Therefore, the need to assist people who are at risk of losing their housing is enormous.

Center for Equal Justice

In keeping with the theme of empowering the homeless and improving access to justice, in May 2006 we will be opening the doors to the Center for Equal Justice (CEJ). CEJ provides computers, a typewriter, copy and fax service, and research materials to the homeless. As we move towards a more digital world and as many courts and agencies utilize online forms, access to the Internet and a computer becomes critical. Through CEJ, we aim to provide not only these technological tools to the homeless, but also brief legal servic-

Emiko L.T. Ryan *AmeriCorps Attorney*
Legal Aid Society of Hawaii—Kauai
4334 Rice Street, Suite 204A Lihue, Hawaii 96766
808.245.4728 emryan@lashaw.org

Emiko Ryan received her J.D. from Seattle University School of Law in 2003. She is an AmeriCorps Attorney for the Legal Aid Society of Hawaii on Kauai. She currently heads the Homeless Legal Advocacy and Prevention Project in addition to carrying a full caseload at the Legal Aid Society of Hawaii.

es. Brief services will include advice and counsel as well as assistance in filling out forms, court documents, and drafting letters. Homeless people will thus have access to online research and printed materials in our office.

CEJ is modeled after the center that currently exists in our Honolulu office. I spent time in the Honolulu office observing the CEJ, and it was evident that the highest rate of users came from the homeless population. They were there for various reasons; some had pending legal issues, and some just wanted to feel connected to the world. Overall, the feeling achieved by the users of CEJ is one of inclusiveness, because they are being allowed to participate not only in the legal world, but also to connect via the Internet to the rest of the world. We have already received very positive feedback from the various agencies on island and presume that CEJ will not lack for participants.

Conclusion

Working with the homeless population has been both challenging and rewarding. As cliché as that sounds, it is still so true. The homeless are a tough population to work with for many of the reasons addressed above. But as the client stories illustrate, there are victories, and help on a small scale can make a difference. I do not think that homelessness will be eradicated on Kauai through legal services. However, if we can make someone's income more secure, ensure that their kids are being taken care of by a legal guardian, bolster safety by assisting with a Temporary Restraining Order, or help a person find public housing, we are making homeless people's lives a little less stressful and chaotic, which in turn may allow them to take the necessary steps to end their own homelessness.

The National Law Center on Homelessness & Poverty

Maria Foscarinis

The National Law Center on Homelessness & Poverty (NLCHP) was established in 1989 to serve as the legal arm of the national movement to prevent and end homelessness. NLCHP works to influence national policy while also ensuring for local level implementation of existing rights and benefits. NLCHP's long-term goal is to help people exercise, realize, and maintain their economic and civil rights so that economic justice is achieved in America and so that no one is homeless or impoverished.

Much of our work centers on implementing and expanding the provisions of the *McKinney-Vento Homeless Assistance Act*, currently the major, and only, federal legislation to address homelessness. Because of my role in the enactment of that legislation (see article in Chapter 1), NLCHP has had special expertise in that law since the organization's founding. Over the years, we have initiated litigation to enforce portions of the Act, and we have also worked to expand its provisions.

Based in Washington, DC, NLCHP works directly with local level groups across the country. In partnership with them, we help implement laws that deliver concrete benefits to homeless men, women and children. We work with policymakers at the national, state, and local levels to educate them about key issues affecting poor and homeless people and to help enact laws and policies that promote systemic, far-ranging solutions. We also educate the public, including the business, legal, and political communities, on homelessness, poverty, and constructive solutions.

Current Programs and Initiatives

NLCHP has a small staff (currently 14), but we are fortunate to benefit from the help of interns and volunteers, including many pro bono lawyers (see article in Chapter 3). To maximize our resources, our programs focus strategically on issues where we feel we can make the greatest impact. Our current focus areas are children's education, housing, benefits, and health care for disabled men, women and children; a new domestic violence project focused on preventing homelessness for women and their children; and protection of the civil rights of homeless people. A new human rights focus promotes advocacy for a human right to housing in the U.S. In addition, we launched a new initiative in response to Hurricanes Katrina and Rita.

Timeline of Success:	
1989 National Law Center on Homelessness & Poverty established.	Founded by lawyer Maria Foscarinis, NLCHP's mission is "*To serve as the legal arm of the national movement to end and prevent homelessness in America.*"
1990 Filed suit against the Social Security Administration (SSA).	NLCHP filed suit citing the SSA's failure to reach out to homeless people with disabilities, 50% of whom may have been eligible for benefits. As a result of the suit, the SSA launched an outreach program educating disabled homeless people about the federal disability benefits available to them.

Hurricane Response Initiative

This is a special initiative and a joint effort of all our programs. It is critically important to our mission; the most severely affected disaster victims were already poor, and the loss of their housing due to the hurricanes put them at risk of immediate and also long-term homelessness. Because of this clear and close connection to our mission, NLCHP decided to focus special attention on the crisis.

A major effort has been litigation against the Federal Emergency Management Agency (FEMA) to extend the hotel program for evacuees pending their receipt of housing assistance and to ensure that they receive that assistance. Working together, the Lawyers' Committee for Civil Rights, the Equal Justice Center, a pro bono law firm, and NLCHP won court orders extending the hotel program and correcting some of the flaws in FEMA's response to disaster victims' housing needs.

During its first year of operation, the project secured local compliance with the federal right to education of homeless children. After pressure from NLCHP, the District of Columbia agreed to provide school bus transportation to homeless children.

NLCHP spearheaded "Beyond McKinney," a nationwide effort to establish long-term solutions to homelessness; efforts included affordable housing, adequate income, social services, and civil rights. Policies developed through "Beyond McKinney" launched the homeless persons' right to vote campaign and prompted a suit filed against the U.S. Census Bureau for failing to include homeless people in the national census count. The undercounting of homeless people deprives many regions of much needed federal funds to help combat homelessness.

Timeline of Success:

1991
Established the Washington Children's Project.

1992
Developed long-term solutions to homelessness.

In addition to collaboration with national partner groups, we are conducting national outreach to disseminate information, focusing our efforts on legal rights. We are working to ensure that children of evacuees have access to education, that disabled evacuees receive disability benefits, and that evacuees are not discriminated against based on disability, domestic violence, or homeless status.

Working in Congress, we are advocating for additional resources to meet the increased housing and social service needs resulting from the disaster. We are working with school districts across the country, helping to ensure that displaced children have access to school. We have also advocated successfully to protect from suspension, immediately after the hurricanes, the federal law guaranteeing the right of homeless children to go to school.

Timeline of Success:

1993
Worked to keep homeless families together.

As a result of a nationwide survey of shelter providers, NLCHP published a report on the extent to which families in the shelter system get separated. Many shelters are so crowded that they can accommodate homeless people only in same-sex, dormitory-style set-ups. Families that are split up often experience longer shelter stays, are more isolated from extended family and community, and have a harder time breaking the cycle of homelessness.

1994
Converted closed military bases to aid homeless people.

NLCHP was instrumental in passing the *Base Closure Community Redevelopment and Homeless Assistance Act of 1994*. The law mandates that when the federal government closes military installations, local homeless service providers are given priority in the redevelopment of the property. Within the next year, more than 12,000 homeless people benefited from housing, job training, childcare, and food programs in converted bases.

Children and Youth Program

This program focuses on ensuring access to school and school programs, including school meals and special education services, for homeless children and youth. Much of this work focuses on ensuring compliance with the McKinney-Vento education provisions.

In a recent victory, we worked with pro bono partner Goodwin Procter (and a team led by partner Jeffrey Simes) on successful litigation to improve compliance with homeless children's right to education under the federal McKinney-Vento Act in the Long Island, New York school system. Brought on behalf of a class of 1,400 homeless children in that system, the suit also reformed state practices to comply with federal law.

We also work legislatively to expand protections for homeless children. Recently, we won new provisions in the *Individuals with Disabilities Education Act* to include and provide services to homeless children as well as favorable regulations to implement the new law. We are currently working on amendments to the Head Start program to include and expand programs for homeless preschoolers.

We follow up to ensure that our legislative victories are actually implemented—and homeless children are helped. Currently we are working on implementing requirements to improve homeless children's access to the *Individuals with Disabilities Education Act* and to

NLCHP won its suit against the District of Columbia when the court ruled that DC was in violation of the McKinney Act and therefore had to provide homeless children transportation to school. Each year, 1.35 million children experience homelessness in the United States. Many are often deprived of their public school education because of barriers such as lack of transportation and difficulties transferring to new schools when their family must move to another shelter.

Timeline of Success:

1995
Protected homeless children's right to education.

NLCHP's staff outside their K Street headquarters in Washington, DC. From left to right: Naomi Stern, Melanie Mullen, Tulin Ozdeger, Lucy Martin, Allison Mitchell, Susan Spellman, Maria Foscarinis, Vibha Bhatia, Michele Frome, Joy Moses, Marion Manheimer, Dara Smith, Terri Keeley, and Jeanine Valles.

enact pending amendments that would improve access to Head Start early childhood programs for homeless toddlers.

In a new initiative, our program is building partnerships with foster care advocates, focusing on issues such as access to education for children in foster care and advocacy to prevent homeless children from being removed from their families and placed in foster care simply because they are homeless.

Housing Program

Our program is currently working to make surplus property available for transitional and permanent housing, child and day care, and food and job training sites for homeless families and individuals.

The McKinney Act, in Title V, makes surplus federal property available on a priority basis for leasing or deeding to groups serving homeless people. This powerful law is often overlooked by service providers and by the federal agencies charged with implementing it. Since its inception, NLCHP has litigated to enforce Title V.[1] A nation-

1 *I originally filed the case while at the National Coalition for the Homeless, and took it with me after I founded NLCHP.*

wide injunction against five federal agencies is in effect, and NLCHP has returned to court several times to correct noncompliance.

In 1994, Congress amended Title V to exempt closed military bases. NLCHP and other advocates worked successfully in Congress to draft defense department legislation requiring that the needs of homeless people be addressed in the process of converting military bases to civilian use and that homeless people and their advocates be included in local processes to plan for the conversion.

As a result of these laws, dozens of former bases and numerous other federal and non-federal properties are now being used for transitional and permanent housing and other services for homeless people. To date, conversion of vacant federal property (over $80 million worth) into housing, job training, childcare and food sites serves more than 100,000 people annually. In a recent victory, we convinced the federal government to allow such property to be used for permanent supportive housing, not just emergency shelter and transitional housing.

Timeline of Success:

1996
Participated in United Nations Habitat II Conference in Istanbul.

In preparation for the historic Habitat II Conference, NLCHP joined forces with other U.S. and international groups to organize forums on international and U.S. homelessness. NLCHP succeeded in including language regarding specific human rights of homeless people in the international document produced at the conference. This conference also resulted in coalition building to begin implementing the right to housing in the United States.

1997
Successfully defended the constitutional rights of homeless people.

NLCHP filed an *amicus* brief in *Benefit v. City of Cambridge*, a successful case on behalf of homeless plaintiffs. The court ruled that prohibiting panhandling is a violation of the right to free speech as well as the right to appeal to other human beings for compassionate aid.

A new round of closures has just been announced, and NLCHP and allied groups are preparing a campaign to ensure that the law is enforced so that homeless people benefit. As part of this effort, NLCHP is recruiting pro bono law firm help to draft model agreements that nonprofit groups can use in negotiating for base property; we are also recruiting pro bono firms to help applicants with negotiating and drafting agreements for particular base properties.

Another program element is advocacy to counter exclusionary laws that prevent developing transitional and permanent housing for homeless families and individuals. While federal anti-discrimination laws do not protect homeless people specifically, the prevalence of protected characteristics, such as disabilities, among the homeless population has been successfully cited to invoke the protection of federal fair housing laws barring discrimination on this basis. NLCHP works with local advocates to challenge such exclusionary laws and policies.

A recent initiative focuses on the growing numbers of people being released from prisons and jails and the barriers they face in

Timeline of Success:

1998
Increased funding for homeless assistance by $152 million.

NLCHP helped secure additional Department of Housing and Urban Development funding for HUD-McKinney Act programs. The nearly 20% increase in funding provided additional shelter, permanent housing, and vital support services for homeless individuals and families.

1999
Defended the legal rights of homeless people.

NLCHP created and distributed over 5,000 *Know Your Rights* informational packets educating service providers, grassroots groups, and homeless individuals on homeless people's rights and the benefits available to them. This information was used to gain school access for homeless children, to receive tax refunds from the IRS for working homeless people, and to convert federal properties into job training, child-care, and housing facilities for homeless people.

securing housing and income—putting them at risk of homelessness. With other organizations, we are working on legislation to address those barriers and to increase the resources available to people reentering society.

Income Program

We advocate removing barriers to disability benefits for homeless individuals, families, and children. This includes: monitoring implementation of a new federal demonstration program that provides outreach funding to help homeless people apply for and receive federal disability benefits to which they are entitled (a program we helped get enacted), helping the Social Security Administration further develop and implement its plan to remove barriers, and working in Congress for additional funding.

We also operate a special program in the District of Columbia focused on helping working homeless people claim the Earned Income Tax Credit—a credit that provides a lump sum case refund that can help people acquire housing and escape homelessness. Our project recruits and trains volunteers as well as operates free tax clinics at service sites across the city.

Timeline of Success:

2000
Successfully advocated for substance abuse programs.

As a result of NLCHP's advocacy work, the federal government's Fiscal Year 2001 budget allocated $10 million for substance abuse treatment programs for the homeless—the first allocation of its kind. Sixty-two percent of homeless persons have had a substance abuse problem at some point in their life.

Won a court decision increasing service providers' access to vacant federal property.

NLCHP won a decision from U.S. District Court Judge Royce C. Lamberth ordering the General Services Administration (GSA) to stop its "circumvention" of a federal law that gives homeless groups priority rights to vacant federal properties across the country.

To date, our clinics for working homeless families and individuals in the District of Columbia have resulted in over $74,000 in federal and DC Earned Income Tax Credits and refunds over two years for those homeless workers. We are exploring the possibility of expanding this work nationally.

Civil Rights Program

Our program works to protect the civil rights of homeless men, women, and children by countering efforts in cities across the country to criminalize the status of homelessness. Since in 1991, we have documented this growing trend in nine national reports that have helped focus national and local attention on the issue.

Working with local advocates, our program has brought legal challenges to such city laws and practices. *Pottinger v. Miami*, a leading case on this issue, was brought initially by lawyers working with the local ACLU. In that case, the court found that there were approximately 6,000 homeless people but only 700 shelter beds in Miami, and that unsheltered homeless people thus had no alternative but to sleep in public. Given these facts, the court held that punishment for

Timeline of Success: **2001** **National membership network launched.**	NLCHP began a National Membership Network aimed at bringing together advocates, service providers, and other members of the homeless community to share resources, educate members, and better assist the millions of homeless men, women, and children in the United States.
DC Homelessness Prevention Project organizes free tax clinics.	NLCHP organized a series of free clinics in the District of Columbia to help the 44% of the homeless population who work to claim the Earned Income Tax Credit. The tax credit can often help fill the gap between income and housing costs. Advocacy by NLCHP has led the IRS to change its instructions to ensure that homeless persons are not precluded from claiming the credit because of their homelessness.

involuntary, necessary, life sustaining, and otherwise innocent conduct—sleeping—was "cruel and unusual" and thus violated the Eighth Amendment to the U.S. Constitution.

NLCHP supported the class of homeless plaintiffs on appeal through amicus briefs and in drafting a strong consent decree. We have also been active in other leading cases, and we continue to mount challenges to such laws and practices, typically in collaboration with local advocates and pro bono counsel.

We also work to prevent cities from adopting laws that criminalize homelessness, testifying with local advocates before their city councils. In one recent success, our program prevented 2,000 people in Manatee County, Florida from being subject to arrest by opposing the adoption of an anti-camping ordinance through testimony at the city council hearing.

We work with advocates and cities to promote constructive solutions instead of punitive policies and to build partnerships with organizations representing cities and police groups to support such

After years of advocacy by NLCHP, SSA removed barriers preventing mentally or physically disabled homeless people from receiving benefits. The SSA also secured federal funding to assist in implementation. An estimated 29% of homeless persons are eligible to receive disability benefits.

Timeline of Success:

2002 Successfully advocated for the Social Security Administration to remove barriers to securing benefits.

NLCHP won major victories in Congress and with the U.S. Department of Education to protect homeless children's right to attend school and receive school meals and other services. In addition, NLCHP won a 50% increase in funding for programs that ensure these rights become reality.

Won a 50% increase in federal funding for the rights of homeless children.

solutions. In one example of this approach, we worked with advocates in Philadelphia to convince the City to conduct outreach to homeless people instead of arresting them and to back up that outreach with additional City funding of aid to homeless people.

Our program also focuses on barriers that homeless people face in gaining access to identification documents, an issue that has become particularly important following September 11 and the heightened security measures that followed it. We recently advocated successfully for state policies that allow homeless people to obtain IDs while also addressing security concerns.

The program also works to ensure for the voting rights of homeless people, who are often threatened by barriers such as highly restrictive ID requirements. In one recent success, we obtained an opinion for the Virginia Attorney General making it clear that homeless people have the right to register and to vote in that state.

Human Rights Program

This new program focuses on developing models for legal and policy advocacy using human rights law, focusing on the human right to housing; building a network of grass roots groups advocat-

Timeline of Success:	
2003 New program launched to protect the housing rights of domestic violence victims.	In response to the growing evidence that domestic violence and homelessness are linked, NLCHP started a program aimed at preventing homelessness among domestic violence victims by preventing evictions and promoting housing access. In a 2002 survey by the U.S. Conference of Mayors, 11 of 25 cities named domestic violence as the primary cause of homelessness for women.
Promoted the human right to housing in the U.S.	NLCHP held a forum of national advocacy organizations that focused on the recognition of the human right to housing for all Americans under international human rights laws. This forum resulted in the formation of a "Right to Housing" working group.

ing for a human right to housing in the U.S., and building alliances with national housing and human rights groups to support this effort. As part of this work, we have organized two national Forums on the right to housing and we are planning a third; we have also organized several regional trainings.

Additionally, we are working with local groups to help them in their campaigns for local recognition of a human right to housing. Two of our local partners have realized significant successes in Chicago and Los Angeles. These include using human rights strategies to secure a County resolution recognizing the human right to housing, leading to increased funding for rent subsidies. We have also joined our efforts with the new U.S. Human Rights Network, chairing its Housing Caucus.

	Timeline of Success:
After advocacy by NLCHP, the Department of Health & Human Services and the U.S. General Services Administration worked with NLCHP to redesign their websites advertising surplus government property available for homeless assistance. The new websites were designed to increase the visibility of surplus property programs and improve service providers' awareness of properties currently available for their use.	**2004** **Increased service providers' access to surplus government property.**
NLCHP initiated a new program of audio trainings for service providers and advocates across the country. The trainings provide participants with tools and information on key issues such as the education of homeless children, how to obtain vacant federal property for providing services to the homeless community, and how to secure the rights of the formerly incarcerated upon their reentry into society.	**Audio training series launched.**

Domestic Violence Program

A new initiative, this program focuses on developing and implementing strategies for domestic violence victims (primarily women and children) from becoming homeless by enforcing fair housing laws to prevent their unlawful eviction, educating domestic violence advocates about the housing rights of domestic violence victims and resources available to assist them, and educating housing and homelessness advocates about domestic violence.

In a recent major victory, we worked with allied groups to draft and incorporate new housing provisions as part of the *Violence Against Women Act*. These provisions will protect victims of domestic violence from losing their housing based on the acts of their abusers. We are now working on implementation strategies to ensure that survivors across the country get the benefits of their protections from loss of housing.

We are also working on a special project in the District of Columbia to enact legislation and implement regulatory changes to protect the housing rights of domestic violence victims.

Key Strategies

Impact Litigation

This work protects and aids homeless people, enforcing and defending their constitutional, statutory, and other legal rights.

Timeline of Success:

2005 Protected victims of the Gulf Coast hurricanes.

Immediately following the hurricanes, NLCHP launched the Katrina Initiative to protect victims of Hurricanes Katrina and Rita. NLCHP is currently co-counsel in *FEMA v. McWaters*, a suit that is fighting to ensure that there is no gap in services to hurricane evacuees, many of whom are currently, or at high risk of becoming, homeless. NLCHP has also worked extensively with local service providers to protect the education rights of child evacuees.

Through our legal expertise and with strong pro bono support from major law firms, we are a powerful resource to local grassroots groups around the country in their efforts to assist homeless families and individuals in their communities.

Policy Advocacy

NLCHP works in Congress and with federal agencies to develop and promote solutions and resources to end homelessness. NLCHP also works at the local and state levels to promote constructive policies, reformed laws, and practical measures to help people out of homelessness.

Public Education and Outreach

This work supports and parallels our litigation and advocacy efforts. Through an ongoing publication effort, we develop and disseminate reports, manuals, fact sheets, and other materials to educate service providers, grass roots activists, policymakers and the public. We also provide informational materials for use by homeless people, including self-advocacy kits. We have published over sixty reports, booklets, articles and fact sheets.

	Timeline of Success:
NLCHP successfully advocated for VAWA 2005 to include provisions that help prevent victims of domestic violence from becoming homeless or being cut off from housing assistance. Prior to the new provisions, domestic violence victims were often penalized or evicted for the violence of their abusers.	**2006 Violence Against Women Act reauthorized.**
NLCHP released a joint report with the National Coalition for the Homeless on the criminalization of homelessness in the United States. The strong media coverage reinvigorated the discussion of homeless people's civil rights and led to several new partnerships between NLCHP and local groups fighting criminalization in their own areas.	**20 "Meanest Cities" ranked by NLCHP.**

National Outreach to Mobilize and Engage Lawyers to Support our Work

Through our national membership network, we seek to strengthen our partnerships with local level providers, advocates, and lawyers working to end homelessness, as well as those with allied national groups. We aim also to build the legal capacity of these groups, and particularly our legal partners, while also strengthening our own capacity for effective advocacy through these partnerships.

We have launched a new initiative to reach out to the private bar to help support our work financially. NLCHP is a not-for-profit organization and receives no government funding. We must raise all our own funding. Even with a modest budget, this is a big challenge, and we have begun an effort to build a diverse base of support.

Specifically, we are:

- continuing to expand our national membership network by adding new members, including grass roots organizations, national, state and local coalitions, and legal services lawyers and groups;
- building the capacity of our partner groups through outreach and training, including regular e-mail updates on important issues and a new audio training series;
- expanding our new Lawyers Executive Advisory Partners (LEAP) Program which brings together law firms to support NLCHP's mission and work through financial and pro bono support;
- building the legal capacity of local groups through pro bono resources of law firms, through our LEAP Program;

For more information on how you can help America's homeless people, please contact:

National Law Center on
Homelessness & Poverty
1411 K Street, N.W., Suite 1400
Washington, DC 20005
(202) 638-2535 nlchp@nlchp.org

- reaching out to new constituencies, such as bar associations and corporate legal departments; and,
- working with the ABA's Commission on Homelessness and Poverty.

The National Law Center on Homelessness & Poverty is committed to serving as the legal arm of the national movement to end and prevent homelessness in America. For more information on how you can help America's homeless people, please contact NLCHP at (202) 638-2535 or visit *www.nlchp.org*.

ABA © NLCHP

Maria Foscarinis *Executive Director*
National Law Center on Homelessness & Poverty
1411 K Street, NW Washington, DC 20005
202.638.2535 mfoscarinis@nlchp.org

Maria Foscarinis is founder and executive director of the National Law Center on Homelessness & Poverty, a not-for-profit organization established in 1989 as the legal arm of the nationwide effort to end homelessness. Ms. Foscarinis has advocated for solutions to homelessness and poverty at the national level since 1985. She is a primary architect of the *Stewart B. McKinney Homeless Assistance Act,* the first major federal legislation addressing homelessness, and she has litigated to secure the legal rights of homeless and poor persons. Ms. Foscarinis writes regularly about legal and policy issues affecting homeless and poor persons, and her work has appeared in legal journals, general audience publications, and books. Ms. Foscarinis is a 1977 graduate of Barnard College and 1981 graduate of Columbia Law School, where she was an editor of the Law Review; she also holds a Masters of Arts degree in Philosophy. After clerking for the Honorable Amalya L. Kearse of the U.S. Court of Appeals for the Second Circuit, she was a litigation associate at Sullivan & Cromwell. In 1985, she led the establishment of the Washington office of the National Coalition for the Homeless until she founded the National Law Center on Homelessness & Poverty.

Public Counsel's Homelessness Prevention Law Project

Paul L. Freese, Jr.

The growing landscape of dispossession, alienation, and suffering that is homelessness bespeaks a disgraceful lack of political will to dedicate the resources and wherewithal to transform our society into one that ensures that no one need sleep on our streets. Public Counsel has endeavored to understand the causes that have made homelessness such an epidemic crisis in the past 25 years and to adapt advocacy strategies to involve the legal profession in being part of the effort to find long term solutions—if not to end homelessness, then at least to reduce its life-shattering reach.

Public Counsel's advocacy efforts have evolved to address the alarming rise in homelessness affecting families, youths entering the foster care system, youths emancipated from foster care or on probation placements with no family support, homeless and runaway youths, individuals discharged from jails, hospitals, and psychiatric wards whose disabilities or poverty prevent them from being housed, and individuals who are infirm, disabled, or elderly who face evictions. Public Counsel has engaged literally thousands of volunteers to advocate on behalf of these vulnerable individuals in a variety of settings that include street outreach, legal clinics at shelters and drop-in centers, and advocacy sessions in county social service offices. The project has evolved from calling itself the

"Homeless Assistance Law Project" to "The Homelessness Prevention Law Project" to reflect our philosophy that homelessness is not an acceptable condition for any human being.

Public Counsel's mission is distinct from most public interest legal programs in that we primarily strive to involve the private bar in providing pro bono services to the poor and marginalized. Thus each year our staff of 50 recruits, trains, and provides technical support or supervision to more than 3,500 volunteer attorneys, law students, retirees, and undergraduate students in helping meet the legal needs of the most vulnerable members of our community.

Our efforts convince us that if we are ever to find a long term solution, we must humanize the plight of our homeless brothers and sisters and help society understand that we are all at risk of ending up among their ranks. When we take our volunteers to shelters and social service centers they are amazed to see engineers, doctors, business owners, teachers, stock brokers, professional athletes, film writers, actors, actresses, and yes—even lawyers—all formerly successful, and all presently homeless (in fact the only profession we haven't seen represented among our homeless clients are politicians—they somehow manage to defy the normal laws of economic gravity). We recognize that not only must the ever-yawning economic divide be bridged for there to be a solution, but also that the ever-yawning divide in perceptions of who the homeless are and who they are not must be bridged as well. There seems to be an increasing hardening of the heart and averting of the eyes that prevent us from seeing the homeless for who they are: human beings fully entitled to a life of dignity and decency no less than any one else's.

Consider one client's story:

As part of a special "cold & wet weather advocacy outreach," Public Counsel led volunteer attorneys and law students to conduct legal clinics on site at National Guard armories that were converted into emergency shelters. At one of these clinics, "Jerry" watched from a distance as his fellow homeless residents sat down with the volunteers. After the clinic was over, he approached one of the attorneys and asked for information about food stamps and public benefits. Pleased to understand how to apply for these benefits, he shared that two years ago he had a six digit income in the defense industry, but then the industry down-sized and massive layoffs ensued. His skills were so highly specialized that he couldn't transfer them to another industry. In short order he had exhausted his savings and unemployment benefits, and the economic distress caused him to go through a divorce and the loss of custody of his children. "Now," he said ruefully, I'm competing for minimum wage work with the rest of the folks you see here in this shelter… and the worst of it is, only two years ago I volunteered with the National Guard to help the people in this shelter…and now here I am right among them."

Perhaps the most important of Public Counsel's efforts is to open the eyes and hearts of our volunteers to see the deplorable need in our community and the inherent injustice of such degradation in this, the wealthiest country on earth. We enable them to have a way to bring their energy, passion, and talent to the fore in order to make a difference.

The following summarizes the primary ways in which Public Counsel recruits and utilizes the services of volunteer attorneys, law students, and paralegals to help prevent homelessness among those confronting its disheartening shadow, while also helping to stabilize the lives of those who are enduring its ravages and desperately striving to keep their hopes and dreams alive.

Public Counsel's General Relief Advocacy Project ("GRAP")

"Sarah," 24, was fleeing a government social services office when she was intercepted by Public Counsel volunteer Maral. Maral was a summer associate with one of L.A.'s major law firms who was spending her day providing General Relief advocacy under Public Counsel's training and supervision. Maral calmed Sarah down and discovered that this distraught woman had not eaten in two days, faced eviction that weekend, and had an urgent medical condition that needed immediate attention. Shockingly, Sarah had been wrongfully informed by a social services employee that she could not receive any assistance that day. Maral spent the afternoon advocating on Sarah's behalf and secured emergency food stamps, aid to prevent eviction, and a medical appointment that day. Six months later, Sarah

called Public Counsel to inform us she had two jobs and permanent housing and to extend her heartfelt thanks to our volunteer for "saving [her] life" at a time of crisis.

Public Counsel's GRAP enlists more than a thousand volunteers annually to advocate on behalf of countless individuals like Sarah who confront homelessness and other crises and have to contend with bureaucratic barriers that block them from the help they need. GRAP enables our volunteers to see first hand the diverse spectrum of individuals who are either homeless or threatened with homelessness and then equips them with advocacy tools to ensure that these needy and anxious individuals receive emergency food, clothing, transportation, and shelter. In one day, many volunteers are able to see how their advocacy efforts truly helped prevent individuals from ending up on the streets. As one client poignantly summed it up for one of our volunteers: "Sir, were it not for your help, the curb would be my pillow tonight."

During the summer months, GRAP trains and supervises more than 500 summer associates from Los Angeles' largest and most prestigious law firms. (During the summer of 2005, 54 of L.A.'s most prestigious law firms had their summer law clerks participate in GRAP). We conduct two hour training sessions in the morning, then break up into groups that meet at public social service offices throughout L.A. County. We enter the offices and announce our presence there to the individuals in the lobbies. Typically, the individuals nearly run to us for help when we arrive. We then advocate on their behalf, helping them cut through the red tape. We do not leave the premises until we are certain that every client who requests our assistance receives all the assistance to which he or she is entitled.

The significance of GRAP can be appreciated when one considers that nearly all of the chronically homeless individuals in Los Angeles County at one time or another came through the doors of the county's public social services department seeking help and yet did not receive such assistance in adequate fashion. A HUD study released in 2000 reinforces how critical the opportunity is to help individuals when they first walk through the public social service office doors. It found that more than 70% of those who experienced homelessness for the first time were able to return to normalcy, provided they received adequate help in a timely manner. Our GRAP project strives to involve lawyers and law students to enter the breach at this critical juncture where their advocacy can make a dramatic difference in helping individuals avoid long-term homelessness.

Homeless Youth Project (HYP)

"Danny" came to Hollywood with stars in his eyes after a blow up with his parents in Florida. He quickly discovered the reality of the streets and ended up homeless. Fortunately, he connected with Covenant House and was able to obtain emergency shelter and support. His case manager had him meet with Public Counsel's volunteer attorneys at their Tuesday night legal clinic. Danny's parents had moved and he had no way of contacting them. Public Counsel was able to find a pro bono private investigator who was able to track down Danny's parents. Public Counsel then made arrangements through Traveler's Aid for Danny to rejoin his parents in time for the Christmas holidays.

For more than 15 years, Public Counsel has overseen volunteer programs geared towards addressing the unique needs of homeless and runaway youth. We train volunteers from local law schools and big firms as well as social work students. We strive to interject our advocacy efforts where they are most accessible to these youth, many of whom fear and distrust adults and authority figures. Thus we conduct street outreach in partnership with Angel's Flight (a youth shelter which employs experienced youth outreach workers). We encounter youth who are fleeing either abusive homes or alienating group homes, and it is not unusual for us to find pregnant teens who are typically victims of sexual assaults or afflicted with severe mental health disabilities.

We also conduct legal clinics staffed by volunteers directly on site at the major drop-in centers and shelters for youth in the Hollywood vicinity, where streets and freeway overpasses are 'home' to the nation's largest population of homeless and runaway youth. Through these legal clinics, youth receive advocacy support to help them access public benefits, health benefits, and emergency housing. They also receive assistance in clearing up minor offenses that interfere with their efforts to obtain driver's licenses or employment. We help them with a myriad of other issues such as locating parents or relatives and reconnecting with their homes of origin after they discover that Hollywood is not the glamorous dream that they were led to perceive it to be. (We were stunned to have youth inform us that many young people flocked to Hollywood in the 1990s after being influenced by the movie *Pretty Woman*. In the movie, Julia Roberts plays a street-walker on Hollywood Boulevard who hooks up with a billionaire john and is subsequently swept off her feet and off the streets).

As with adults, intervening to help youth in crisis in a timely manner is critical to help prevent their ending up among the ranks of the chronically homeless. Our programs strive to utilize our extensive volunteer base in ways that make advocacy support readily available to our most at-risk homeless youth in a timely manner and within a youth friendly environment.

Juvenile Court Advocacy and Intervention Project

"Eddie" was serving a four month juvenile disposition at Camp David Gonzalez when he learned of the legal clinic offered on site there by Public Counsel and its volunteers. He shared that his girlfriend had just had his baby and that he wanted to be a responsible father but that he was not being allowed to have her and her child come visit him. Public Counsel discussed this with the Camp Director, who made arrangements for Eddie to see his child. Eddie's morale and school performance greatly improved. Then Eddie learned his best friend had been killed in a drive by. When he shared his desire to revenge his friend's death, we spent several sessions reminding him of his obligations to his little girl and her need to have a father that she could grow up with in her home—he would be putting all of that at risk. We helped Eddie enroll in the 'Dad's Program' where he received further counseling, and he ultimately swore to us that he would not seek revenge. Instead, he would dedicate himself to ensuring his daughter had a father there for her in a way he had never experienced growing up.

Public Counsel's Juvenile Justice Intervention & Advocacy Project seeks to give encouragement, hope and opportunity to youth like "Eddie" who are at extremely high risk of spending most of their adult life in correctional facilities. We launched this effort after discovering that fully 60% of the youth we engaged in our Homeless Youth Project legal clinics had been in foster care at some point before becoming homeless. We began tailoring legal services to address the needs of foster youth, with special focus upon those preparing to emancipate themselves from the foster care system or those who had crossed over into the probation system in which they were no longer treated as victims, but as perpetrators instead.

Our attorneys have been actively involved in helping shape community based supportive housing arrangements for youth with mental health disabilities or with needs for special education or regional center services. In the fall of 2006, we will have a fellow focus her energy upon helping such youth transition from foster care group homes and probation camps back to their communities with appropriate support and after care.

At the public policy level, we have been actively involved with county task forces and work groups that design independent living program (ILP) benefits and transitional housing options for former foster youth. Presently, we are intensively involved in helping shape services for homeless youth with mental health disabilities that will be funded via the special *Mental Health Services Act* (Proposition 63). We have also advocated for these services to be available in settings that are youth friendly and that they be staffed by individuals with proven capability of effectively engaging youth and garnering their trust.

Housing Advocacy/Eviction Defense Project

Existing affordable housing in the City of Los Angeles under the Rent Stabilization Ordinance ("RSO") and/or Section 8 [voucher] Housing Benefits are currently being eliminated, resulting from the rapidly rising cost of rental housing and drastically reduced funding of the Section 8 Voucher Program. Moreover, affordable rental housing that exists in the city of Los Angeles due to the protections of the RSO is rapidly being eliminated, due to the increase in the market rate for rental housing. Many low income tenants whose affordable rental housing is protected by the RSO are being unlawfully evicted by landlords, who are then able to re-rent such units at market rates (often increasing rent by over 100%). These trends are putting approximately 50,000 individuals who are either elderly and/or disabled at risk of ending up on the streets.

Public Counsel's Housing Advocacy/Eviction Defense Project was established in 2005 to equip our volunteers with advocacy skills that enable them to play a vital role in helping preserve affordable housing. The following illustrates the specific ways in which we are utilizing their advocacy to advance this goal:

(1) The tenant outreach/education component strives to empower large numbers of low income tenants to preserve existing affordable rental housing by educating tenants about (a) their legal rights, obligations and protection from actions by landlords, such as protections afforded by the Rent Stabilization Ordinance as well as Section 8 tenants' protection under Fed and State Law; (b) the procedural protections of proper notice requirements and the importance of obtaining immediate legal assistance; and (c) information regarding not only their respective rights and duties as tenants, but the landlords' duties and responsibilities as well.

(2) The litigation component provides tenants with legal representation in unlawful Detainer cases and "impact litigation" for selected wrongful eviction cases, especially targeting Property Management Companies that engage in illegal "self-help" eviction, and/or violation of tenant rights (breach of warranty of habitability). In 2005, HPLP successfully defended evictions of low income tenants through development and use of a variety of creative defenses that were devised as a result of the dynamic involvement of our volunteers.

(3) The housing benefits advocacy component utilizes volunteer resources in the form of law students and volunteer attorneys. These volunteers advocate for persons being terminated from housing benefits (Section 8), represent them in termination of (Section 8) ben-

efit hearings, and pressure city and county government for systemic reforms of the local housing authorities' administrative plans that affect Section 8 tenants. They work in partnership with other great public interest legal organizations (such as Bet Tzedek and Legal Aid Foundation of Los Angeles) as well as grass roots organizations (such as the Save Section 8 Coalition).

Public Counsel staff acts extensively through a wide array of working committees and task forces that are dedicated to ending homelessness, including one that is helping shape reforms in the Discharge Planning from hospitals, jails, and psychiatric wards, as well as one developing the blueprint for the Ten Year Plan to End Homelessness. In all of our efforts, our volunteers bring dynamism, passion, and vision to inspire our efforts. And we would be remiss if we neglected to mention the ongoing inspiration that our clients provide, as best illustrated by the following:

ABA © TED ZEPEDA

Paul L. Freese, Jr. *Director of Litigation & Advocacy*
Public Counsel
P.O. Box 76900 Los Angeles, CA 90076
213.637.3809 pfreese@publiccounsel.org

Paul L. Freese, Jr., is the Director of Litigation & Advocacy for Public Counsel, the public interest law office of the Los Angeles County and Beverly Hills Bar Associations and the largest provider of pro bono legal services in the United States. He has been a member of the California State Bar since 1988. From 1988 to 1994, he worked as a litigation associate with the law firm of Perkins Coie. He joined Public Counsel in March, 1994, and acted as Directing Attorney of the Homelessness Prevention Law Project for more than six years before being promoted in January 2001 to his current position in which he supervises more than 20 attorneys and their staff. He serves on a vast array of working groups and task forces that address the needs of the poor and marginalized, particularly those of emancipating foster and probation youth and the homeless.

"Nafeeshah" came to Public Counsel's legal clinic at Covenant House, L.A. County's only emergency shelter for youth ages 18-20, to seek help resolving a minor traffic citation that she could not afford. She also showed a lot of curiosity about law school and shared that she hoped to be a lawyer one day. When asked what it was about the legal profession that attracted her interest she replied to the effect that she saw the good that lawyers could do through this clinic and added, "I feel like I've been given a lot in my life, and I feel a need to give back." Here she was, no home to turn to for love or support, living in a homeless shelter in Hollywood, and she felt the need to give back.

Humbled and inspired by the example of amazing clients like "Nafeeshah," Public Counsel strives to call upon the entire community to share her spirit of wanting to give back. We are heartened by the legions of individuals who, without any affiliation, come forward to answer the call. Their spirit can be summed up as "we love justice, and want to serve." It is that spirit that gives us hope that the disgraceful spectacle of human suffering that is homelessness will one day come to pass.

Ending and Preventing Homelessness for Victims of Domestic Violence

Robin R. Runge

Domestic violence is an epidemic—it is the leading cause of homelessness for women and children in the United States. Nearly half of the 24 cities surveyed in 2005 by the U.S. Conference of Mayors identified domestic violence as a "primary cause" of homelessness. Ninety-two percent of homeless women have experienced severe physical or sexual abuse at some point in their lives,[1] and 63% have been victims of domestic violence as adults.[2] Currently, 38% of domestic violence victims have been homeless at some point in their lives.[3] In fact, fear of homelessness is one of the primary reasons why survivors do not leave violent relationships.

It may be obvious, but it needs to be stated: in order to escape violence at the hands of a loved one, one will most likely be forced to leave one's home. Domestic violence victim advocates recognized

---

1 *A. Browne & S. Bassuk, "Intimate Violence in the Lives of Homeless and Poor Housed Women: Prevalence and Patters in an Ethnically Diverse Sample," American Journal of Orthopsychiatry, 67(2), 261-278, April 1997; A. Browne, "Responding to the Needs of Low Income and Homeless Women Who Are Survivors of Family Violence," Journal of American Medical Association 53(2), 57-64, Spring 1998.*

2 *Id.*

3 *Charlene k. Baker et al., "Domestic Violence and Housing Problems: A Contextual Analysis of Women's Help-Seeking, Received Informal Support, and Formal System Response," Violence Against Women 9(7) (2003): 754-783.*

that by offering safe housing for survivors and their children, more survivors would be able to leave their violent homes—thus ending the violence without causing homelessness. Initial housing assistance efforts focused on the development of emergency shelters at confidential locations where a survivor and her children could stay for anywhere from a few days to three months. Over time, however, it became clear that after their stay in the emergency shelter, victims found themselves at risk for homelessness yet again, forcing them to return to the home they shared with the abuser or to become homeless. This led advocates to ask a key question—why should a survivor of domestic violence be forced to leave her home and risk becoming homeless in order to obtain safety?

Attorneys representing victims of domestic violence in many instances are lawyers working to end homelessness. Every state in the country enables a victim of domestic violence to obtain an order of protection, civil protection order, or restraining order against her husband, live-in intimate partner, or person with whom she has a child in common. In many states, one form of relief is evicting the perpetrator of the violence from the residence shared with the victim and her children. In many jurisdictions, the victim's name must appear on the mortgage or lease in order for the judge to be able to order this relief. This "kick out" order is regularly requested by attorneys representing survivors of domestic violence and is frequently granted. This advocacy regarding housing for victims of domestic violence in protection order hearings is standard and is often an effective way to both end domestic violence and prevent homelessness. However, removing the batterer may also mean removing the person from the home who had the means to pay the rent or mortgage. Moreover, the batterer may continue to harass, stalk, and abuse the victim at the residence—tearing down the door, throwing rocks in the windows, and otherwise disturbing the peace—leading the police to be called and the landlord to take retaliatory action against the victim in the form of eviction proceedings. Moreover, if a survivor decides to leave her home and seek housing on her own, more than two-thirds of domestic violence service providers surveyed identified "discriminatory practices by landlords" as a barrier that survivors face in their effort to obtain housing.

Examples of Effective Legal Advocacy on Behalf of Victims of Domestic Violence to Obtain and Maintain Housing

Pine Tree Legal Aid of Maine provides legal assistance with a particular focus on the unique challenges facing survivors of domestic violence in obtaining and/or maintaining housing.[4] There are three ways in which Pine Tree Legal Aid handles housing cases on behalf of victims of domestic violence: (1) survivors call the office because they have received an eviction notice, and through the intake process, domestic violence is identified as an issue, (2) Pine Tree Legal Aid hosts a "kids project" at the local hospital through which it also receives some domestic violence cases involving housing issues, and (3) referrals come in from the Family Crisis Center, a multi-service organization that assists survivors of domestic violence. The primary types of cases that Pine Tree Legal Aid attorneys handle on behalf of survivors of domestic violence are providing representation in eviction proceedings and filing actions against landlords. Pine Tree Legal Aid also recognizes the need to raise awareness of the housing issues facing victims of domestic violence among housing providers and therefore provides education presentations on a regular basis.

Examples of the types of issues raised in representation of survivors of domestic violence in housing cases include the enforcement of protection orders that require eviction and stay away of a batterer who is a former tenant. In those circumstances, the landlord or public housing authority can obtain a no trespass order against the evicted batterer. This becomes complicated, however,

4 *The author thanks Frank D'Alessandro for his generosity in taking the time to provide this description of the phenomenal services he and his colleagues at Pine Tree Legal Aid provide to victims of domestic violence.*

when the survivor takes the batterer back and permits him to return to the premises.

Pine Tree Legal Aid attorneys also assist survivors of domestic violence through their Fair Housing Project by arguing discrimination against the victim based upon her status as a victim as a form of gender discrimination. Pine Tree Legal Aid attorneys assist survivors of domestic violence in cases involving non-payment of rent by helping them identify short term sources of funding, including accessing public benefits such as general assistance and TANF. Finally, in one location, Pine Tree Legal Aid has an attorney placed in an emergency shelter for victims who goes to the court to pick up eviction cases, many of which involve victims of domestic violence. This attorney has reported a drop in the number of people staying in the emergency shelter and attributes it to the eviction cases that he is successfully handling. Pine Tree Legal Aid has also successfully integrated pro bono attorneys into its work on behalf of victims of domestic violence with housing issues. Pine Tree Legal Aid refers cases to a Pro Bono Panel based in Portland.

Another organization that demonstrates how attorneys are successfully advocating for the housing needs of victims of domestic violence and thus ending homelessness is the Community Legal Aid Society, Inc. (CLASI) in Delaware.[5] CLASI is a statewide program with three offices in Wilmington, Dover, and Georgetown. CLASI handles housing cases on behalf of victims of domestic violence in three of its programs: (1) fair housing, (2) eviction defense, and (3) public housing. In addition, CLASI has worked with the Delaware Coalition Against Domestic Violence to draft an amendment to the Landlord and Tenant Code to allow a survivor of domestic violence to terminate a lease within 30 days if it is necessary to ensure her safety. The attorney in the fair housing program for CLASI has handled several ground-breaking cases on behalf of survivors of domestic violence. In one, she represented a victim who was being

5 *The author thanks Kathaleen McCormick, Emily Farley and Debbie Gottschalk for their generosity in taking the time to provide this description of the exemplary services that they and their colleagues at the Delaware Community Legal Aid Society, Inc. provide to victims of domestic violence.*

evicted from her public housing at least in part because of numerous police calls to her unit. The survivor had called the police because of her abusive husband, who was ultimately arrested. In a second case, a private landlord took steps to evict a victim of domestic violence right after she obtained a no contact order against her boyfriend and former co-tenant. The batterer had broken the door to the house and the victim requested that the landlord fix the door, but the landlord did not (although it was later discovered that he had collected money from the batterer for this purpose).

Pine Tree Legal Aid and the Delaware Community Legal Aid Society, Inc. are two examples of the exceptional advocacy that

ABA © SARAH KAYSER

Robin R. Runge *Director*
ABA Commission on Domestic Violence
740 15th Street, NW Washington, DC
202.662.8637 runger@staff.abanet.org

Robin R. Runge is the Director of the Commission on Domestic Violence at the American Bar Association. Robin has been a domestic violence victim advocate for fourteen years and practiced employment law for five years with a focus on women's rights in employment, specifically the Family and Medical Leave Act, Title VII, the Americans with Disabilities Act and employment protections for victims of domestic violence, sexual assault, and stalking. Robin is a nationally-recognized expert on the employment rights of victims and speaks and provides trainings regularly on these issues. She has co-authored several articles on employment law and domestic violence, and has worked on state and federal legislation providing job-guaranteed leave from work, unemployment insurance, and anti-discrimination in employment for domestic violence and sexual assault victims. Robin currently serves on the advisory board of the Corporate Alliance To End Partner Violence and the Women's Information Network. Robin is currently an Associate Professorial Lecturer in Law at The George Washington University Law School teaching *Public Interest Lawyering* and an Adjunct Professor at The American University Washington College of Law where she teaches *Domestic Violence Law.*

attorneys are providing to victims of domestic violence to prevent them from becoming homeless. Across the country, housing has increasingly been recognized as a priority to ensure long term safety for victims of domestic violence and their children. In recent years, state legislatures have recognized the need to increase protection for victims, and a few states have passed laws prohibiting discrimination in housing against victims of domestic violence or permitting them to break leases quickly without penalty if they are forced to flee for their safety. Moreover, the Violence Against Women Act of 2005 contains extensive protection for victims of domestic violence in public housing, including prohibiting victims from being evicted from or denied housing because of their status as victims. Attorneys are needed to ensure that we continue to raise awareness of the obstacles survivors of domestic violence face when attempting to maintain or obtain housing.

CHAPTER 6

Courts Working to End Homelessness

Making Jail the Last Resort

Judge Steve Leifman

According to statistics reported by the Florida Department of Children and Families, Miami-Dade County is home to the largest percentage of people with serious mental illnesses of any urban community in the United States. It is estimated that 210,000 people, or 9.1% of the general population, experience mental illnesses. Among individuals who are homeless, the prevalence is even higher. Of the estimated 5,000 people who are homeless on the streets, in emergency shelters, or in transitional housing in Miami-Dade County, one in five experiences a mental illness and one in four experiences a co-occurring mental illness and substance use disorder. The prevalence of these disorders serve not only as a contributing factors to homelessness, but also as significant barriers to those seeking to break the cycle of homelessness and move toward successful community integration.

Compared to other homeless subgroups, people with serious mental illnesses tend to be homeless more often and for longer periods of time. Untreated, their psychiatric symptoms are often chronic and severe. The majority of individuals with mental illnesses who are homeless have limited opportunities to access mental health treatment and support services that may lead to recovery and improved life-health outcomes. Those who do access services tend to do so under aversive and distressing conditions such as during crisis episodes, while incarcerated, or under involuntary civil commitment. Unable to access continuing care services upon community re-entry, many of these individuals inevitably decompensate and slip back into episodes of acute psychiatric illness, which makes it extremely difficult to negotiate even the most basic demands of daily living such as finding food, shelter, and safety.

Similar to the experience of many other communities around the country, law enforcement and correctional personnel in Miami-Dade County have increasingly become the lone responders to people in crisis due to untreated mental illnesses. Homeless individuals with mental illnesses are twice as likely as other homeless subgroups to be arrested or jailed as a result of encounters with law enforcement officers. On average, law enforcement officers in Florida handle more mental health calls than burglaries, assaults, and DUI cases, yet these officers rarely receive any kind of training to deal with this population.

On any given day, the Miami-Dade County Jail houses between 800 and 1,200 defendants with serious mental illnesses, many of whom are homeless. This represents approximately 20% of the total inmate population and costs taxpayers millions of dollars annually. The Miami-Dade County Jail now serves as the largest psychiatric facility in the state of Florida. People with mental illnesses remain in jail eight times longer than people without mental illnesses for the exact same charges, and at a cost seven times higher. With little treatment available, many individuals cycle through this system for the majority of their adult lives. Consequences include an increase in the number of people who become chronically homeless, increased injuries to law enforcement officers responding to mental health calls, increased police shootings of people with mental ill-

Homeless individuals with mental illnesses are twice as likely as other homeless subgroups to be arrested or jailed as a result of encounters with law enforcement officers. On average, law enforcement officers in Florida handle more mental health calls than burglaries, assaults, and DUI cases.

nesses, wasted tax dollars, and the reality that untreated mental illness has essentially been made a crime.

Almost six years ago, I sought to address this problem by convening a two-day summit meeting of traditional and non-traditional stakeholders to review how the Miami-Dade community dealt with individuals entangled in the criminal justice system due to untreated mental illnesses. The stakeholders were comprised of law enforcement agencies, the courts, public defenders, state attorneys, mental health professionals, community mental health providers, consumers, and families. What we found was both interesting and alarming. We found that, although none of us were acting out of deliberate malice, almost all of us were complicit in helping to perpetuate what was an embarrassingly dysfunctional system. The problem was that everyone was so busy doing his or her job that no one was looking at the larger issues of how individual roles come together to support or inhibit the welfare of the system as a whole. The police were policing. The judges were judging. The prosecutors were prosecuting. After spending time together, it became apparent that we were fragmented and disconnected as a community. We knew very little about the ways in which our professional lives intersected, and we found that we were literally paying a hefty price for our ignorance. Many of us were shocked to find out that a single person with mental illness was accessing the services of almost everybody in the room, not just once, but again and again as the individual revolved in cycles of disenfranchisement and despair between a criminal justice system that was never intended to handle overwhelming numbers of people with serious mental illnesses and a community-based system of mental health care that was ill-equipped to provide the necessary services to those most in need. We began to realize that people with untreated serious mental illnesses may be among the most expensive population in our society, not because of their conditions, but because of the way we treat them.

The result of this summit was the establishment of the 11th Judicial Circuit Criminal Mental Health Project (CMHP), which was designed and implemented to divert people with serious mental illnesses who commit minor, misdemeanor offenses away from the criminal justice system and into community-based care. The program operates both a pre-booking and post-booking jail diversion program and brings together the resources and services of healthcare providers, social-service agencies, law enforcement personnel, and the Courts. It has resulted in substantial gains in the effort to reverse the criminalization of people with mental illnesses and serves as a testament to the value and potential of true cross-systems collaboration. The idea was not to create new services, but to merge and blend existing services in a way that was more efficient, pragmatic, and continuous across the system. We sought to eliminate gaps in services by forging productive and innovative relationships among all stakeholders who have an interest in the welfare and safety of one of our community's most vulnerable populations.

Miami-Dade County has seen dramatic reductions in arrests among misdemeanant offenders in acute psychiatric distress. Recidivism rates among individuals arrested while in the midst of acute psychiatric crises have dropped from over 70% prior to the program's implementation to 22% last year. Individuals with mental illnesses are spending less time in jail and more time engaged in treatment. Crisis Intervention Team (CIT) training, a collaborative effort between law enforcement agencies and the mental health community to teach officers how to respond to incidents involving people with mental illnesses more effectively and to divert individuals to crisis-oriented services in lieu of making an arrest, has been

The Criminal Mental Health Project diverts people with serious mental illnesses who commit minor, misdemeanor offenses away from the criminal justice system and into community-based care through a collaboration of resources and services of healthcare providers, social service agencies, law enforcement, and the Courts.

adopted by 22 of Miami-Dade County's 32 law enforcement agencies, with nearly 1,000 officers trained to date. CIT officers at the City of Miami Police Department, who respond to over 3,600 mental health calls annually, have not discharged a firearm, experienced a police injury, or been involved in an incident resulting in the use of deadly force on a person with mental illness since the implementation of this program four years ago. The burden of providing psychiatric services through our jails has been eased, and Miami-Dade County is saving millions of taxpayer dollars annually.

Because a vast majority of the people served by the CMHP are either homeless or live in unstable housing arrangements at the time they enter the program, residential placement is a primary concern as individuals begin to reintegrate into community living following a period of crisis stabilization. Without access to supportive housing options which are equipped to provide appropriate levels of assistance and care, many individuals are at significant risk of falling into the insidious pattern of chronic homelessness interspersed with periods of criminal justice system involvement that have plagued this community for years. Through cooperative relationships developed with various community based partners, the CMHP has been successful in accessing a wide range of housing resources across the continuum of care, including beds in residential treatment facilities, homeless assistance programs, and transitional and permanent housing.

I do not pretend to take credit for the hard work performed by those in the community who strive every day to improve the lives of people with mental illnesses. These are the real agents of change. My role as a member of the judiciary, however, has afforded me the ability to bring together the people and resources that are necessary to effect significant change. As a group, we are engaged in a process of seeking solutions to problems that, on the surface, often seem unsolvable. None of us created this problem alone and none of us will be able to fix this problem alone. We all must be a part of the solution.

I have been fortunate to have the opportunity to sit down with professionals, family members, and consumers to understand where the system works and where it begins to break down. This, in turn, has enabled me to bring a voice to these issues, and to deliver the message that change is needed. The voice I use is not mine alone. It is the voice of a community that has come to recognize that the health and well being of our community is inextricably linked to the health and well being of our residents. Perhaps most importantly, it is the voice of those most vulnerable in our community, who have been historically marginalized and overlooked by the system.

As judges we are in the unique position to help bring communities together to deal effectively with difficult and complex problems. I am not alone in this effort. Along with Justice Evelyn

ABA © STEVE LEIFMAN

Judge Steve Leifman *Associate Administrative Judge*
11th Judicial Circuit of Florida
1351 NW 12th Street, Room 617, Miami, FL 33128
305.548.5394 sleifman@jud11.flcourt.org

Judge Leifman serves as the Associate Administrative Judge of the Miami-Dade County Court, Criminal Division. In the most recent Dade County Bar Poll, Judge Leifman received the highest exceptionally qualified rating of all the Miami-Dade County Court Judges. Judge Leifman chairs the Mental Health Committee for the Eleventh Judicial Circuit of Florida and was responsible for creating the Eleventh Judicial Circuit Criminal Mental Health Project. This highly successful program diverts non-violent misdemeanor defendants with mental illnesses to appropriate mental health facilities and provides Crisis Intervention Team training for law enforcement agencies in Miami-Dade County. The program has substantially reduced recidivism and saved the county and state critical funds. In recognition of this program, the Project was awarded the 2001 Council of State Governments Innovations Award and was recently awarded a SAMSHA Jail Diversion Expansion Grant. Judge Leifman serves on the ABA Commission on Homelessness and Poverty.

Stratton of the Ohio Supreme Court, I currently serve as co-chair of the Judges' Criminal Justice/Mental Health Leadership Initiative. Our goal is to reach out to members of the judiciary around the country in an effort to enlist more judges in this important effort. Our experience shows that as members of the judiciary, we can play a critical and helpful role in bridging the gap between the many different and diverse individuals and systems that make up our "mental health system," thereby making jail the last resort for people with untreated mental illnesses.

The Homeless Court Program:

Taking the Court to the Streets

Steve Binder

"Recall the face of the poorest and the weakest man whom you may have seen, ask yourself if the step you contemplate is going to be of any use to him. Will he gain anything by it? Will it restore him to a control over his own life and destiny?"

Mahatma Gandhi, 1947

Homeless People Smile Too(th)

Looking at a wall of people's faces in contrasting photographs, with and without teeth, the judge pointed his finger and said, "I'd sentence that person different from that person." The only difference between the two people pictured were their smiles—one toothless and one full of teeth. While Medicaid pays to pull teeth, it does not pay to put teeth back into a person's mouth. The dentists who volunteer their services at St. Vincent de Paul Village restore the smiles to people who reside at the homeless shelter. Our tour guide turned to the judge and said, "That's just the physical change that takes place here."

This moment of candor occurred during a tour of St. Vincent de Paul Village in preparation for the Homeless Court Program (HCP) hearings being held there in the community room. The full team of

HCP key players was touring the Village to better understand the program activities that homeless people can access while also checking that the community room provided a safe courtroom environment. We had all heard of St. Vincent de Paul Village. We knew the tremendous effort Father Joe Carroll had undertaken for funding their programs. Over the years, we had worked with staff and people who had successfully overcome homelessness with assistance from the Village. Yet despite these interactions, few from our group had actually touched the building and grounds or seen it in action.

Throughout the tour, the HCP key players observed the child care center, kitchen (where 4,000 meals are served each day), assessment center, and medical clinic. In the back of the medical clinic sits the dental clinic, with photographs of faces, no teeth and teeth. The lesson from this tour highlighted the challenges we all face in understanding our community, the lives of the dispossessed, and the obstacles we all face in life. During the tour, a number of us said, "This really is a Village." Many times over, we heard people say, "There but for the grace of God, go I."

How does this relate to *Lawyers Working to End Homelessness*? What part does this play with the Homeless Court Program?

Homeless Court Program

Homeless Court Program is a special Superior Court session for homeless defendants—convened in a homeless shelter—to resolve outstanding misdemeanor offenses and warrants. The HCP builds on partnerships between the court, local shelters, service agencies, homeless participants, the prosecutor, and the public defender. It works to resolve the problems that homelessness represents with practical solutions. Initial referrals to Homeless Court originate in shelters and service agencies. The prosecution and defense review the cases before the court hearing, and the court order for sentencing substitutes participation in agency programs for fines and custody. The HCP is designed for efficiency; the majority of cases are heard and resolved in one hearing.

Frustration and Despair

In 1989, I was working in the San Diego Office of the Public Defender as a deputy public defender in the misdemeanor arraignment department. I was responsible for explaining to the defendants courtroom procedures, the charges against them, their rights and possible defenses, and the proposed plea-bargain and sentence. Misdemeanor offenses at that time accounted for 80% of the criminal caseload in the Office of the Public Defender.

In 1989, it was not unusual for a person who was homeless to carry a pocket full of 20 or more citations. There were more than a handful of people on the streets with 50 to 100 warrants for "disturbing the peace." The police issued citations as an invitation to get out of town—a clear signal the homeless were not wanted in San Diego. In practice, the police and the homeless were engaged in a game of cat and mouse. The police would conduct a sweep of the streets in downtown San Diego, issue citations, and force the homeless into Balboa Park. In an effort to clear out the park, police would then issue a new round of citations. Another round robin of citations and movement ensued.

The vast majority of citations issued were for Penal Code section 647(j), commonly known as illegal lodging. Penal code section 647(j) defines Disorderly Conduct, a misdemeanor, as the actions of anyone who "lodges in any building, structure, vehicle, or place, whether public or private, without the permission of the owner or person entitled to the permission or in control thereof." When issued a criminal citation for illegal lodging, the homeless person would receive a 4 by 7 inch piece of pink paper, a demand for a total bail payment of $135.00, and the threat of a maximum of six months incarceration and $500.00 fine.

During this period, the police complained that the people they arrested were released after serving a few days in custody. Judges were frustrated by the backlog of warrants that accumulated when defendants failed to appear for court. These same judges realized the futility of handing out sentences and issuing orders that would not be obeyed.

Homeless defendants often fail to appear in court not because of a disregard for the court system, but due to their status and condition. They struggle daily for food, clothing, and shelter. They are not in a position to adhere to short-term guidelines. They do not carry calendars. They are scared. In the past, court orders and sentences guaranteed their failure. They could not pay fines. Custody left them, society, and the court no better off than before they attended court.

When homeless people did appear in court, they tried to explain to the judge the sorry set of circumstances that had taken them from families, homes, and jobs to sleeping in the dirty bedrolls that lay beside them in court. Some were articulate and educated, and some were even working but unable to afford a rent deposit or a room.

"How do you plead to the charge?" the judge would ask.

"Guilty," they invariably answered.

They would come before the court and walk away with a sentence that required them to pay a fine, perform public work service, or spend time in custody. They picked up their court orders at the clerk's office and walked back to the streets, adding legal burdens on top of their other troubles.

The prosecutors, judges, and even the police were uncomfortable and frustrated with the futility of this revolving-door approach. A person who could not afford a room to rent could not afford a fine for being homeless. At the time, however, there were no alternatives. The criminal justice system had an established routine that unfortunately did not adequately meet the needs of this population with special issues.

We are supposed to call the police when things get out of hand so that the police can solve crime and restore order to our community. Officers wear the motto, "To Serve and Protect" on uniforms and patrol cars. In an attempt to answer complaints from the citizenry and guide them to action, the San Diego Police Department Crime Prevention Unit published a pamphlet entitled "A Citizen's Guide To Transient-Related Crime" that is a compilation of laws commonly violated by some transients, defined as "chronic law violators who infringe upon the rights of others." The violations listed include being drunk in public, illegal lodging, urinating in public, camping on the beach or park, and habitation in a vehicle. While the community turns to law enforcement to bring order to our community, the citation, arrest, and incarceration of homeless people with public nuisance offenses pushes homeless people further outside society while also belittling law enforcement.

The illegal lodging citation represents the shortcomings of turning to law enforcement and a criminal justice system that relies on fines and custody to address the problems homelessness represents. Typically, the homeless defendant will appear in custody, enter a plea bargain, spend the weekend in custody, and be released to the streets on Monday morning. With no means to break this cycle, the person remains homeless.

For me, the inspiration that led to the Homeless Court Program grew from the frustration and despair I felt when I first started as a defense attorney. Counseling homeless individuals in misdemeanor arraignment is an intense review of an individual's case, conveyance of the proposed plea agreement, and their option of going to trial.

Oftentimes, misdemeanor arraignment was populated by two very different groups of defendants. One group included the growing homeless population in San Diego, a then estimated staggering 5,000 persons (current estimates are 8,000 people living on the streets of San Diego). The other group contained middle class defendants. They were cited for actions such as keeping a dog off a leash and the improper use of cable services. The middle class clients would often come with evidence of their middle class status. Pictures of their dog and letters saluting their contributions to Little League were common. The implicit plea in their actions was, "I'm middle class. I don't deserve this. Please go after real criminals."

When the homeless defendants appeared in court, I heard tales of hardship and renewal. Some people came to court telling me they had recently found a place to live. Others came in talking about the CIA and FBI. Many carried their worldly belongings in bags. A number were malodorous. All struggled with problems that the criminal justice system ignored. Invariably, the judge would sentence them after taking a plea for an array of public nuisance offenses. They would be sentenced to fines they could not afford along with terms and conditions that frustrated their continued participation in society.

Clearly, the criminal justice system was failing to bring order to society and was perpetuating the pain and suffering of homeless people. I started attending the local bar association's homeless subcommittee meetings. At one meeting, two Vietnam veterans, Dr. Jon Nachison and Robert Van Keuren, addressed the civil attorneys and asked for their assistance at an event they created called "Stand Down." They explained that Stand Down is a military term signaling the removal of exhausted combat soldiers from battle to provide them an opportunity to rest and recover in a place of relative safety and security. They emphasized the importance of creating a community that transformed the frustration and despair of homelessness to self-respect and opportunity for integration back into society. They built a three-day tent community with a cornucopia of services and applied this concept to 700 homeless veterans doing battle on the streets. They distributed an eight page exit survey, tallied by the Veteran Administration (VA), from the first Stand Down, wherein 116 of 500 homeless veterans stated that their greatest need was to resolve outstanding bench warrants. This meeting and the Stand Down event were "eureka" moments for the Homeless Court Program.

Serving Justice on a Handball Court

Homeless veterans of San Diego inspired the misdemeanor criminal court to leave the courthouse and join the Stand Down effort. In 1989, San Diego started the first Homeless Court Program in the nation, a special Superior Court session held on handball courts at Stand Down's three-day tent city for homeless veterans. At the court's location, three gray concrete walls at San Diego High School's athletic field surrounded foldout tables and chairs. Desert camouflage netting sheltered the court from the sun. The flag of the United States anchored one corner; the State of California's the other.

Stand Down Homeless Court Program San Diego, CA

ABA © STEVE BINDER

The defendants appearing before this outdoor Homeless Court were veterans who live outdoors on the streets of San Diego, but for three days they would be sheltered in tents, receive employment counseling, housing referrals, medical and mental health care, and other social services.

The Veterans Village of San Diego, sponsors of Stand Down, established a three-day tent city designed to relieve the isolation of homeless veterans while assisting their re-entry into society. The annual event provides comprehensive services for homeless veterans, including employment, housing, medical, legal (civil and criminal), physical and mental health treatment, and numerous social services. But the event is more than a collection of services. The sponsors also concentrate on building community and developing the strengths of the participants as members of the community.

Following this first Homeless Court session at Stand Down in 1989, 130 defendants had 451 cases adjudicated. Between 1989 and 1992, the court resolved 4,895 cases for 942 homeless veterans.

The continued large numbers of homeless people participating in the HCP, coupled with their efforts to overcome the obstacles their condition represents, fostered the program's expansion from an annual, to a quarterly, then finally to a monthly schedule. Over the years, the HCP expanded to serve battered and homeless women (1990), residents at the city-sponsored cold weather shelter (1994), and the general homeless population served at local shelters (1995). In 1999, the HCP started holding monthly sessions, alternating between two shelters (St. Vincent de Paul Village and Veterans Village of San Diego). In short, everyone was looking for order and control of their community, a way to make society fair and just.

While I do not remember the name of the first HCP participant or the substance of his case, I do remember the audible sigh that came from the crowd when this brave soul walked before the judge on the handball court and proceeded to get his court docket from the court clerk's office.

The HCP is about more than just the resolution of criminal cases. It is as much attitude as it is process. The HCP practitioners do not simply move and resolve cases—they help to move people from the streets through their chosen program to self-sufficiency. While the HCP's primary focus is the adjudication of criminal cases, the movement of case files alone does not begin to describe the fundamental challenges and change that occurs when a homeless individual stands before the court, walks back into the audience, and returns to the shelter with successful resolution of his/her case. The effect of the HCP and its power to challenge and change participants extends to the key players that comprise the criminal justice system as well.

It was the second or third year of Stand Down's HCP when we noticed that a number of participants who had resolved their cases still carried outstanding cases throughout San Diego County. We counseled them to take care of these outstanding cases, saying, "if you do not go to court on these matters, you will still be looking over your shoulder, worried about being picked up by the police on warrants." Politely, sometimes with nervous laughter, they would respond by saying, "That court will not help or take care of us like the court did here." We persisted, "You know these cases will not disappear or go away, go with a friend, take someone from your tent, but by all means go to court on your case." Shortly thereafter, the South Bay court called the downtown courthouse, asking what Stand Down was and why so many people had shown up there.

The following year, the outlying courts joined in the Stand Down HCP.

From day one, the HCP at Stand Down was a court and community effort. Early on, local attorneys on the homeless subcommittee approached the court, presenting a sound proposal to move the court to Stand Down. The lead clerk of the court, D. Kent Pederson said, "Yes, we can pick up the court and move it to a handball court," making sure to transport case files without losing them. The court provided an on-site computer and its court docket, and clerks volunteered to help. And so, the HCP conducted its first session—mirroring exactly what would happen inside a courthouse, only this time it came to order under camouflage netting on an outdoor handball court at San Diego High School.

Access to Court

In time, the HCP developed a monthly session to meet the growing demands of homeless participants working with local homeless service agencies. The Homeless Court Program provided access to court for homeless defendants while working with shelter service providers, holding proceedings in shelter community rooms, and recognizing individual effort for purposes of sentencing. The Homeless Court Program's greatest achievement to date is the contribution of the service providers and homeless participants that resulted in the creation of a more inclusive criminal justice system and stronger community. The Homeless Court Program is a community working together, finding opportunity in adversity.

Homeless people voluntarily sign up in shelters—the first step in taking responsibility for their offense(s). By taking the initiative to sign up, the participants of the Homeless Court search for justice and a way to reconcile their past with their future. The Homeless Court Program enables homeless individuals who are engaged in an organized program or shelter to participate in a court session at a homeless shelter.

An experienced Homeless Court Program prosecutor said, "We want what is best for the community. We reward the positive efforts they have made, efforts that indicate they are less likely to re-offend." This prosecutor continued, "They give more than traditional court participants. It is not because we have asked for their rehabilitative efforts. Their incentive to participate in the program activities is their own, not from the court."

The Homeless Court Program recognizes that each defendant is an individual working to overcome the wreckage of his/her past. A judge who presided over numerous Homeless Court sessions said, "It is important for those who work in the criminal justice system to understand that many people who find themselves in the system are just in a phase of their life, and the incident which brings them before the court does not reflect their entire life. Many of our homeless have contributed to society, and perhaps for all these individuals, the best is yet to come."

The HCP innovation promotes access to court for people who have experienced homelessness. To counteract the effect of criminal cases pushing homeless defendants further outside society, this court combines a progressive plea bargain system, alternative sentencing structure, assurance of "no custody," and proof of program activities to address a full range of misdemeanor offenses and bring the participants back into society.

The HCP "sentences" participants to activities in the shelter program. Local homeless shelters and agencies are the gateway for participants to enter this court. Homeless persons who want to appear before this court must sign up through one of a number of local shelters.

The HCP is structured to maximize the participant's representation in court. The participant voluntarily signs up for the HCP from his/her chosen homeless shelter or agency. The participant decides which shelter and what program activities best meets his/her needs in their transition from the streets toward self-sufficiency.

Core Elements

HCP is a Voluntary Program

Homeless participants voluntarily sign up for the HCP, and the participant voluntarily enters the homeless shelter or agency. The HCP does not order participants into a program. If a participant who has signed up for Homeless Court decides to challenge his/her case, be it through a trial or motion, the case is set for a certain date in the courthouse. The HCP homeless participant is entitled to all protections afforded by due process of law. No one gives up the right to go to trial or pursue motions challenging the allegations against him/her.

HCP Addresses a Full Range of Misdemeanor Offenses

The HCP addresses a broad spectrum of misdemeanor offenses including charges of being under the influence of a controlled substance, theft, and driving under the influence. The HCP recognizes that people can overcome great obstacles and serious misdemeanor offenses, and it realizes that these cases represent but one part of a life, not the whole of an individual. Participants who appear in Homeless Court with serious misdemeanor cases submit proof of completion of significant program activities. In many circumstances, the participants' program activities voluntarily exceed the demands a court might order for treatment for low-term felony cases (e.g. certain drug and theft charges).

HCP Uses a Progressive Plea Bargain System

The HCP offers a different plea structure from the traditional court proceedings. The HCP plea agreement responds to the cases or offenses the homeless participants receive due to their condition and status of living on the streets. Additionally, the HCP agreement acknowledges the efforts that the participants undertake before their appearance in court. The plea agreement recognizes that the participant has completed the court order before the court imposes a sentence. The participant performed the program activities without the threat of custody or a larger fine. The participant completed the order before it was given because that is what he/she needed to do to make a move from the streets, through the shelter program, to self-sufficiency.

HCP Employs Alternative Sentencing

The HCP "sentences" participants to activities in the shelter program. Local homeless shelters and agencies are the gateway for participants to enter this court. Homeless persons who want to appear before this must sign up through one of a number of local shelters.

The alternative sentencing structure is not coercive or punitive in nature, but rather designed to assist homeless participants with reintegration into society. With alternative sentencing, the HCP gives "credit for time served" for the participant's accomplishments in shelter activities. These activities include life-skills, chemical dependency or AA/NA meetings, computer and literacy classes, training or searching for employment, medical care (physical and mental), counseling, and volunteer work. These activities replace the traditional court sentence options of fines, public work service, and custody.

The Homeless Court recognizes that each shelter has its own requirements and guidelines to allow residents to access the Homeless Court. Some shelters require a resident to complete an assessment, an initial phase of the program, or attend specified meetings. The shelters introduce potential participants to the Homeless Court through a variety of means. These agencies will address the Homeless Court as an option after the homeless person has completed a certain course, phase, or activity. The Homeless Court does not interfere with the shelter requirements.

The shelters perform assessments of clients and provide for their basic needs (food, clothing, and shelter) while building the motivation and support that lead clients to the services which, in turn, fulfill the court orders for alternative sentencing. The shelter is in the best position to evaluate the client's needs and design a plan with attainable goals and benefits. Most shelters offer emergency and transitional beds for their clients. Some provide independent living for clients who successfully complete their program. Other shelters provide basic services or support for clients seeking to access benefits, counseling, group meetings, identification cards, clean clothing, and a meal. Clients who actively select their services and goals are more likely to benefit from the program. The Homeless Court and shelters share the desire to empower the individual and enable that person to overcome the adversity that fosters or causes homelessness.

The shelter representatives write advocacy letters for each client. The advocacy letter is symbolic of the relationship between the client and the agency and includes a description of the program, the client's start date and accomplishments, programs completed, and insight into the client's efforts. The HCP sentence strengthens and advances the efforts of the participant and agency representatives.

When participants work with agency representatives to identify and overcome the causes of their homelessness, they are in a stronger position to successfully comply with court orders. The quality, not the quantity, of the participant's time spent in furtherance of the program is of paramount importance for a successful HCP experience. A person who signs up for the HCP is not limited to the sentencing alternatives provided by the homeless agency that referred him/her to court. Rather, the participant is encouraged to participate in a program that will best meet his/her needs.

No One Goes into Custody

The HCP key players (judges, prosecutors, defense attorneys, and homeless shelter/service agencies) agree, "No one goes into custody against his or her will." This does not mean that the prosecution gives up its power to ask for custody, nor does the court relinquish its authority to incarcerate. Rather, this agreement acknowledges both that the participants have committed offenses and have met court requirements through their work in their programs. This agreement respects the relationship and the trust that the homeless service agencies hold with the participants who appear before the HCP and also acknowledges that time spent working with these agencies is equivalent to and more constructive than time spent in custody.

Distinctions between the Traditional Court and Homeless Court

In San Diego, the traditional court sentence for a municipal code violation is a fine of $300. In the traditional court setting, a defendant will receive a $50.00 "credit" against a fine for every day spent in custody. The defendant who spends two days in custody receives credit for a $100.00 fine. To satisfy a fine of $300.00, the court requires a defendant spend six days in custody. Thirty days in custody is the equivalent of a $1,500.00 fine.

The court might convert this fine to six days of public service work or the equivalent time in custody. The traditional punishment for a petty theft is one day in custody (for book and release), $400 in fines, victim restitution, and an eight-hour shoplifter course. When someone is convicted of being under the influence of a controlled substance for the first time, he/she faces a mandatory 90 days in custody or the option of completing a diversion program. The diversion program includes an enrollment orientation, 20 hours of education (2 hours a week for 10 weeks), individual session (biweekly for 3 months, 15 minutes each), drug testing, weekly self-help meetings, and an exit conference.

Typically, the HCP participant has *already* been in a shelter program for at least 30 days (from the initial point of registration to the hearing date) before standing before the judge at the shelter for Homeless Court. By this point, their level of activities in the shelter or a service agency *exceeds* the requirements of the traditional court order. While the program activities vary from one shelter to another, they usually involve a greater time commitment than traditional court orders and introspection for their participants. Shelter staff ensure that the homeless participants are already successful in their efforts to leave the streets before they enter the courtroom.

The HCP builds community and justice by working with homeless service agencies to lay the foundation for homeless participants to prepare for a court hearing after having already completed their "sentence." There, they show significant strides from the streets and through their program activities; they exhibit self-sufficiency. Building from the ground up, the HCP provides a foundation for homeless participants to stand before the court and resolve their cases successfully, with finality, in one hearing.

The HCP illustrates that homeless participants do want to address their cases and lead law-abiding lives, just as the court wants to resolve cases in an efficient and cost effective manner.

Process

Each month, staff from the public defender's and prosecution's offices, various shelters, and the San Diego Superior Court carry out a series of synchronized steps that ultimately culminate in the HCP hearing.

Step One: Outreach/Roadshow

Initially, to help staff and case managers understand and visualize the HCP, an attorney from the Office of the Public Defender visits local shelters and service agencies to explain the HCP's purpose and process. In turn, the case managers introduce their clients to the HCP. The case managers' challenge is to encourage participation in the HCP. They use their ability to convince potential defendants that this program is designed to be a positive experience in their lives. The case managers use examples of successful participants to illustrate the importance of clearing one's record and being able to access government services.

The outreach program begins with a viewing of the HCP half hour documentary video, *And Justice for All: Taking Courts to the Street*. The video shows the frustration and despair on the streets of San Diego. It explains how the HCP started and shows the HCP in action at the shelters. The public defender presents the video, explains how to use the monthly calendar, "Interest List," and "Agreement to Appear," and answers questions or responds to issues raised during the session. When possible, a representative from one of the host shelters joins the outreach meetings.

Step Two: Interest List

After learning about the program through an outreach session or from the shelter staff, shelter residents sign-up on the "HCP Interest List." Potential participants provide their name (including aliases), date of birth, gender, and ethnicity for purpose of identification. The agency fills out contact information (agency name, case manager, and contact person's phone number) and forwards the list to the Office of the Public Defender for a search of case files. The Office of the Public Defender coordinates the participation of those whose names appear on the interest list, delivering the list to the prosecution and court. Participants receive an agreement to appear calendar, which acts as an organizing device for those who cannot afford day planners. This also serves as a notice to show the police that the participant has a future court date.

Step Three: Plea Offers and Negotiations

The prosecutor reviews the case files of the defendants on the court calendar and then generates a list of cases, relevant discovery and an offer (plea bargain) for resolution of the cases. The prosecutor makes offers for resolution of the cases based on criminal history, the impact of criminal behavior on the community, and the number of outstanding cases. The city attorney offers a plea bargain in anticipation of proof and an acknowledgement of each participant's involvement in his or her respective program. Cases outside the city of San Diego are negotiated between the deputy public defender and deputy district attorney on a case by case basis.

The public defender may negotiate further with the prosecutor after learning more about the defendant's individual situation during a pre-hearing consultation. In most instances, these negotiations end with an agreement reached.

Step Four: Records Search

Using the information on the Interest List, the Deputy Clerk of the San Diego Superior Court conducts a criminal history search for open cases, further proceedings, warrants, and pending civil assessment penalties. Active cases are placed on the next HCP calendar if they are criminal cases within the jurisdiction of the San Diego City Attorney's Office (i.e. persons cited for misdemeanors committed in the City of San Diego). Cases from the County of San Diego in the jurisdiction of the District Attorney are addressed on the HCP calendar when negotiations are final. No felony charges are calendared for HCP. However, attorneys with the Office of the Public Defender coordinate the surrender of felony clients into the courthouse as referrals from the Homeless Court Program with proof of participation in program activities.

Step Five: Active Cases Set for Hearing

The San Diego Superior Court clerk prepares a court calendar/docket for the HCP hearing. This docket includes those who signed up on the Interest List and who were found to have outstanding active, non-felony, city of San Diego cases with the court. The court calendar lists each defendant and all of his/her open cases, warrants, fines, civil assessment penalties, and any other pertinent information.

Step Six: Defense Attorney Consultations

One week prior to the hearing, the public defender meets participants at the host shelter. Case managers notify each defendant who has open cases to come to the meeting so that they can review the case(s) and prepare for the next week's court hearing.

The public defender meets with the defendant to review his/her case(s). The public defender presents each individual's case(s) and proposed plea agreement as the worst-case scenario in order to help the participant face his/her greatest fears about the judicial process. The public defender learns about the individual's participation in a shelter or other type of program (i.e. community college, technical school rehabilitation, and outside medical treatment), which the court can use as an alternative sentence to fines, community service, probation, or in some cases, custody. During the consultation, the public defender also explains the importance of the advocacy letters each participant is required to bring to court. These letters show proof of participation in classes, counseling, and community service. These letters highlight individual accomplishments with specific information, including the total number of hours that the defendant participated in treatment or counseling. The public defender also explains the history of the HCP program. The defense attorney uses the shelter programs and the recovery process to involve clients in successful court hearings. The defense attorney tells the clients to bring back proof of program activities and advocacy letters to ensure a successful resolution to the individual cases.

The one-week lapse between the initial interview and the court session allows the attorney time to confirm the participant's activities and identify difficult cases.

The consultation meeting between the public defender and the defendant a week before the HCP hearing is unlike the process in a traditional misdemeanor court. Usually in a traditional misdemeanor court, the public defender only meets with the defendant just prior to an appearance in court. The HCP consultation provides the public defender with important information to negotiate a settlement with the prosecutor. If the defendant cannot attend the initial meeting, phone counseling can be arranged during that week. Occasionally, the defendant and the public defender meet on the HCP day. The pre-hearing case review is an unusual and unique feature of the HCP program.

Step Seven: The Hearing

The hearing is scheduled for the third Wednesday of each month. Hearings are alternately held at one of the two largest shelters in the San Diego area (St. Vincent de Paul Village or Veterans Village of San Diego) to accommodate the defendants, shelter staff, court personnel, and visitors. Due to advanced planning efforts by all involved parties, the hearing moves rather quickly. The California and American flags are placed in the front of the room. The sheriff calls the court to order as the judge—dressed in traditional court attire—enters the room. This careful preparation generates an atmosphere similar to the "traditional courtroom."

The defense attorney formally calls each defendant to come before the judge. The public defender, prosecutor, and defendant all stand at the front of the room. The judge takes the bench, either standing at a podium or seated at a table. The defense attorney states the agreement, says whether the recommendation is a dismissal or a plea, and then presents the letters. The court clerks give the case files to the judge, and the public defender asks that advocacy letters be formally entered into evidence.

When the participant stands before the HCP, he/she stands before the court as a human being. The court sees the participant as someone who has struggled through hard times and is making great efforts to overcome hardship, be it problems with addiction, mental health, economic calamity, or a host of other issues. The court acknowledges each participant's accomplishments. It is with this understanding that the HCP states, "No one is going into custody." At the HCP, it is not uncommon for the court and participant to engage in conversation or for the judge and participant to shake hands at the conclusion of proceedings.

Unlike a traditional court, the judge communicates more often with the defendant than with the public defender. The judge asks the defendant about what brought him/her to the court, his/her participation in programs, counseling, or classes. The judge consults the prosecution about the offer for disposition and, in most cases, the charges, warrants, and penalties are formally dropped as previously agreed. The defendant's record is clean. On average, 90% of the Homeless Court cases are dismissed.

As in traditional court, the judge may continue a case until the defendant provides appropriate documentation to satisfy the alternative sentence agreement (such as advocacy letters). If a defendant fails to appear for the hearing, the case is taken 'off-calendar' and any agreements that have been negotiated between the prosecutor and public defender are withdrawn.

Step Eight: Follow-Up

The deputy court clerk transfers the case disposition information written on the court calendar at the hearing into the court's database, files the advocacy letters, and closes the case files if necessary. Defendants who fail to appear are not automatically placed on the HCP calendar for the following month. They must begin the process again at step one, signing up with the public defender.

Replication of the Homeless Court Program

In July 1999, 10 years after starting with Stand Down, the Homeless Court received a grant from the Department of Justice Bureau of Justice Assistance to hold monthly court sessions. This grant funded all the key agencies that comprise the Homeless Court: the Office of the Public Defender, City Attorney of San Diego, San Diego County Superior Court, Veterans Village of San Diego, St. Vincent de Paul, and an evaluation by SANDAG (San Diego Association of Governments). In April 2001, at the grant's end, all the key players integrated funding of the monthly court sessions into their regular budget.

The American Bar Association Commission on Homelessness and Poverty asked me to conduct an HCP presentation for their business meeting in San Diego on February 17, 2001. The Commission conducted an Internet search on innovative homeless services in San Diego prior to the meeting and found a mock up of an HCP website prepared by a volunteer. While this web site was never launched, it provided vital exposure to the HCP. This website led to my presentation at the business meeting, which in turn led to my joining the Commission, the publication of an HCP how to manual (2002), an ABA resolution supporting the HCP (2003), and a national conference (2004).

The ABA Commission on Homelessness and Poverty is a key collaborator and major impetus for the replication of the HCP. In addition to being the sponsor of the national Homeless Court conference, the Commission coordinates and funds other conference presentations and hosts the Homeless Court website.

The October 8, 2004 conference, held at the University of San Diego's Joan Kroc Peace and Justice Institute, was attended by more then 130 persons and featured panelists from a number of Homeless Court Programs. The Commission published a conference book with articles from 10 Homeless Courts, each developed from the San Diego model, highlighting individual perspectives of all the key players and features from national homeless advocacy organizations based in Washington, DC. This book was published with generous support from the Commission, Oklahoma's Crowe & Dunlevy PC, and QUALCOMM.

In 2004, the Commission launched a new website on homeless courts that includes background information along with various resource materials and a listserv. The site is located at *http://www.abanet.org/homeless/Homeless_Courts.html.*

Plans for this website include the addition of tool kits designed specifically for judges, court administrators, prosecutors, defenders, and service providers as well as video clips from interview and productions from other HCPs.

Currently, the HCP has been replicated in 14 communities in California (while 7 communities are in the developmental stages) and 13 jurisdictions across the United States, and Stand Down events occur across the country. HCP serves as a model of how other jurisdictions can establish a program to better serve homeless defendants and meet their special needs. The following communities illustrate the growth and development of the HCP over the years.

Alameda, California

The Alameda County Homeless & Caring Court Program held its first regular session one week after the Commission conference in October. The Hon. Gordon Baranco of Alameda Superior Court and Alameda County Public Defender Diane Bellas participated in the Commission's October 2004 conference panel. They developed a detailed protocol: Intake Form, Calendar, How HCP Works, and Chronology of its evolution from February 2003 to April 2006. The Alameda HCP was featured in numerous newspaper articles. Its future efforts will focus on building provider services. Additionally, it will host the HCP Roundtable in October 2006.

Ann Arbor, Michigan

Judge Elizabeth Hines contacted the Commission after learning about the Homeless Court on the ABA website and requested copies of the manual, conference course book, and video. Judge Hines, affiliated with the community team charged with drafting a plan to end homelessness, developed interest in information about addressing the special legal problems of homeless people into the Street Outreach Court. The Street Outreach Court expanded upon the San Diego model developing a protocol that focused on an "action plan" over treatment plans and accepting clients who are at risk of becoming homeless.

Arizona (Phoenix, Tucson and Flagstaff)

A group of Arizona judges, court administrators, lawyers, and law students attended the Commission's National Conference on Homeless Courts in San Diego. The attendees from Arizona were impressed with the concept of courts geared to homeless populations and the benefits they provide to their communities. A handful of attendees followed up with the Commission to seek additional resources after the conference. They developed a white paper for homeless court pilot projects in Arizona. This collaborative effort was led by Judge Louraine Arkfeld, Jeremy Mussman, Special Assistant Maricopa County Public Defender, and Patience Huntwork, Chief Staff Attorney, Arizona Supreme Court. Judge Arkfeld requested an article on homeless courts for the Winter 2005 edition of the Judicial Division Record. The site for this article is *http://www.abanet.org/jd/publications/jdrecord/2005winter.pdf.*

Tucson already has a Homeless Court and has plans to expand its scope. The City of Phoenix held a hybrid Homeless Court at its local Stand Down event in a warehouse in South Phoenix. One of the primary obstacles to the development of a complete Homeless Court Program in Phoenix is the challenge of integrating the cases from 23 jurisdictions into one courtroom. This challenge, coupled with the need for a central authority, makes it difficult to find a decisionmaker to implement a Homeless Court across the city.

Albuquerque, New Mexico

The Albuquerque court has worked hard to build community exposure and trust. Eight members of the Albuquerque court traveled to meet with the San Diego HCP in January 2001. Presiding Criminal Judge Victoria Grant held the first Homeless Court on June 5, 2002, with two participants appearing. In time the court grew from quarterly to bi-monthly sessions with an average of 25 referrals each session.

Houston, Texas

I met with Lynda Greene, Community Director for the DeGeorge at Union Station, a supportive housing community for veterans, judges, and advocates on Veterans Day to discuss the possibility of creating a HCP in Houston. This meeting coincided with my Affiliation in Ashoka Innovators for the Public during their Induction ceremony held November 11-14, 2003.

In March 2006, Andre Simpson (long standing HCP coordinator, Vice President and C.O.O. of Veterans Village of San Diego) and I were invited to Houston by Scot More, the Community Resource Manager for the Coalition for the Homeless of Houston/Harris County, who coordinated a one day workshop on the Houston Homeless Court. The workshop for service providers, government officials, and court personnel spread the word, refined the program screening and the application process, and increased the scope of cases heard. All of this was combined with efforts to strengthen and build representation for the clients.

Kern County, California

In March 2002, I traveled to Bakersfield to consult on the HCP. I met with staff from the Greater Bakersfield Legal Assistance, Inc. (GBLA), Judge Staley (judge at Stand Down), Judge Wallace (presiding judge), shelter providers, and court staff. The day of meetings culminated with Judge Wallace giving approval for an HCP pilot project. One month later, Judge Staley and Josh Rudnick (staff attorney with GBLA) came to San Diego to observe a session of the HCP and to meet the San Diego HCP key players.

On November 27, 2002, Bakersfield held its second HCP session in the dining room of the Bakersfield Homeless Center, owned by the city, operated by Bethany Services since 1991 (which leases the facility for $1.00 a year). The Bakersfield HCP holds to the premise that no one is going to jail. Additionally, the court recognizes participation in program activities when sentencing. Child Support Services sends an outreach officer to meet with homeless participants. On that day, over 10 people stayed to talk with the outreach officer after the court hearing.

Reno, Nevada

After attending the Commission's HCP conference in October 2004, Judge Janet Berry returned to Reno and discussed the homeless court concept with her fellow judges and administrators at a regional judicial council. The Commission provided Judge Berry with copies of the conference course book along with a VHS video on homeless courts in preparation for a meeting with the Specialty Court Coordinator, Mental Health Court Coordinator, and Specialty Court Judge on January 28, 2005. Judge Berry's office followed up with the Commission to request additional materials and determine how to pull the prosecution into the process while developing the provider role in the HCP. Judge Berry notes cases are resolved in their HCP through "reverse sentencing," when the court orders credit for time served to clients who have already completed their activities in homeless service agency programs.

Seattle, Washington

Commission member Casey Trupin and Ishbel Dickens (a former Curtin fellow) presented the Homeless Court to King County Coalition for the Homeless, city council members and court personnel. This introduction led to the Seattle Homeless Court for Veterans Forum on Collaborative Justice on June 27, 2005. In the spring of 2006, the Seattle HCP held its first session with an eye on expanding to the general homeless population.

San Joaquin County, California

On Friday, January 27, 2006, San Joaquin held its first Homeless Court session at St. Mary's Interfaith Community Services, serving a total of 7 defendants and resolving 29 cases. This effort was spear-

Interested in learning more about the Homeless Court Program or creating a similar program in your community?

Contact the ABA Commission on Homelessness & Poverty at (202) 662-1694 or visit the Commission's website at **www.abanet.org/homeless**.

headed by Hon. Barbara A. Kronlund. The court renewed its efforts for the development of an HCP after attending the HCP court session, and the full panel presented a workshop at St. Vincent de Paul Village for the State Judicial Branch Conference on September 8, 2005. After four sessions, the San Joaquin HCP is at maximum capacity. Building on the San Diego model, San Joaquin's Homeless Court opted to accept referrals of people who are borderline homeless and address probation conditions in felony cases.

Vancouver, Washington

Vancouver created an HCP after receiving materials from the Commission. I was contacted by a reporter doing a story on the new court and was then put in contact with the defense attorney affiliated with their HCP. While Vancouver does not have a public defender office, they rely upon private defense attorneys to staff their traditional and homeless court. The defense attorney who volunteers at the Vancouver Homeless Court said their efforts have taken on a life of its own as other attorneys come forward to volunteer their time. They currently have 10 volunteer attorneys. The Columbian newspaper ran the article as the front-page story on Sunday, December 26, 2004.

Ventura, California

"While court outreach and restorative justice programs are important, that consideration is secondary to the simple practical advantage of finding alternatives to the traditional cycle of arrest/jail/reoffense for those society must serve in some way," said John E. Dobroth, Judge of the Superior Court. The Ventura HCP built off the efforts of Tina Rasnow, Self-Help Legal Access Center–Coordinator for the Superior Court of Ventura. Their first session on July 28, 2000 was a pilot project in conjunction with an annual Stand Down event. They had 17 defendants with a total of 55 open cases. Two months later, all but one defendant had completed or exceeded the court's expectations. In 2001, the Judicial Council of California presented the Kleps Award to the HCP of Ventura County.

The Ventura HCP compiled a Statistical Report from April 2001 through March 2002 which states:

Number of cases 428

Number of cases cleared[1]..344

Number of defendants (122 male; 114 female) 236

Number of defendants who
successfully completed 189 (80%)
the sentence imposed in Homeless Court[2]

Number of community service hours performed 8,322.5
(4,821 hours were documented as community service performed over and above sentence requirements.)

Number of defendants who achieved sobriety[3].......................32

Number of defendants who found housing[4]............................25

Number of defendants who regained custody of 9
their children

Number of defendants who found employment 23

These Homeless Court Programs illustrate people are willing to work, extend themselves and find innovative ways to deal with the obstacles homeless people face in dealing with the criminal justice system. They find a way to reach outside the confines of their regular 8 to 5 work day, leave the creature comforts of the courthouse and serve justice in the community. Each has a story to tell.

---

1 *Most of the offenses involved drinking or sleeping in public and various traffic-related infractions.*

2 *Many of the defendants who did not complete their sentence by the cut-off date for compiling these statistics (March 31, 2002), were still working toward successful completion. Thus the 20% who did not successfully complete their sentence by March 31, 2002 includes those who are performing their community service hours and are expected to satisfactorily complete their sentences.*

3 *Sobriety is defined as living clean and sober following release from in-house treatment program. An additional 6 defendants were identified as being clean and sober, but did not have a known history of substance abuse.*

4 *Housing is defined as living in an owned unit or rental unit under a term lease or month-to-month tenancy. An additional 3 defendants had arranged some form of housing with a relative, but did not occupy under a lease or rental agreement.*

Conclusion

Each of us has a story. Stories fill our lives. Art and literature give us stories that inspire us to look beyond ourselves, to see the world in a different way, in a new language or context. Charlie Chaplin gave us the Little Tramp. Innocent and misunderstood on first appearance, the Little Tramp is *literally* seen in the end of the

ABA © STEVE BINDER

Steve Binder *Deputy Public Defender*
San Diego County Office of the Public Defender
233 A St., Ste. 800 San Diego, CA 92101
619.338.4708 steve.binder@sdcounty.ca.gov

Steve Binder is a deputy public defender with the San Diego Office of the Public Defender, where he has practiced since 1989. Steve represented clients in the mental health and welfare fraud specialty units. He founded the Homeless Court Program (HCP) in 1989 and authored a grant request for Dept. of Justice/Bureau of Justice Assistance funding for it. Mr. Binder has received many awards for his work on it. In 2004, the HCP was selected as one of fifteen finalists for the Innovations in Government Awards by the Ash Institute/Kennedy School of Government-Harvard University, and Binder received the Outstanding Community Service Award (2004) from the San Diego Bar Association. In 2002, the Board of Directors of Defense Programs in San Diego presented him the E. Stanley Conant Award. The National Coalition for Homeless Veterans presented him with the "Unsung Hero Award" in 2000, the Veterans Village of San Diego presented him the "Volunteer Attorney of the Year" in 1990, and the Public Defender Association presented him the "Community Service Award" in 1999. The American Bar Association presented the "Hodson Award" to the San Diego County Office of the Public Defender for outstanding service by a public agency with the Homeless Court. He is a Fellow with Ashoka Innovators for the Public, working fulltime to further replication of the Homeless Court Program. He currently serves with the San Diego Regional Task Force on the Homeless. He is Chair of the ABA Commission on Homelessness and Poverty. He was a Eureka Communities Fellow (2000-2001).

movie *City Lights* as a person. In *Les Miserables*, Victor Hugo introduced Jean Valjean, a character who is imprisoned for stealing a loaf of bread, but who is later given a second chance when the Monsignor hands him two silver candle sticks saying, "Go in peace. By the way my friend, when you come again...you can always come and go by the front door." In *The Wizard of Oz*, an uncertain and vulnerable Dorothy called out "There's no place like home" and eventually found hope and dreams on the other side of the rainbow. Each of us has a story. Some long to be understood, others want or need a second chance, all seek hope and opportunity.

Recently, the San Diego HCP has been the focus of the media. More than once, we have been asked whether the homeless participants who appear will have teeth. This inquiry serves as an important reminder that the story we receive and convey must reach people in a place and time when they can accept it. This applies equally to those who watch the news and those who are subjects in the news segment, be they housed or homeless. Meet them where they are and bring them to understand the community they live in, their place and importance in it...how we are all in this together. United we stand! The promise and spirit of these words fill the Stand Down event, the Homeless Court Program, and the streets of communities across the nation.

When homeless people request help with criminal cases, they seek justice and respect. They want to take responsibility while looking for opportunity. While the continued problems homelessness represents are discouraging and frustrating, it is important to remember: it is the condition of homelessness that is undesirable, not the people.

The challenge and opportunity facing us today is to find art and breathe life into our daily lives and commitment in delivering justice for all, thus bringing law to the streets, the court to shelters, and homeless people back into society.

Preventing Homelessness of Elder Disabled Tenants:

Creating a Holistic Eviction Diversion Project

Rhonda Dahlman

A very wise friend recently told me that the next civil rights movement in the United States would be that of the elders. The chord of that prophetic statement stuck in my throat. It was then that I realized that the work done on behalf of elder disabled tenants at risk of being evicted would require a voice like none ever heard. Elder disabled tenants are of all walks of life and include millionaires as well as those living without the entitlements they deserve. The aging process does not discriminate.

This chapter is written from my years of experience in working with elder disabled tenants who, through no fault of their own, are at risk of eviction. Throughout my twenty-year career as a legal service lawyer, I rarely saw elder tenants appear personally in landlord tenant court. Elder disabled tenants are challenged by the processes necessary to navigate eviction proceedings. Such legal proceedings are often effectuated without the tenants' presence, without the legal services of a lawyer, or without the Court even being aware that the tenant is a disabled elder. Included are stories of struggle for continued dignity and independence of a few from the hundreds of elder tenants my staff and I have worked with to prevent the indignity and fear of an elder tenant facing homelessness.

Many readers may remember when their great grandparents, or great-grandparents were cared for by family members until their passing. However, due to our current societal transience, familial proximity with its elders is becoming less and less prevalent. More often, sons and daughters live far from their aging parents and other relatives, and frequent, regular visits are less common. Moreover, within the next twenty-five years, the elder population will more than double.[1] Thus, this chapter has present and future relevance. It is about our parents, our uncles and aunts, our friends of advanced age, and one day it will be about us. Our own children will likely not live in close proximity to us and will lead their own lives. In such a transient society, we must look to the ways of the past in which families were able to care for their aging family members, as well as to learn and grow from the wisdom of our elders.

AARP/Legal Counsel for the Elderly (hereinafter, LCE) has embraced the immense and growing problem of elder disabled tenants facing evictions and, as a result, has founded a city-wide holistic eviction diversion project: The Alternatives to Landlord/Tenant Court for the Elderly Project (hereinafter, the Alternatives Project). The Alternatives Project, founded six years ago, was formed as a multidisciplinary city-wide coalition and partnership which included the Court, attorneys representing landlords and tenants, housing providers (including our public housing authority), social workers, medical and mental health service providers, scores of youth, as well as community and church volunteers.

Within this diverse group of professionals and nonprofessionals, a common goal was shared—to divert the evictions of elder tenants from landlord tenant court. It was also agreed that housing providers needed to be aware of such an eviction diversion project and understand the warning signs identifying the underlying problem(s) from which an elder tenant may suffer before receiving an eviction summons.

1 Washington Post, *March 10, 2006: A9.*

With aging—no matter how this society struggles against embracing it—generally comes disability of some form or another. There are very few elders who are not subject to the aches and pains, including mental, emotional, and physical, of the aging process. The disabilities often come in the form of incontinence, arthritis, sensory loss and impairment, dementia, Alzheimer's disease, depression, as well as symptoms of hoarding (the amassing of "stuff"), just to name a few. None of these disabilities are the fault of elders—they are merely forms of aging in action.

How do these disabilities affect one's tenancy and the possibility that such disabilities and symptoms will lead to eviction? Within the context of landlord/tenant relations, as well as condo and cooperatives rules, each resident must follow a set of rules set up by the governing body, such as the landlord, co-op, or condo board. Many of these rules pertain to the quiet enjoyment by all the residents and the necessity to maintain a healthy, safe living environment. Each tenant must follow the rules or risk eviction. The aging process can compromise elder tenants' abilities to comply with the rules of their tenancy through restriction of movement, smell, sight, hearing, and memory. As one ages, the dulling of senses can become a downward spiral in which time becomes a singular enemy as it relates to independent living.

Let us envision three common scenarios faced by elder tenants. The first involves the disability of arthritis. As one ages, for one suffering from arthritis, it becomes more difficult for a tenant to clean an apartment and complete chores such as taking the trash to the dumpster—even if it is as simple and accessible as a dumpster chute located in the building.

When it becomes physically difficult for a tenant to even get out of bed in the morning because of arthritis pain, many elder tenants think, "Well, maybe tomorrow I will be better and I'll do what needs to get done." After a few weeks of trash build-up, the cockroaches find their gold, the mice find their meals, and the elder tenant is on a path to eviction. The housing provider will often look the other way given "the age" of the elder and issue the tenant a verbal warning, but in this instance the additional time resolves nothing—nothing. In fact, the additional time only compounds the problem, for with the added time, the odors of the garbage begin to seep through the hallways and into the common areas of the apartment building. It is often the complaints from other tenants that bring the matter to the attention of management. In the past there was one road this dilemma would follow—the road to court, the eviction of the elder, and life on the street.

I once worked with a 93-year-old elder who lived in a cooperative who was at grave risk of eviction and was referred to the Alternatives Project by his co-op board. This elder gentleman had absolutely no physical ability to take his garbage to the disposal, though it was merely steps from his apartment. It took him nearly two painful minutes to walk ten steps and, along with his continuing loss of sight, he could no longer see his trash building up. He wanted to remain in his cooperative apartment where he was, as he had lived there for more than 40 years. However, because of the trash build-up and the resulting infestation of roaches, he was facing eviction. Through a holistic assessment, the elder was able to remain in his home by receiving necessary support services.

Housing providers may feel at a complete loss to find ways to resolve such a solvable problem. From my experience of providing legal services to poor people, I've noticed a distinct difference in how housing providers view the younger tenant population versus the elder tenant population for whom they provide housing. Countless times while working at LCE, I received referrals from housing providers who, while making referrals on behalf of their elder tenants to the Alternatives Project, are brought to tears as they share their own personal experiences regarding their own struggles in trying to keep their own elderly family members from being evicted. This commonality of personal experience has become the thread of LCE's eviction diversion program. Many members of this society will face similar struggles keeping their own elder family members living independently, along with the frustration due to the lack of integrated holistic support services.

Another common scenario that places elder disabled tenants at risk of eviction is nonpayment of rent. This may occur for a variety of reasons, including dementia, Alzheimer's disease, or a sudden undiagnosed stroke—the inherent effects of which can create an absolute impediment for an elder tenant in paying timely rent. Another reason for rent nonpayment is the existence of financial abuse. A "friend" or family member may be "assisting" the elder tenant in paying their rent when in fact they are pocketing the money for their own use. These situations are often the easiest cases to resolve through the Alternatives Project, though it is incumbent on the housing provider to call for eviction diversion services immediately and not wait three or four months as unpaid rent accumulates.

One of the aspects of the Alternatives Project has been to train housing providers in recognizing the "red flags" and contacting the Project before situations get out of hand. For example, if an elder tenant has always paid their rent in a timely fashion and suddenly stops making payments, housing providers are trained to make immediate referrals to the Project. The Project will send out a social worker to meet with the "at-risk" tenant, assess the underlying problem(s), and discuss with the elder tenant the risk of eviction, as well as suggest possible solutions such as obtaining a Power of Attorney or set up the tenant with a voluntary trained bill payer from the community.

The third situation that often precedes the threat of eviction is that of hoarding. In the past, these cases have been nearly irresolvable. The Alternatives Project has met these difficult situations head-on through the most innovative and successful of means. The Elder Buddies Program, the volunteer component of the Alternative Project, performs near miracles in its goal to assist elder tenants with de-cluttering. Elder Buddies matches high school students, who are

Interested in learning more about Legal Counsel for the Elderly?

Visit **http://www.aarp.org/states/dc/dc-lce/.**

required to complete community service hours, with elders who are at risk of eviction because of the hoarding. Elder Buddies over the past two years has extended into the religious community including many denominations and groups of all ages. Trained adult mentors are also integrated into this volunteer project.

At times, when one first enters an apartment of a tenant who suffers from hoarding, there may be accumulation of "stuff" all the way to the ceiling. There may or not be paths through the advanced clutter, and often it is unclear where the elder tenant is sleeping. The hoarded items may be books, clothes, papers, food and furniture, or other belongings.

In preparation for the de-cluttering, a trained professional works closely with the tenant. Hoarding can be a symptom of depression and often obsessive-compulsive behavior. I worked very closely with one tenant who in the past was a very productive federal employee. She was adamantly opposed to the removal from her apartment of mostly boxes of papers piled to the ceiling throughout her apartment, in which there was a single path to her bed. I spent hours with this tenant. Once she trusted me, she shared with me the reason for her hoarding behavior. She collected things because all of her friends had passed away and her "stuff" was her only connection to this world. In her isolation, her belongings became her only connection. However, when she and I made a "heart to heart" connection, her "stuff" lost its meaning to her and allowed her to shed her excess belongings.

This story is representative of the tenants with whom the Elder Buddies work. One of the problems faced in the District is the lack of city-paid cleaning services. Many tenants have to wait up to six months for a city-paid cleaning aide. Many housing providers are not willing to wait that long due to the potential fire hazard. Elder Buddies can often provide these much needed services to the tenant while waiting for city-paid services.

Moreover, many of the elders have less fear of youth. They often welcome their visits. While initially, tenants may be apprehensive at the thought of their beloved belongings leaving their apartment, as their connection with the youth develops, their connection to their hoarded belongings becomes less and less important. It is imperative to note, however, that it is the decision of the tenant which belongings are to be discarded and which belongings the tenant will keep. It is often an arduous process, but the youth volunteers have patience that adults may lack. The de-cluttering may take many visits, but eventually, the apartment passes inspection. Before and after pictures of the apartment are taken, as well as pictures of the elder tenant and their "Elder Buddies." The youth volunteers, who may not have their grandparents living in close proximity, have the added benefit of connecting with the elder. And while the students may initially share trepidation, they most often come away with a changed perception and a new-found compassion for the aging process. The stories the elders are able to share with the students are heartwarming and an incredible learning experience for the Elder Buddies.[2]

As mentioned, city-wide partnerships are crucial in developing an effective holistic eviction diversion project. In what are often very difficult cases, it is imperative that all necessary partners work very closely together and for services to be integrated and coordinated. While LCE has obtained funding for a part-time Elder Buddies coordinator and social worker, the social worker's duty is to put out the immediate fire and make a referral to the necessary partner(s), which can include a community social worker, a mental health professional, medical services, bill payer services and if needed, an attorney. It is only through such an ongoing and coordinated partnership that each tenant will be guaranteed all the support services necessary to remain living independently. And independent living is always the goal.

The landlord tenant court in the District of Columbia has been a critical partner in the eviction diversion work of the Alternatives Project. While many housing providers utilize the project, there are still those that either are not yet aware of it or choose not to use the benefits the project provides. Soon after the project was firmly established and we began to experience the positive results of pro-

2 *All parents of Elder Buddies sign waivers as well as each tenant who receives such services.*

viding holistic assessments and services, I approached the Court with two goals in mind. The first was to educate landlord tenant court judges of the "fair housing" nature of these types of cases that come before them as well as the purpose of the Alternatives Project. The Court was very enthusiastic about the project and agreed to become a partner, being quite aware that the problem with disabled elder tenants facing eviction through no fault of their own is a social issue—not necessarily a legal problem. Soon thereafter, judges began diverting eviction cases involving elder tenants to the project.

One example of this involved a case of an elder disabled tenant who could not keep her apartment clean. The landlord involved was not aware of the Alternatives Project and had instituted an eviction action against the tenant. While the case was in the middle of trial and the judge saw the pictures presented by the landlord evidencing the conditions of the apartment, he stayed the proceedings, called the project, and sent the tenant to LCE. The Alternatives staff immediately provided an assessment and began providing holistic services for the elder tenant, which included cleaning services, as well as obtaining a voluntary bill payer for the tenant (who had missed a rental payment during the litigation). What was most interesting about this case was that once the clutter was removed, it was apparent there were many housing code violations for which the landlord was responsible and had to rectify. In such instances, the Alternatives Project becomes a Friend of the Court, and while not formally litigating on behalf of the elder tenant, more often than

Rhonda Dahlman

elders have so much to say
in the voicelessness of speech
elders hold the wisdom
the elders' voice must speak

our aging is not shameful
our aging is not weak
our aging is not our process
it is this gift to seek

not, it rectifies the matter on behalf of the Court and more importantly, the tenant who is facing eviction.

The tenant is the most critical partner in any eviction diversion work. No service is utilized without the tenant's knowledge and consent. Each tenant decides how to proceed. Partners do not act upon what they "think best" for the tenant. Partners do not patronize tenants. It is respect for and dignity towards the tenant that always remains the first and foremost priority. The Alternatives Project informs each tenant of his/her options and secures the services the elder will accept. Also, it is imperative that any housing provider who participates in the project understands that while the tenant is at risk because of lease violations, the housing provider has the absolute duty to make all necessary repairs in the tenant's apartment within the "alternatives process."

There are times when elder tenants—especially when they are suffering from dementia or Alzheimer's disease—may not have the capacity to understand the consequences of their decisions. For example, there are occasions when an elder is facing eviction because of nonpayment of rent due to financial exploitation. Because of the tenant's mental impairment(s), her or she may have no understanding that rent nonpayment will result in eviction. It may be at that time, after the completion of a thorough assessment is completed by a trained professional, that the community partners will meet and make a decision to initiate a protective arrangement action.

There are two different legal actions that can be taken for the protection of incapacitated individuals—those being guardianship, which protects the person; and conservatorship, which protects the assets of the person. There is little question that such an action will have bearing on the decision-making rights of any human being. In the District of Columbia, the decision to go forward with a guardianship or conservatorship is made by a "protective arrangement panel"—a multidisciplinary team composed of social workers, a lawyer, and a geriatric medical professional. The mandate of the panel is to have before it a full medical, mental health, and social work assessment as well as a risk assessment for each individual case brought before it. Family members are often also present.

For example, a tenant's case may be brought before the protection arrangement panel, and it is clear that the tenant has no capacity to understand the risk of eviction. However, if there has not yet been provided a written notice to the tenant of an impending legal action and the tenant poses no harm to her or himself, the panel will decide to keep working with the tenant in hopes that the tenant will eventually accept available support services that will ameliorate the eviction risk. If, however, the risk has become too great, such as ongoing fires or floods in the building resulting from his or her disability, or an action has already commenced toward eviction proceedings for nonpayment of rent, then the panel may decide to pursue the legal action of obtaining a guardian or conservator. The panel always decides on the least restrictive alternative, and in each and every case, the goal is to attempt to keep the elder tenant in his or her current living arrangement.

In some instances where a tenant, having capacity, makes a decision that will lead to his or her eviction, such as not accepting support services, the tenant's decision will stand even if that decision will lead to their eviction. In other words, each tenant with capacity has the right to make his or her choice—no matter the consequences. When such a situation arises, the team will take every step to ensure that another placement is available to the tenant if he or she chooses.

The cases resulting in guardianship or conservatorship for the tenant make up for less than five percent of the eviction diversion work of the Alternatives Project. There are many in the legal service community who cringe at the thought of this legal approach, since it encroaches on the decision-making right of the individual. However, intervention proceedings exist in every jurisdiction for the protection of the most vulnerable in our society. While as an attorney, this can be an uncomfortable situation, it is an attorney's duty as an officer of the court to assist the court in ensuring protection for the most vulnerable of our society. However, such proceedings should be used only when all other alternatives have been exhausted. Even through these proceedings, the attorney should always seek the most creative and least restrictive means of providing for the needs of the incapacitated individual while protecting his or her rights threatened by the possibility of eviction. For example, if a tenant has had a number of smoke fires because he or she is forgetting to turn off the stove burner, the attorney could request that a guardian be appointed for the sole purpose of replacing the stove with a microwave. Or, if a conservator is needed for purposes of paying rent, then the lawyer should request that a temporary conservator be put in place until a representative payee is obtained through the Social Security Administration. The conservatorship should be terminated when a representative payee is established and all extra money, after payment of rent, should be given to the tenant. The most important point in terms of protection arrangements is that the team involved with the tenant seek every creative avenue to allow the elder tenant to live independently and with dignity.

Holistic eviction diversion programs must be based upon reasonable accommodations within the *Fair Housing Act of 1988* and Section 504 of the *Rehabilitation Act of 1973*. While the law is clear that housing providers are not responsible for providing reasonable accommodations to disabled tenants, housing providers are required to allow reasonable accommodations to occur when such a disability is creating the eviction risk. The most common reasonable accommodation requested by the lawyer involved in such cases is one of time.

I was involved in a case in which a disabled elder tenant was caring for three grandchildren. The tenant was three months behind in his rent with no present accessible income. The Alternatives Project required nothing but time in order to obtain necessary benefits. After completing a full financial assessment with the tenant, it was concluded that the tenant was neither receiving entitlement benefits for his grandchildren nor was he receiving benefits to which he was entitled from the federal government resulting from his wife's death—both of which were needed to pay back rent and maintain his current rent. The housing provider who had worked with the project in the past, was well aware of the projects integrity, and allowed the necessary time to achieve resolution. The housing provider, who had had only past success with the project in the past, stated that if it took a year, he would consent. Such a time extension would not in all probability be allowed through the court process.

This example highlights the need and importance of integrity in a community-developed holistic eviction diversion project. In developing such an eviction diversion project, never promise to rectify a situation if it can't be done. Never "string along" a housing provider with the hope that the problem will go away, because it won't. And ultimately, any such holistic eviction diversion project will fail.

If situations arise in where litigation needs to take place, secure a signed retainer agreement and litigate. The law of reasonable accommodations pursuant to fair housing law for disabled tenants needs to be used in conjunction with such an eviction diversion project. No lawyer should shy away from this litigation responsibility. However, familiarize yourself with what is "reasonable" and what is not through a thorough review of prior litigation. Don't be afraid to be creative and don't be afraid to "push the envelope." As a litigator representing elder tenants, I have used a fair housing defense in 95 percent of my housing litigation cases involving elder disabled tenants. I am also aware of the time it takes to litigate such cases. During the last five years of the project, LCE has not shied away from litigation. However, the project, which is completely voluntary for housing providers, has obtained more extensive "reasonable accommodations" outside of the court room than what we could obtain from fair housing law itself.

The Alternatives Project has created an environment in which all partners win. It allows a tenant attorney to successfully resolve hundreds of "fair housing" cases within a brief amount of time without litigating. It saves housing providers attorney fees and time in court. But most importantly, it allows our elders to live independently and with dignity.

It is absolutely incumbent upon any advocate attempting to prevent homelessness in a holistic manner to be proactive when representing elder disabled tenants. We must look to the resources within our own communities and work in partnership to best utilize those resources. We must begin to see housing providers as partners for the sake of elder disabled tenants—both nationally and on a grass roots level. This society cannot socially or economically afford the costs associated with the evictions of elder disabled tenants. LCE, through its Alternatives Project, has saved our local government hundreds of thousands of dollars in Medicaid funding by keeping disabled elder tenants in their homes rather than being placed in nursing homes or assisted living facilities. As such, your community government should have great economic incentive to become a very willing partner in this endeavor.

The time has come that family must be bolstered by "community" as it relates to the care of our disabled elders. That will be the basis upon which elder tenants may continue to live in their apartments with necessary holistic support services involving the entire community. This is already being accomplished within the District of Columbia and must, for the sake of all disabled elder tenants, become a national perspective. We, as a society, must begin to see elder disabled tenants at risk of eviction not as "problem ten-

ABA © EILEEN COVEY

Rhonda Dahlman
rdahlman@ns.sympatico.ca

Rhonda Dahlman was formerly a staff and supervising attorney at Legal Counsel for the Elderly. An accomplished litigator and advocate, Ms. Dahlman created the Alternatives Project, which provides a holistic approach to the resolution of landlord-tenant disputes on behalf of elder disabled tenants. She authored a manual outlining the project as a model for use by other jurisdictions across the country and provided trainings at both the local and national level. Rhonda was awarded the District of Columbia Bar Foundation's Jerrold Scoutt Prize in 2002 in recognition of her commitment to providing legal services to low-income elderly clients. Rhonda is a graduate of Antioch School of Law and previously served as a staff attorney for 13 years at Neighborhood Legal Services Program. She is presently an artist and writer living on Cape Breton Island in Nova Scotia, Canada.

ants" but "tenants with problems" that can be resolved through holistic assessments and the provision of community-wide integrated services.

We have great challenges ahead in changing the societal perceptions of the aging process of our most fragile elders in this country. If we do not begin to meet these challenges head-on, we will experience a pandemic of homeless elders in the future, and it will be a burden this government will not be financially able to bear.

The seed of changing perceptions regarding disabled aging tenants has been planted in the District of Columbia. Out of that seed has grown the strongest of trees, with its roots in an eviction diversion project reaching far into the ground and its branches continuing to expand into the community further than most would have envisioned.

Each reader of this chapter must begin to see the possibilities of setting up an eviction diversion project on behalf of disabled elder tenants within their own communities. It must start with changing our own perceptions of the aging process. Homelessness of elders is unacceptable. It is this voice that must be heard on behalf of the voiceless. Each of us within our own communities must take the responsibility of speaking the voice of, and caring for, our most vulnerable elders. It is their stories, and one day, our stories that must have a voice.

American Bar Association Commission on Homelessness & Poverty 2005-2006

Chair

Steve Binder
San Diego, CA

Members

Lynne Barr
Boston, MA

Robert Downs
Chicago, IL

Maria Foscarinis
Washington, DC

Paul Freese
Los Angeles, CA

Jerome Holmes
Oklahoma City, OK

Patricia Julianelle
Santiago, Chile

Michael Karwoski
Detroit, MI

Hon. Steven Leifman
Miami, FL

Kara Nyquist
Anchorage, AK

J. Peter Sabonis
Bangor, ME

Casey Trupin
Seattle, WA

Cindy Wang
Atlanta, GA

Board of Governors Liaison

Sharon Stevens
Keizer, OR

Staff

Amy Horton-Newell
American Bar Association
740 15th Street, NW
Washington, DC 20005
Tel. (202) 662-1693
Fax (202) 638-3844
Email: homeless@staff.abanet.org